Road to Nowhere

Road to Nowhere

What Silicon Valley Gets Wrong about the Future of Transportation

Paris Marx

VERSO

London • New York

First published by Verso 2022
© Paris Marx, 2022

1 3 5 7 9 10 8 6 4 2

Verso
UK: 6 Meard Street, London W1F 0EG
US: 20 Jay Street, Suite 1010, Brooklyn, NY 11201
versobooks.com

Verso is the imprint of New Left Books

ISBN-13: 978-1-83976-588-9
ISBN-13: 978-1-83976-591-9 (US EBK)
ISBN-13: 978-1-83976-590-2 (UK EBK)

British Library Cataloguing in Publication Data
A catalogue record for this book is available from the British Library

Library of Congress Cataloging-in-Publication Data
A catalog record for this book is available from the Library of Congress

Typeset in Sabon by MJ & N Gavan, Truro, Cornwall
Printed and bound by CPI Group (UK) Ltd, Croydon, CR0 4YY

For Jacques and Christina

Contents

Introduction

I have seen the future.

From April 30, 1939, to October 27, 1940, five million people walked through the doors of General Motors' Futurama exhibition at the New York World's Fair. As they left, they were each given a pin inscribed with those five words—and they believed it.

Coming out of the depths of the Great Depression, people had lost their hope for the future. Poverty was a widespread reality, and there was no time to think about grandiose visions of a transformed society when every day was a struggle just to put food on the table. The World's Fair, and in particular the Futurama, was an attempt to change that.

When guests entered the General Motors pavilion, they entered the world of 1960—one of wealth and opportunity beyond many of their imaginations. It was a world where wide expressways ran through cities peppered with tall skyscrapers and surrounded by vast parks. Slums had been leveled to make way for the future, and pedestrians used new elevated walkways that allowed them to get around without slowing the flow of vehicle traffic.

The expressways extended out from gleaming cities into the vast suburban expanses of single-family homes filled with all manner of new consumer goods and appliances that families would enjoy in 1960. As these new neighborhoods continued into the rural fringes, one discovered an agricultural landscape transformed by mechanization and the application of new scientific techniques—and the entire trip could be made without manually steering at all, as one's vehicle was guided by radio control signals embedded in the highways.

It is no surprise that people were awed by the world on display. But who did this vision of the future actually serve? General Motors and the other companies at the World's Fair did not go and ask the people of the United States what kind of lives they wanted to lead. Instead, what was dreamed up internally served a different set of goals—one they successfully sold to the public through their grand exhibitions.

Industrial designer Norman Bel Geddes was behind the General Motors pavilion, but many of its key details came from a project he had developed several years earlier: the Shell Oil City of Tomorrow, which was also an auto-oriented vision of the future with wide urban expressways and tall skyscrapers. After the World's Fair, Geddes was sought out by President Franklin D. Roosevelt to advise his administration on transportation policy and on the Federal-Aid Highway Act of 1944, effectively ensuring aspects of his plan—the same one he had been paid by oil and automotive companies to develop—became public policy.

While the World's Fair had plenty of companies showing off new technologies, what ultimately drove the remaking of society along the lines imagined by those corporate interests was not the simple fact that those new inventions existed. Rather, the convergence of the public and private sectors around a plan for a vast transportation infrastructure for automobiles enabled a new way of life that generated economic expansion and large corporate profits.

When we look back at the Futurama, it is wrong to say that the exhibition, or Bel Geddes himself, correctly predicted a lot of what was to come. The suburban, auto-oriented future offered market opportunities for automotive companies, property developers, and consumer goods manufacturers—to name just a few. Their combined influence, paired with a brilliant marketing campaign, was enough to get political leaders to respond to their demands and direct significant resources into realizing their vision of the future. The corporations didn't *predict* a car-centric, consumerist future—they made it a reality.

But that vision, designed to give US consumers—or at least some of them—hope for the future, conveniently ignored the drawbacks. Highways tore through cities, displacing poor and often Black communities. Wider roads accommodated more vehicles, but the promised pedestrian infrastructure never materialized. Skyscrapers were erected in cities, but the green space was paved so people could park their vehicles. The use of cars exploded, but the radio signals to guide them without human drivers never made it beyond a few pilot programs.

More than eighty years later, we can see the folly in the grand plan laid out in the Futurama. We built communities that are located far from workplaces, retail centers, and key services, which often require people to drive long distances. For many residents, suburban neighborhoods are not idyllic communities, but places that breed loneliness as they are cut off from others.

Our dependence on automobiles causes us to waste long periods of time in traffic, which also brings the risk of a whole host of adverse health conditions. All those vehicles, the inefficient nature of suburban living, and the mass consumption of goods have significantly contributed to the greenhouse gas emissions that threaten the future of every being on the planet. And as we quickly cycled through low-quality goods, we also littered the lands and oceans with our trash. But it is not just the environment that has been affected.

The death toll of the automobile is astronomical. In the United States alone, 3.7 million people have been killed by motor vehicles since 1899.[1] That does not count the millions more who were injured, or all the people who died prematurely from air pollution spewing from tailpipes; nor all those who continue to die every day in cities and towns around the world because they are hit by a motor vehicle. Those details conveniently never made it into the Futurama. They would have spoiled the fantasy.

As the current climate crisis escalates and the contradictions of our real transportation system become too great to continue ignoring, there are growing calls for change. People are demanding better public transit, more infrastructure for bicycles, and communities that have the services they rely on within walking distance. But the distribution of power within the economy has shifted, and in the past several decades new industries have accumulated the power—and the capital—to unleash their own grand visions for the future. The modern tech industry is chief among them.

After restructuring how we communicate with one another, entertain ourselves, buy consumer goods, and far more, the companies that have prospered as the internet expanded to every corner of the globe are now setting their sights on the physical environment, with a particular focus on the transportation system. While they are called technology companies, what they mean by "tech" is a very narrow understanding of the concept. It refers only to the so-called high-tech industries that are on the cutting edge of technological development, seen most often in the digitization and automation of even more aspects of social and economic life.

The astronomical growth of the tech industry has made its investors and top executives billionaires many times over, and they want to use their newfound wealth to build a future centered around the technologies that they believe will solve society's problems, at least as they experience them. Over the past decade, some important industry players have turned their attention away from the digital realm to the streets we travel every day to lay out visions for how we should move in the future—visions that all too often continue to center around the automobile. But after a century of living in cities built for cars, we must be wary of embracing sweeping

4

masterplans that fail to properly consider the full effects of what elite proposals will likely mean for the rest of us.

The World's Fair helped renew New Yorkers' faith in the future when many people had lost hope that things could get better, and the tech industry has sought to do the same. As the neoliberal political system gave up on bold policies in favor of managing a worsening status quo, they left the door open to techno-utopians to fill the void. In the aftermath of the 2008 financial crisis, Silicon Valley was embraced as the driver of economic growth, and that included valorizing its key figures and buying into its big plans to remake the world—regardless of how poorly they were thought through.

Transportation was perceived to be ripe for disruption. Elon Musk graced the covers of major magazines and was profiled repeatedly as the entrepreneur who was going to "save the planet" with his sexy electric sportscars, before promising trains in vacuum tubes and a large-scale tunnel system to solve traffic congestion. But he was not the only one with big plans for mobility. Uber's chief executive Travis Kalanick had a measurable impact on how we get around after he introduced a taxi service hailed from a smartphone, and then used that success to build grander visions where drivers were automated and flying cars finally became a reality. Google also got in on the future transport hype as its co-founder, Sergey Brin, promised cities completely transformed by autonomously driven pods, and as those companies were praised and rewarded with venture capital, they inspired a whole host of other founders to dream up big ideas of their own and try to make them a reality.

However, just as the World's Fair showed only the positive side of the automotive future, the tech industry's visions also glossed over many problems, including the key question of whether they could ever be properly realized. As Musk received high praise, Tesla workers were suffering with high injury rates, while his green vehicles had to rely on a dirty mineral supply chain. Uber was embraced by tech workers and the journalists who gave it such good press, but in reality cities were swamped with new vehicles and Uber's driver workforce was exploited. Meanwhile, Google's self-driving team had internal problems, and as time passed it became clear that it placed far too much faith in the technology—a common theme not just in the present, but throughout the long history of the innovations chronicled in this book. Not only are visions of electric, hailed, autonomous, or even flying cars not new, but, rather than addressing the problems that have arisen from mass use of the automobile, tech's purported solutions serve only to entrench them.

In the coming chapters, I will make the case that we need a better transportation system and by extension better cities—but that Silicon Valley and its various global permutations will not deliver an equitable version of automobility simply by upgrading it with new technologies. Rather, improving our mobility systems requires going deeper to address the inherently political questions that the tech industry prefers to avoid about the way we build those systems in the first place. Technology alone cannot resolve the inequities of the existing transport system, especially when the visions in question are constrained by the elite perspectives of the people dreaming them up.

Before analyzing the solutions that tech executives and engineers are proposing for our cities, we first need to understand the context of their proposals. I start by digging into the history of automobility to illustrate how transportation systems—both in cities and beyond—were reconstructed through the twentieth century to make way for the automobile and how that change was not one that was demanded by the public, but rather was implemented against their wishes by capitalist interests who saw great profits in the future they sought to make reality. My focus is primarily on the United States, given that it is the country where automobility is most entrenched and whose model served as inspiration for cities and countries around the world. It is also where many (though not all) of the technological solutions to transport problems are emerging and being implemented, so we can see whether they are truly able to deliver the promised benefits.

Examining the history of transportation, however, only gets us part of the way to understanding the problems with the tech industry's proposals for the future. And so I then move on to outline the evolution of Silicon Valley and how it fused its faith in technology to neoliberal economics to hide its deep links to the US government and military. Its adherents' belief in the power of technology alone to transform any industry or system for the better, without considering the political and social implications, is the product of that techno-utopian ideology.

In the central chapters of the book I apply those histories to critically dissect some of the most prominent of tech's proposals for the future of transportation and cities. I cover electric vehicles, ride-hailing services, and self-driving cars; the Boring Company's tunnel system and Uber's vision for flying cars; along with the implications of micromobility services and the delivery robots increasingly staking a claim to the sidewalks. I outline the problems that all these ideas face in achieving mass adoption—assuming their technology can ever be perfected— but also how they are in fact unlikely to deliver the benefits that are often claimed. While I do refer to supply chains, logistics, and delivery, my focus is primarily on the transportation of people, not of goods.

My argument is not that we do not need a significant over- haul of the way transportation works, nor indeed that we do not need to reimagine how we approach urban planning. In recent years, there has been a lot more discussion about the need to challenge auto-oriented development in favor of prioritizing pedestrians, cyclists, and public transit to enable denser, greener, and more walkable communities. But progress is far too slow given the harms and inequities of the current system. Where changes do happen, it is not uncommon that they benefit only the wealthy while excluding the poor and the working class. This is untenable, and must change.

Finally, I outline what we should take away from the failings of the technological solutions to our urban crises, and lay out a vision for a more equitable future of transportation and of urban life. That vision is not anti-technology. But it recognizes that technology is not the primary driver in creating fairer and more equitable cities and transportation systems; that will require much deeper and more fundamental change to give people more power over the decisions that are made about their communities.

1

How the Automobile
Disrupted Mobility

Throughout much of the world, the automobile dominates. In the postwar era, especially in the West, cities sprawled with low-density housing, making it increasingly difficult to get anywhere without owning a vehicle of one's own. Now, after successive generations reinforcing that process, many people struggle to even imagine an alternative to the auto-oriented city. Owning a vehicle is not a choice, it is a necessity, and to suggest otherwise would be silly.

That perspective has been reinforced by glossy advertisements and entertainment that centers around the desirability of automobiles, all bolstered by sympathetic media coverage. Our auto-dominated cities seem natural. The car seemingly embodies our values, offering unparalleled speed and individual freedom. We are told our cities must be this way because this is the best way for them to be; because that is what people want. Why would we give that up for an unreliable or uncertain alternative?

Meanwhile, technology is positioned as having developed along a linear trajectory—the wheel all the way to the smartphone was part of a long march of innovation—but that perceived inevitability only comes after a process of disruptive and often violent change. The billionaires who profited from that innovation want us to believe that it is ultimately leading us to a utopian existence, perhaps even life in outer space or on Mars. But this is a sanitized retelling of history, constructed to serve the ends of the modern capitalist tech industry that wants us to believe there was no other path. Silicon Valley's dominance and the type of technological development it undertakes, its executives report, is the natural outcome of that linear progression. To question that idea is to question the very notion of progress itself.

Before computers and the internet, the automobile was the dominant technology that "disrupted" our society. It transformed the way we move around, but it also overturned the ways we live and work, and had a massive impact on the climate of our planet as one of the largest sources of carbon pollution. Looking through the rear-view mirror of history, it can seem like all these developments were predestined: the invention of the automobile led to engineers reconfiguring streets to privilege motor vehicles. The development of new manufacturing methods meant that cars were more affordable, and in time they were adopted en masse, with the result that while the city center was jammed with traffic, the suburbs expanded on the urban fringes. People moved there to get away from the city, hollowing out the urban core.

This pattern can be seen in the cities and towns of the United States, Canada, and parts of Europe in the years following World War II, but it certainly was not set in stone as soon as the first Model T was built in 1908. Such a technological determinism, one that positions the technology as the primary driver of the last century of urban development, ignores all the interests that were fighting over the future direction of streets, cities, and even countries. These interests had different visions for the role of the new automotive technology within the broader urban landscape. Groups of urban residents were worried about what the automobile was doing to their communities and the people who lived in them. They were concerned about the public good and wanted to maintain the collective health of their neighborhoods.

Powerful business interests, however, did not live in the affected communities, and they saw not only personal mobility benefits from the automobile but the opportunity to earn incredible profits by selling as many of them as possible. They would stop at nothing to achieve that goal. In such hands, the forward march of technology was also the direction of travel of capitalism.

This book looks at the future of this entwined and complex relationship. But before critiquing the tech industry's visions for the future of transportation, we need to understand how we got here and how the mobility problems they claim to be concerned about arose in the first place. That requires not just tracking how communities and the role of the automobile have evolved since the turn of the twentieth century but understanding the interests that were involved in those developments. It is only through acknowledging the role of powerful groups in commanding changes in the past that we can clearly see the present-day efforts of the tech industry to alter urban transportation as part of a much longer trend of elites remaking the city to serve their interests.

The city streets of the late nineteenth century and early twentieth century were nothing like those we use today. Pavement was rare, as the mixing of tar and stones was not patented until the early 1900s. Most streets were covered in dirt, cobbles, or gravel, and while they were still used to get around, they worked very differently. Streets were not the exclusive domain of the automobile, with colored lights at every intersection and parking spots lining many streets—indeed, there were few motor vehicles to speak of. Instead, the street was shared by horse-drawn carriages, streetcars, bicyclists, and pedestrians. People could walk in the street, linger for a conversation, or buy something from a vendor. It was even a space where children could play, especially on the side streets. They were a shared space where everyone moved at a relatively slow speed, compared to the present, and that allowed people to navigate their interactions despite all the different users on the same stretch of road. But urban life had already begun to change.

Walking was still the primary means of getting around, so that meant the places where people lived, shopped, and worked all had to be within close proximity of one another. But as people continued moving into cities, they were packed closely together, often in inadequate housing, and the lack of access to toilets and provision of sewer systems remained problems into the early twentieth century. Outside, many of the streets were narrow, while ineffective drainage contributed to the spread of waterborne illnesses. It did not help that horse manure and dead animals were a common sight.

By the 1890s, streetcars and bicycles were disrupting urban transport patterns and some aspects of city planning. Transport researchers John Falcocchio and Herbert Levinson wrote that every time a new transport technology has taken hold, it has tended to increase travel speeds, "and each time travel speed has increased, the amount of land used for urban growth has increased and population density has decreased."[1] We can see this in the present day with the automotive infrastructure and suburban landscapes that have been constructed over many decades. But the response to new transport technologies by governments and commercial interests helped to set cities on a path toward accommodating speed and, over time, expanding their boundaries.

Before the arrival of the streetcar, the railway, and the omnibus, the outskirts of cities were places for the wealthy, who reached their homes with private horse-drawn carriages. But collective transportation made it feasible to develop that land, creating communities centered around the stops on streetcar and train lines that freighted the growing number of commuters to and from their jobs. In larger urban areas such as New York City and London, the underground subway was also an option.

Given the concerns about overcrowded living conditions

in cities, expanding the urban footprint was attractive to reformers who wanted to address sanitation, overcrowding, and other issues, but also to streetcar operators and private construction interests who profited from building the new communities. Streetcars were run by private companies, and streetcar suburbs gave them reliable passengers. The suburbs of the time looked nothing like their modern counterparts since they did not need to make room for cars, but they began a trend that continued as new and faster transport options became available.

Bicycles had been around for much of the nineteenth century, but until the late 1880s they were primarily used by men, with women often restricted to using two-seater tandem or sociable bikes with a man. The popular penny-farthing bicycle had a large front tire that was directly pedaled by the rider, but it could be hard to control and was too high for the rider's legs to reach the ground. The invention of the safety bicycle with two tires of similar size and pedals connected to a chain drive—effectively the same style of bicycle in use today —led to a boom in bicycle use in the 1890s and made them accessible to virtually everyone. Women, in particular, gained a new sense of freedom from owning their own bicycles.

As bicycles surged in popularity, riders demanded road improvements to make cycling safer, faster, and more enjoyable. In 1904, a national road census found that only 7 percent of roads in the United States were covered in stone or gravel; the other 93 percent were dirt.[2] Bicyclists found common cause with motorists when the Ford Model T and other early automobiles came on the market. Even though those paved roads allowed automobiles to go much faster than a bicycle and eventually push the bicyclists, along with the other road users, off the street almost entirely, it was not clear how automobiles might transform mobility in their quest for supremacy.

In the cities of the early twentieth century, automobiles "gave their wealthy owners the freedom of a rapid, flexible and individual form of mobility, unencumbered by the collective regimentation of railway timetables and itineraries."[3] Carriages already provided a degree of flexibility and individuality, but the addition of the motor to replace horses gave them unparalleled mobility in comparison to the rest of the urban population. The automobile was not a mass product, but a luxury one, and the key luxury it provided—to go faster than anyone else on the road—was one that could only be realized while their numbers remained low. As social philosopher André Gorz explained, all train passengers traveled at the same speed, as did horse-drawn carriages and carts, but the arrival of the automobile was a notable break where "for the first time class differences were to be extended to speed and to the means of transportation."[4]

Gorz explained this by using the example of a seaside villa, which "is only desirable and useful insofar as the masses do not have one." There simply is not space for everyone to own their own piece of the coast, especially with access to the beach. Villas cannot be democratized through private, individual ownership; the only effective solution is "the collectivist one. And this solution is necessarily at war with the luxury of the private beach, which is a privilege that a small minority takes as their right at the expense of all."[5]

We have been taught not to see this as a problem with automobiles. Everyone can own a car, a truck, an SUV, or maybe one of each, and there will always be room for that private luxury. They will always provide speed and freedom, even as those promises have evaporated with the unending traffic congestion and longer commute times that result from everyone owning their own personal vehicles to get around. Even though these contradictions can be tough to recognize in the present, they were once undeniable. Indeed, they drove the creation of the physical world in which we live today. The late urbanist Peter Hall wrote that "at the end of the 1920s, it was still possible to see the car as a benign technology,"[6] in the sense that the environmental toll, the sprawling suburbs, and its later near-monopoly on mobility were not at all apparent at that time. But as more were sold, and their speeds rose, automobiles presented an irreconcilable challenge to urban residents.

Henry H. Bliss is a name few people might recognize today, but in 1899, it was plastered across the front pages of US newspapers. Bliss had stepped off a streetcar at the corner of West Seventy-Fifth Street and Central Park West in New York City and turned to help his companion step down. As he did so, a motor vehicle knocked him to the ground and ran over his head and body, crushing his skull and chest. He died of his injuries the next day, making him the first person ever recorded to have been killed by a motor vehicle in the United States.[7]

In 1900, there were an estimated 8,000 motor vehicles on US roads, but by 1920 that number was closer to 8 million.[8] The expansion of automobile ownership created congestion on urban streets, but growing the customer base was essential for automakers. Some capitalists "hoped that auto ownership would overcome class tensions by turning workers into 'property owners,' thus giving them a stake in capitalism."[9] By 1912, traffic counts in New York City registered more vehicles powered by internal combustion engines than drawn by horses, and the use of horses continued to drop as automobile sales grew.[10] A decade later, large US cities reported that only 3 to 6 percent of all vehicles still used horses.[11] Meanwhile, streetcar ridership started to fall as some passengers bought their own automobiles and increased congestion made streetcars less reliable. Since they were run by private companies, declining ridership and revenue affected their ability to keep operating.

Freeing horses from having to haul vehicles across cities for their entire lives was a positive development, and while streetcars were beginning to feel the consequences of the automobile's proliferation, they were still operating. The problem that became quickly apparent as automobile numbers grew was that their size and speed were a deadly combination that did not fit within existing norms of the street as a shared space where all users moved relatively slowly. Breaching those norms did not just affect people's ability to get around the city; it cost lives, and in particular the lives of children.

In 1920, the population of the United States was a little over 106 million, but the death toll from automobiles was staggering and on the rise. In the four years following Armistice Day in 1918, it was widely publicized that "more Americans were killed in automobile accidents than had died in battle in France," and through the 1920s more than 200,000 lives were lost to cars.[12] Urban residents and pedestrians were most impacted by this carnage, and the majority of the deaths were among children and, to a lesser degree, young women. While Bliss's death received attention, the growing death toll—especially because it was disproportionately affecting such innocent young people—became a sensation that may be difficult to comprehend by looking back with present-day values.

In the 1920s, a movement grew to draw attention to the mounting death toll and demand action. According to historian Peter Norton, mothers whose children were killed by automobiles were considered white- or gold-star mothers, like those who had lost children fighting in the war, and it did not stop there. Posters and cartoons depicted the automobile as a "modern Moloch" that demanded child sacrifice, while others showed mothers cradling dead children or kids asking after their fathers who would never return home. In cities around the United States, groups held events to draw attention to the lives being lost. Children were memorialized with funereal parades, public ceremonies, and landmarks honoring the dead. In 1919, a campaign by Detroit's safety council had the bells at City Hall, every school, and even a church and a fire station tolled eight times twice daily on every day that a life was lost to a motor vehicle. The names of the dead were also read out to school children by teachers or police officers.

These reactions to pedestrian deaths might seem unimaginable today, but that is because the mass death caused by automobiles had not yet been normalized. Thousands of people, especially children, were being mowed down; automobiles, not pedestrians, were the intruders. In the early twentieth century, pedestrians had a right to be on the roads if they chose to be. The street was still a public space and children were allowed to roam and play, as had been normal before the arrival of the automobile. There was a moral clarity in the recognition that when a driver killed a pedestrian in the 1920s, they were seen as a murderer. Today, if a pedestrian dies when venturing onto the street, people often respond by questioning why they had been there in the first place.

The campaigns to restrict automobile traffic came to a head in the early 1920s. Deaths increased by 20 percent in 1922–3 alone, and in the following years car sales stagnated, even dropping by 12 percent in 1924, which caused unsold cars to fill lots and some manufacturers to go out of business.[13] It seemed that not only was the gruesome messaging of safety campaigners suppressing sales, but within the prevailing streetscape and dense cities, there simply was not exponential demand for vehicles that had begun to get stuck in traffic and proved inconvenient to store since they could not simply be parked on the street. The promises of speed and freedom were being impinged upon. Trade journals started publishing articles about market saturation, suggesting that the market for automobiles was already tapped out. But the industry knew the real problem was not that there were not enough buyers; the problem was that the streets did not properly accommodate their product.

At the time, police and traffic engineers were still figuring out the best way to manage automobiles and ensure they could coexist with other street traffic. They were encroaching on space that pedestrians and other transport modes still had a stronger claim to. Many of those early actions were not so much about how to enable the swiftest, most efficient movement of automobiles as possible, but how to keep pedestrians safe and stop automobiles from killing people, including early experiments with traffic lights and directing how drivers should turn in intersections. But those actions conflicted with what automakers were selling their wealthy customers: if cities successfully limited motor vehicle speeds, the main selling point of the automobile would be negated.

Spurred by the growing body count, campaigns arose in the early 1920s with demands for exactly what the auto industry most feared. In Cincinnati, more than 10 percent of the city's residents signed petitions calling for an ordinance to require speed limiters—devices that set a top speed that vehicles could not exceed—on all motor vehicles in 1923.[14] As a result, the local government decided to hold a referendum. There was not a national highway system, so intercity trips were far less common than they are today, and it was not too difficult to ensure that most automobiles entering the city would be limited to a maximum speed of twenty-five miles per hour. Such a measure could have made streets safer, but it would have threatened future sales. Automotive interests knew it had to be stopped.

Between the mounting opposition to automobiles and the slowing sales, companies that profited from them formed organizations to push more effectively for visions of transportation and the city that served their bottom lines. This group included the automotive manufacturers, their dealers, and local auto clubs, but it also extended to other industries that had a stake in the automobile: oil companies whose product might be in greater demand if motor vehicle sales took off; suppliers of key materials such as steel and rubber; and the real estate and construction industries who built the roads and suburban communities.[15] Those interests only expanded as more industries became dependent on automobility and suburbanization for their sales growth.

The speed limiter referendum in Cincinnati was an early example of the influence that corporate players could have when they worked together to forward their business goals. The local newspapers became one of the primary allies of the auto industry in Cincinnati, imploring readers to vote against the proposal. This alliance was born out of the money automakers paid newspapers for advertising; it is a relationship that largely continues to this day. One of the organizations supported by the industry also printed posters calling for voters to reject the referendum, including one that referred to it as "The Great Wall of China against Progress."[16]

There are two ways of seeing the speed limiter referendum and other efforts of the time to make the automobile conform to the existing norms of the street. As suggested by the posters, any attempt to slow down or constrain the automobile, on the level of the individual vehicle or the entire automotive mode of transportation, could be seen as an opposition to progress—specifically, what the automotive companies defined progress to mean. Yet many residents saw it a different way. While campaigns to require speed limiters did not, for example, go as far as the Luddites' smashing of the mechanized looms in English textile mills, they expressed a similar desire: to limit technologies that made the lives of the poor and working-class majority worse while serving a small, wealthy segment of the population.

The automobile provided few benefits to the average city dweller, yet their children and family members were being killed in the street, their access was being revoked, and the benefits of this dangerous new technology were almost exclusively captured by the wealthiest residents—both in the sense of their personal ownership of automobiles, and in how they were often reaping profits from associated industries. Residents had no power to shut down the companies, so they used spectacle to draw attention to the violence of the automobile, which was effective for a time. Then they attempted to seek regulatory changes to constrain the automobile and remove some of the benefits of ownership. Even limiting cars to twenty-five miles per hour would have been a compromise, more than anything a straightforward attempt to save urban lives, but the growing power of the auto industry got in the way of achieving even that.

The industry claimed success in Cincinnati, but the fight did not end there. With automotive interests working together to reorganize streets and reconstruct communities to serve their profit margins, the coming years and decades saw more initiatives to build new highways and encourage people to leave cities, along with counter-movements to halt their progress.

By the early 1930s, pedestrians were increasingly being pushed off the streets as the boundaries of public space were redrawn, so that "just a few years later streets were more often treated as a half-public, half-private territory where the pursuit of efficiency could not justify state intrusion."[17] Nearly every state had passed a gas tax by 1925, and the increased revenue for road infrastructure paired with the auto industry's growing influence over traffic engineers led to a shift where they began to see their role as meeting the demand for street space rather than shaping how the streets were used.

That had the effect of granting more attention and infrastructure spending to automobiles even though they were the least efficient means of transporting people on urban roads. Technically, pedestrians could still use the street, but in practice their rights were curtailed long before laws changed because if they did not get out of the way, the speeding automobiles could take their lives or severely injure them. Parents, teachers, and police officers advised children to be more cautious around roads for their own safety because automobiles were not being properly kept in check.

Meanwhile, the old forms of transit were also under threat. The streetcars many pedestrians once relied upon were in jeopardy as they struggled with falling ridership and revenue. Whereas growing sums of money were being invested into road infrastructure made freely available to automobiles, streetcars were treated as businesses, not as public services, and the rare attempts to get voters to approve new transit funding did not receive enough support. Not only did street-car companies begin to fail, but automotive interests helped to accelerate their decline.

General Motors, Standard Oil of California, and Firestone Tire Company formed a bus company called National City Lines in the 1930s to buy up streetcar networks around the country, dismantle them, and replace them with buses. The consortium was convicted of conspiracy under US antitrust laws in 1949, but it was too late; by the late 1950s, nearly all the streetcars across the country had been dismantled. Gorz argued this was a key strategy to make people dependent on automobiles: as people began to realize that the key promise of speed could not be fulfilled by the motorcar, they considered going back to their old ways of mobility; so those options had to be removed.

It was not enough to just take away the alternatives, however; cities and transport networks had to be remade for the automobile, and that required major programs to expand road infrastructure and build suburban housing.

To make space for all the new motor vehicles, cities looked to controlled access highways, also known as freeways or motorways, as the answer. By limiting access, highways were presented as a means to reduce pedestrian injures, while allowing vehicles to move at higher speeds. Highway engineers also promised they were going to solve the growing problems of congestion and vehicle crashes.

Given that most trips were still within the boundaries of the greater urban area, not between different cities, the priorities determining freeway development were quite different than those of the later networks to connect the country. Cities were the primary forces behind urban freeways, not the state or federal governments, so they were conceived to serve urban residents and make it easier for them to get from one part of the city to another. Those early freeways were "designed to accommodate short intraurban trips, to disperse traffic widely across a dense network of roadways, and to increase the speed of transit vehicles as well as autos, all while weaving through the urban fabric with the least possible disruption."[18]

They were meant to fit into the city, not to be rings on their outskirts, and proposals usually included rail lines, bus lanes, and truck lanes, recognizing the multimodality of the city. Examples of this kind of highway planning include Detroit's 1924 superhighway plan that combined 225 miles of freeways with a rail rapid-transit system, and Los Angeles's 1939 freeway plan that combined regional rail with a "dense grid pattern as opposed to a sparse ring-radial system in order to spread traffic across the city."[19] These urban freeways were not only seen as a way to alleviate congestion, but also to promote urban growth through a land use component whose goal was to reduce suburbanization by keeping people within cities.

This vision of freeways still favored automobiles and Detroit automakers saw them as a way to increase automobile use in cities, but they were in many ways superior to the highways that ended up getting built later. Some of these plans were implemented across the United States, but they ultimately got supplanted by a different vision for a very important reason: cities did not have the money to build them.

After the stock market crash in 1929, the Great Depression persisted throughout the 1930s. Among its many impacts, local governments were starved of funds, meaning many cities could not afford to build freeways on their own. At the same time, the revenue from gas taxes was flowing to state and federal governments, which had different priorities. States were far more focused on rural highways than urban highways, and "with state money came state control," so freeways were redesigned to focus on state goals.[20]

That meant that instead of embracing multimodal transportation and facilitating trips within the city, freeways were instead reconceptualized to connect rural communities and facilitate intercity transportation. With suburbanization not then seen in the negative light it has taken on over time, state governments were not interested in trying to keep socioeconomic activity concentrated in the cities. Rather, they pursued an intentional development program positioned "as a strategy for allowing people in congested cities to escape to areas where they could enjoy higher quality housing, healthier lifestyles, and parks and open space."[21] This vision was also embraced by the federal government.

After World War II, the automotive lobby and President Dwight D. Eisenhower's administration were coalescing around a major infrastructure program to build the national highway network the country was lacking. Eisenhower "believed that he had won the war on the German Autobahnen" and that freeways were essential for the national defense of the United States, especially as it was entering into its decades-long Cold War with the Soviet Union.[22]

That was not the only reason the government was interested in the program, however. General Lucius D. Clay, whom Eisenhower had appointed to draw up a proposal for the national highway system in 1954, described why the system was needed: "It was evident we needed better highways. We needed them for safety, to accommodate more automobiles. We needed them for defense purposes, if that should ever be necessary. And we needed them for the economy. Not just as a public works measure, but for future growth."[23] In service of those goals, the Federal-Aid Highway Act of 1956 proposed an initial investment of $25 billion to construct 41,000 miles of highways across the country, making it the largest public works projects in the country, if not the world.

It may seem difficult to imagine the present-day US government embarking on such an ambitious public venture, but at the time the massive public works programs of the New Deal were recent history and political leaders still saw a role for the government to make the necessary investments in public infrastructure to promote economic growth, general prosperity, and higher living standards. Earlier in his career, General Clay had even spent four years as part of the US Army Corps of Engineers overseeing the construction of New Deal public works.

The amount of work necessary to construct all the roads and highways involved in the Interstate Highway System, not to mention the new suburban communities they allowed developers to build, created an economic boom and aligned even more interests with the auto industry, including "business organizations, Keynesian economists, the U.S. Department of Agriculture, the U.S. Department of the Interior, public utilities, local development and planning interests, and labor groups."[24] Once construction began, the Interstate project helped halt the US economy's slide into recession in the mid-1950s, and the economic benefits continued to be reaped through the 1960s.

The huge scale of the program meant there were debates about how the system should be funded and designed. The first attempt to pass the bill through Congress failed in 1955 because Democrats were not willing to fund it through general revenue. Instead, the revised proposal sought to pay for it through a series of taxes on motor vehicles, including on fuel, tires, and heavy vehicles. This angered part of the auto industry's coalition.

Automakers were behind the proposal either way—they knew the highway system would promote automobile sales and saw the benefits of gas taxes in the 1920s—but "the rubber, petroleum, trucking, and intercity bus industries" opposed the tax increases.[25] When the Federal-Aid Highway Act was finally passed in 1956, it established the Highway Trust Fund that used the dedicated tax revenue to pay for highway construction, and most of the funds came from taxes on gas and diesel. After the brief fight was over, the industries that initially opposed the additional taxes became major supporters (and beneficiaries) of highway construction. In April 1972, an article in the *New York Times* declared that "since World War II, few special interests have been so spectacularly successful, few pressure groups have had such a secure half nelson on Government expenditures, as the collection of businesses and officials that make up the highway lobby."[26]

With funding out of the way, planners and lawmakers then had to figure out where these new highways were to be built. Unlike the urban freeways of the 1920s and 1930s that were designed by cities to better balance the interests of urban residents and the auto industry, the Interstate was designed to serve the needs of the federal government and the powerful interests that had its ear.

One of the consequences of using taxes on motor vehicles to fund the highways was that planners felt little need to consider other modes, so multimodality was dropped. The government also wanted to minimize the mileage of the system, so instead of dispersing traffic over networks of roads as the urban highways had proposed, the Interstate "concentrated traffic on relatively few, high-speed, high-capacity freeways."[27]

This was not an issue on the intercity sections through rural parts of the country, but when the program was expanded to include expressways through cities, it became a major problem. The system's urban routes were drawn up in just eight months with little local input over what they looked like or how they would affect existing communities. Even General Clay, who was not involved after putting together his initial plan in 1955, later acknowledged that the highway segments cutting through cities were not popular and had vastly increased the cost of the system. They were not in his original plan.

However, the problems created by the urban expressways cannot just be attributed to neglect. Influential planners such as Robert Moses in New York City and Harland Bartholomew in St. Louis pushed for highway plans that extended into the very heart of US cities.[28] Not only were these highways more convenient for suburban residents, but they allowed the planners to use them to destroy Black neighborhoods by removing "blighted" areas, which became a major focus of the urban renewal agenda that had already begun demolishing poor and minority neighborhoods to concentrate their residents in isolated public housing projects. In just one example of how racism was built into the physical environment of major cities, Moses ordered the overpass bridges on the Southern State Parkway to be low enough so that buses could not drive under them, thus ensuring that poor and Black bus riders could not reach Jones Beach.

The highway construction boom slowed by the end of the 1960s as costs rose faster than inflation, but their construction had also created a new coalition to challenge them: environmental activists, civil rights groups, the consumer movement, and urban residents. The most prominent figure to come out of this movement was none other than activist and author Jane Jacobs. From the late 1950s through the 1960s, Jacobs was a leader in the campaign against Moses's urban renewal strategy—in part because of how it affected her neighborhood of Greenwich Village—and his planned Lower Manhattan Expressway that would have cut through Manhattan to connect the Manhattan Bridge and the Williamsburg Bridge to the Holland Tunnel. But she was also not alone; similar campaigns against urban highways were occurring across the United States in the 1960s.

Jacobs's seminal critique of modernist urban planning in *The Death and Life of Great American Cities*, published in 1961, outlined the importance of the diversity of urban communities and argued against the effort to encourage more people to move to suburbs on the urban fringe. Yet, as sociologist Sharon Zukin has explained, Jacobs directed her ire at urban planners, not at the forces of capital that were really driving the reconstruction of the American city to suit their interests. As Zukin put it, planners are "a relatively powerless group compared to developers who build, and banks and insurance companies who finance the building that rips out a city's heart."[29] Jacobs supported efforts to "unslum" urban communities and the very aesthetic she prized of "small blocks, cobblestone streets, mixed-uses, local character" has been adopted as "the gentrifiers' ideal."[30] Greenwich Village may have been maintained for people like Jacobs, but the failure of campaigns against urban highways to contend with larger economic forces did not stop the suburban trend, and eventually caused the working class to be forced out of downtown neighborhoods by rising prices, robbing them of the very cultural diversity Jacobs sought to preserve. While Jacobs's campaign in New York City was successful, most of the highways proposed elsewhere in the United States were built as planned.

Around the same time as people were trying to stifle highway projects, Ralph Nader was also gaining attention as a consumer advocate with a focus on the automobile. In his 1965 book *Unsafe at Any Speed*, Nader exposed the automotive industry's disregard for safety, which included ignoring clear safety hazards, investing more in vehicle styling than safety features, and efforts to blame drivers for harms that could have been avoided through better practices on the part of the automakers.

Nader's book, paired with the escalating number of road deaths in the 1960s, finally forced the federal and state governments to address the automotive safety crisis. Every state but New Hampshire implemented seatbelt laws, and the federal government passed the National Traffic and Motor Vehicle Safety Act in 1966 to establish new safety regulations and monitoring for roads and motor vehicles. There is no question that Nader's intervention saved countless lives over the years by, at least for a time, shaming industry and government into making automobiles safer. Yet, once again, his and his followers' work did not challenge the economic forces driving the mass adoption of automobiles. It is one thing to make cars and trucks safer, but it is quite another to reduce automobile usage altogether and eliminate the risks they pose in the first place.

These movements successfully defeated freeways, won new environmental protections, and established new safety standards, but they failed to undo the much deeper legal and regulatory structures that were promoting the exodus to the suburbs, automotive supremacy, and the gentrification of cities to serve capital. We can build more livable and sustainable communities that address those problems, but dismantling the regime that created them requires us to understand how it got this way in the first place.

Over the course of the past century, state policy has been essential to the remaking of cities for the automobile. One of the most important of those incentives was the mortgage insurance provided by the Federal Housing Administration (FHA), which gave many Americans access to cheap mortgages. Established in 1934 as part of the New Deal, the agency insured long-term mortgages provided by private lenders for the construction and sale of homes, and there was a rapid uptake.

> In 1934 more than 70 percent of the nation's commercial banks had FHA insurance plans. By 1959, FHA mortgage insurance had helped three out of every five American families to purchase a home and helped to repair or improve 22 million properties.[31]

Given how important mortgage insurance was to facilitating homeownership, the FHA had a lot of influence over the standards for housing construction, and since the agency was largely run by people from the real estate and banking industries, those standards were designed to serve their interests. The FHA's guidelines promoted suburban, car-oriented development over urban, transit-oriented construction, but beyond that they enabled a practice called "redlining" that gave favorable status to white communities and effectively barred Black communities from the program.

This had the effect of ensuring that Black people had a much more difficult time accessing mortgages and, by extension, homeownership. As white people fled the cities for their new homes in the suburbs, Black people were unable to make the same journey and urban services deteriorated as their tax basis left. Since it was harder for Black residents to buy homes, they also did not share in the wealth that came with rising property values throughout the twentieth century, further cementing the gap between white and Black Americans.

However, the FHA's standards were not the only initiative taken by various levels of government to promote a car-oriented society. Zoning policies that were originally embraced because they were perceived to be good for business homogenized different areas of cities, regulated the built environment as a means of excluding undesirable people from certain neighborhoods, and were ultimately justified in the name of increasing property values. They had the effect of breaking the city up into distinct zones designed for specific uses, such as separating residential neighborhoods from where people worked and where they engaged in leisure activities. In pulling apart aspects of urban life that were once integrated, the city was sanitized. It became difficult to get anywhere without a car, and a side effect of that was the severing of social and community bonds that were much more common before the entrenchment of suburban living.

But there is far more to it than that. Roads and freeways were, in part, constructed with gas taxes paid by motorists, but maintenance is also required on every road and highway that gets built. The Interstate is estimated to have cost over $500 billion in 2016 dollars,[32] but that does not include the ongoing cost of maintaining all those highways. Meanwhile, only 11 percent of the cost of maintenance on local roads has been estimated to be covered by motorists, while the other 89 percent is covered by general tax revenue, which amounts to a large subsidy for drivers that comes to half a trillion dollars every thirteen years.[33]

All the free parking that abounds in cities constitutes another major taxpayer-funded benefit amounting to between $148 billion and $423 billion in 2019 dollars, and up to 96 percent of it is paid from general revenue, not by motorists.[34] Parking also has significant implications for cities themselves as the edges of streets were handed over to parked vehicles, while housing and businesses were leveled to make room for large paved areas where people can leave their vehicles. But beyond roads and parking, there are countless ways the legal system subsidizes the use of automobiles.

Law professor Gregory Shill outlined many of the legal structures that uphold automotive supremacy, including "traffic regulation, land use law, criminal law, torts, insurance law, environmental law, vehicle safety rules, and even tax law, all of which provide incentives to cooperate with the dominant transport mode and punishment for those who defect."[35] These are ways that the legal system has been designed, over the course of many decades, to privilege drivers above everyone else, and they have created a transportation system that is not only a danger to everyone who uses the road, but which promotes a set of values that makes this danger difficult to address.

Around the world, an estimated 1.3 million people are killed every year in road traffic crashes—that is, more than 3,500 people every single day. Among those killed, pedestrians, cyclists, and motorcycle riders are at far greater risk than car drivers, and motor vehicles remain the leading cause of death of people aged five to twenty-nine years old.[36] Cars, trucks, and SUVs present a deadly obstacle for people trying to get to work, pick up food, or simply visit a friend or family member. Ninety-three percent of those deaths take place in low- and middle-income countries, despite having only 60 percent of the world's vehicles, but that does not make it solely a problem for the Global South.

In 2020, 38,680 people were killed by automobiles on US roads, an increase of 7.2 percent from 2019.[37] Yet that is not the full picture. There are more than a hundred severe injuries for every person killed in a vehicle crash, and the air pollution from the hundreds of millions of vehicles in the United States is responsible for a further 53,000 annual deaths.[38]

While driver deaths have generally been declining for two decades, pedestrian and bicyclist deaths have been increasing to such a degree that the pedestrian death toll in 2018 reached its highest level since 1990. Even though vehicles are increasingly filled with new technologies such as lane-keeping systems and emergency braking, they are not making streets safer for pedestrians. This is, in part, because over that time automakers have been promoting large trucks and SUVs that not only make them more money, but are heavier, taller, and have broader front ends that are two to three times more likely to kill pedestrians.[39] And, like in the 1920s, those deaths fall disproportionately among certain groups.

The old, the poor, and people of color are more likely to be killed by automobiles than other road users, and living in an area of concentrated poverty places one at greater risk of dying in a crash. But children and youth are still incredibly vulnerable. Even as parents have become concerned about kidnappers and pedophiles targeting their children and the number of kids walking to school has plummeted, the biggest threat to their lives is actually the very vehicles that are perceived to be keeping them safe.

More young people die from vehicle crashes than are killed with guns in the United States, yet while guns get ample media attention and there is a robust movement to bring in new regulations to try to reduce those deaths, there is comparatively little attention paid to vehicle deaths because they have been normalized. In 2016, Janette Sadik-Khan, a former commissioner of the New York City Department of Transportation, wrote, "Transportation is one of the few professions where 33,000 people can lose their lives in one year and no one in a position of responsibility is in danger of losing his or her job."[40] Sadly, the numbers have since gotten worse.

In the early twentieth century, traffic deaths might have been cause for protest. But after a century, our values have changed to make us less concerned about the other people in our communities and more focused on what is best for us as individuals. In 2019, researchers in Australia found that 55 percent of non-cyclists perceived cyclists as "less than human,"[41] which justified the aggressive actions taken by drivers when they encounter cyclists on the road.

Even as the automobile was promoted as the pinnacle of individual freedom, the reality was that congestion had negated the supposed benefits of mass car ownership. In this way, Gorz called it "the paradoxical example of a luxury object that has been devalued by its own spread"—the more cars there were, the less attractive it was to buy one—but "this practical devaluation has not yet been followed by an ideological devaluation."[42] While the supposed benefits of owning a car were curtailed as commutes kept getting longer due to sprawling suburbs and heavier traffic, people still believed in the individualist benefits it provided.

Gorz's observation is connected to sociologist John Urry's claim that the automobile was the "'iron cage' of modernity" in both a literal sense due to how it enclosed the driver, turning people into "anonymized flows of faceless ghostly machines," but also because of how it constrained people "to live their lives in spatially stretched and time-compressed ways."[43] The truth was that, far from offering individual freedom, the automobile made drivers incredibly dependent on a whole host of commercial interests.

> Unlike the horse rider, the wagon driver, or the cyclist, the motorist was going to depend for the fuel supply, as well as for the smallest kind of repair, on dealers and specialists in engines, lubrication, and ignition, and on the interchangeability of parts. Unlike all previous owners of a means of locomotion, the motorist's relationship to his or her vehicle was to be that of user and consumer—and not owner and master. This vehicle, in other words, would oblige the owner to consume and use a host of commercial services and industrial products that could only be provided by some third party. The apparent independence of the automobile owner was only concealing the actual radical dependency.[44]

The geographic expansion of cities to make room for cars, the construction of auto-oriented suburbs, and the dismantling of public and rail transport only increased that dependency, even as it was sold to the automotive consumer as individual freedom. Once that dependency was established and cemented, all the interests centered around the automobile were able to reap their profits at the expense not just of the driver but the whole of society. Meanwhile, the damage caused by all those vehicles—in maimed bodies, atomized communities, and a defiled environment—was downplayed through changing social norms and a compliant media that rarely drew attention to that array of problems so as not to risk losing large sums of advertising revenue from automotive interests.

With the reconstruction of the self as an individual with their own vehicle and self-contained home whose power was exerted not through collective action but individual consumption, the means to push back against the unending traffic and the dangers of road travel were limited. With everyone owning their own vehicle, if not more than one, "the roads become so jammed that driving becomes an experience of frustration, not liberation and individuality," and the roads themselves "become battlegrounds for limited space."[45] The individual response creates a circular pattern that not only makes those problems worse but results in more consumption that benefits automotive interests.

> To secure individual advantage in the Darwinian struggle for space, some drivers up the ante by buying large, powerful, military-like sport-utility vehicles, lording it over the lower species of the road in an aggressive grandeur that only makes driving more competitive and dangerous.[46]

As vehicles get larger, roads get more dangerous, the risk for pedestrians grows, and the harm to the climate, our health, and the communities we live in accelerates. There is a growing recognition that something needs to change, as even the increase in the size of automobiles has once again failed to solve the contradictions that are built into a transportation system where everyone requires their own personal vehicle. For some, the response has been to return to the city and to promote walkability, a greater use of bicycles, and improved public transit systems, but the financialization of the housing market has caused urban rents and home prices to soar. Some people in the tech industry take this view, but others are not ready to give up on the automobile or accept the inherent spatial constraints of urban areas that make mass automobile use unworkable.

The history of automobility is hardly a natural progression. Its present-day dominance of transportation systems in North America, Australia, parts of Europe, and increasingly in parts of the Global South is the product of a concerted effort by invested interests to completely overhaul the way we live and get around to serve their bottom lines. Instead of living within close proximity of our workplaces and the services we rely on, everything has been spread out so that we have to buy an automobile, insure it, get frequent maintenance, fill it up with fuel, and waste a growing amount of our time in traffic.

There were opportunities to take a different path. Had the automobile been more successfully restricted in the 1920s, we would likely live far more urban lives that are less dependent on driving everywhere. Even a different outcome in the 1970s could have limited further suburban growth, as was the case in some parts of Europe. But instead, powerful interests won out and got the support of the state to subsidize and entrench their vision for the future.

We can observe the impact that the dominant interests of the twentieth century have had on our lives, our communities, and the planet—and there is a lot that is not to like. However, the twenty-first century has a new set of powerful interests born out of the commercialization of the internet, and after amassing great fortunes of their own, they too want to make us dependent on their products, not just when we browse the web but when we are out in our communities too.

Despite promises that their visions for transportation and the city will serve everyone, it is already becoming clear that those claims are nothing more than marketing material meant to build public support for products that will ultimately serve their companies, their shareholders, and themselves. It is a repetition of how automakers and real estate companies successfully used advertising and the media to convince us to accept our dependence on their industries. We now risk a further deployment of luxury mobility into an already broken transportation system by industry leaders who downplay political problems in favor of technological solutions that fail to grapple with the complexity of the situations into which they are intervening. We cannot allow them to determine our future.

2

Understanding the Silicon Valley Worldview

On August 13, 1980, Apple Computer placed an ad in the *Wall Street Journal* that compared the personal computer to the automobile. It was the first in a three-part series where co-founder Steve Jobs ostensibly set out to explain "the personal computer, and the effects it will have on society," but it might be better seen as one fragment of a much larger attempt to set the narrative of this new technology.

Jobs and other key figures in Silicon Valley's computing industry had high hopes for the kind of society personal computers might usher in, and they wanted as many people as possible—especially the influential and wealthy readers of the *Wall Street Journal*—to buy into their vision.

The ad copy, framed as an interview with Jobs, asked readers to:

> Think of the large computers (the mainframes and the minis) as the passenger train and the Apple personal computer as the Volkswagen. The Volkswagen isn't as fast or as comfortable as the passenger train. But the VW owners can go where they want, when they want and with whom they want. The VW owners have personal control of the machine.

In these few sentences, Jobs linked the personal computer to the most important ideological aspect of the automobile: its association with individual freedom. The personal computer was being positioned as a device that "offers its power to the *individual*." In the same way that the automobile could take the driver anywhere they wanted to go, the personal computer would put its "electronic intelligence" at the disposal of its individual owner to help them "deal with the complexities of modern society." These new machines were "tools, not toys," and would "do as much for the individual as the big computers did for the corporation in the 60s and 70s."

In focusing on the personal computer as something that was used for work, Jobs was also alluding to ideas about a less bureaucratic form of organization that revolved around the entrepreneurial spirit of the individual instead of the hierarchy of the corporation. This was not an idea that originated with Jobs, but one that had been gaining ground for nearly two decades. As we seek to understand the impact that the tech industry is having on our transportation systems, its history— and how it has been recast through a particular lens to suit its dominant companies—provides insight into the market-oriented worldview and techno-solutionist approach to problem-solving that it seeks to apply beyond the digital realm.

The story that Silicon Valley likes to tell about itself is one that comes out of the ideological foundations that were being laid through the 1970s and 1980s. It lauds the entrepreneurialism of the individual—one who drops out of college, starts a company in their garage, and goes on to create a multibillion-dollar empire or sell their company to one of the private monopolies that have become the dominant institutions of the industry. In this telling of the history of California's tech industry, which has come to shape other tech hubs around the world that seek to emulate its success, the supposed innovation that emerged from the San Francisco Bay Area is the product of the free market: the founders with their bold visions, the venture capitalists who identify promising start-ups, and the dominant companies whose size comes from providing products that transform our lives for the better—certainly not in service of their own interests.

There is no doubt that this is an attractive story. It fits perfectly within the neoliberal economic narratives that have come to dominate since the 1970s, when governments began slashing tax rates, privatizing public services, and deregulating the economy with the promise that unleashing the free market would leave us all better off. In the same way that the neoliberal miracle has failed to materialize outside the upper echelons of the income distribution, the story that the billionaires of Silicon Valley and those who hope to follow in their footsteps tell us about the foundations of their industry's success purposefully leaves out where their ideas came from and the role of government in making it all possible.

Rather than being the scrappy underdog whose fortunes exploded thanks to the entrepreneurialism of tech's visionary founders, San Francisco has played a central role in the United States' efforts to keep its technological edge over its geopolitical foes for nearly a century. As technology historian Margaret O'Mara described:

> The whole enterprise rested on a foundation of massive government investment during and after World War II, from space-age defense contracts to university research grants to public schools and roads and tax regimes. Silicon Valley hasn't been a sideshow to the main thrust of modern American history. It has been right at the center, all along.[1]

Due to the public funds that flowed into the Bay Area to make it the research hub that modern Silicon Valley companies would profit from, O'Mara called the US government "the Valley's first, and perhaps its greatest, venture capitalist"[2] —a position it held for decades.

During World War II, the civilian and military arms of the US government spent immense amounts of money to develop new military and communications technologies to keep up with and defeat Nazi Germany. Some of that money was doled out to defense contractors, but a lot of it went to universities to train the researchers and build the facilities that undertook the necessary work to keep the US military ahead of its adversaries. Among the biggest beneficiaries of that government spending were the Massachusetts Institute of Technology (MIT) and Stanford University, which made Route 128 in Boston—a twenty-seven-mile stretch of highway that became home to a cluster of technology firms—and Silicon Valley the country's electronics hubs. Even after the war ended, state funding ensured the Bay Area continued to be one of the leading research centers in the United States because it had already developed the infrastructure and cultivated the talent that the government needed as it headed into the Cold War.

Military spending dipped after the end of World War II, bringing down research spending with it, but that did not last for long. In 1957, the Soviet Union successfully launched the Sputnik 1 satellite, and by the early 1960s the United States had sent tens of thousands of troops to Vietnam in its attempt to stop communist forces from controlling the country. For the US government, it was clear that the Soviet Union was not only an ideological rival, but a technological and military one. Funding for defense research was scaled up to help with the war effort and President Eisenhower created the Advanced Research Projects Agency (ARPA) in 1958 to challenge the Soviet Union's technological prowess outside the military sphere, directing a new wave of public funds for basic research to private contractors and university research labs.

The Bay Area was once again a major beneficiary of federal spending on research and development as local defense and electronics companies, along with University of California, Berkeley and Stanford University, received new government contracts. While MIT had a history of keeping close ties with business and industry, of encouraging its faculty to consult in the private sector, and even of spinning off start-ups out of the university, Stanford took its industry partnerships even further. That included graduate courses for engineers at local electronics companies that could be taken through televised instruction without leaving work. Thirty-two companies were on board by 1961.[3]

A decade earlier, it had also established the Stanford Industrial Park, where prominent companies such as General Electric, Eastman Kodak, and Hewlett-Packard set up research centers with easy access to students and faculty, while bringing in revenue for the university. The industrial park removed the barrier between basic research and corporate research, blending the two in a preview of the important role that commercialization of public research would play as personal computers and later the internet became defining technologies fueling the growth of the modern tech companies.

The cooperation between the university and the corporate sector could also be seen as a reflection of the conservative culture that was present in the Valley through the 1960s. Major employers in the Bay Area high-tech industry were vehemently anti-union and, despite the key role women had played in early computation and programing, white men took over and ensured future corporate leaders would be just like them. The entrepreneurs they funded tended to have a number of common traits, including "engineering degrees from certain programs, some service in the military, conservative in their bearing and their politics, and utterly consumed and fascinated by technical challenges."[4]

By the mid-1960s, the industry was facing criticism over its relationship with the military as the counterculture gained traction and opposition to the Vietnam War grew. Reflecting that conservativism, Robert Noyce, who co-founded Fairchild Semiconductor and Intel, saw the hippies as opponents of technology and, indeed, of progress itself. Tom Wolfe described this all-too-familiar narrative in a 1983 profile of Noyce for *Esquire*. "They wanted to destroy the new machines ... They wanted to call off the future," he wrote of Noyce's stance on *the youth*. "If you wanted to talk about the creators of the future—well, here they were! Here in the Silicon Valley!"⁵ Yet as young people voiced criticism of corporate hierarchies and decisions made by their government, some of their number became key to the next stage of the industry's corporate evolution.

The counterculture was one of many oppositional move- ments of the 1960s that influenced the people who would go on to shape the ideology of the modern tech industry, but it was by far the most consequential. Historian Fred Turner has explained that the 1960s saw the rise of the New Left and the New Communalists, but the two movements had very differ- ent ideas about how to change the world.

The New Left was associated with the Civil Rights Movement, the anti-war protests, and the student protests of the Free Speech Movement that gripped college campuses in the mid-1960s. Those who participated in it generally believed that political struggle was essential to tear down the oppressive structures of contemporary capitalist society and build a better world. But the communalists saw a dif- ferent route to address similar problems. Instead of turning "outward, toward political action, this wing turned inward, toward questions of consciousness and interpersonal inti- macy, and toward small-scale tools such as LSD or rock music as ways to enhance both."⁶ This is not to say that the New Left did not engage in these aspects of the counterculture, but that the key difference was in the groups' stance on political engagement.

While political action was central to the New Left, the com- munalists were hostile to the notion of protest or engagement with the political system. Their response to the social and political challenges of the sixties was to abandon politics alto- gether and seek out individualized solutions, even going so far as to retreat from society and build their own communities modeled on how they believed their ideal world should work.

But their communes displayed the fundamental problems with their approach, and those issues would be echoed in the institutions that were inspired by them.

In 1967, former Stanford biology student and US Army soldier Stewart Brand set up the *Whole Earth Catalog* with his wife, Lois Jennings. The *Catalog* brought together Brand's countercultural, scientific, and academic interests in the pursuit of enhancing individual freedom and went on to create an influential nexus of ideas and personalities that inspired the worldview of Silicon Valley. The inside cover of every issue contained a statement that set out the Promethean ideology behind the worldview Brand was creating in bringing together his various interests. It read:

> We are as gods and might as well get good at it. So far, remotely done power and glory—as via government, big business, formal education, church—has succeeded to the point where gross defects obscure actual gains. In response to this dilemma and to these gains a realm of intimate, personal power is developing— power of the individual to conduct his own education, find his own inspiration, shape his own environment, and share his adventure with whoever is interested. Tools that aid this process are sought and promoted by the WHOLE EARTH CATALOG.

There is a clear line between Brand's thinking in the *Catalog* and how Jobs was promoting the personal computer thirteen years later. Brand positioned individuals as being akin to gods and promised the *Catalog* would equip them with the tools they needed to wield their power toward whatever end they saw fit, and some of those tools were small-scale technologies designed to serve individuals instead of major corporations. The magazine was designed as the place where "the technological and intellectual output of industry and high science met the Eastern religion, acid mysticism, and communal social theory of the back-to-the-land movement."[7]

In bringing these communities together, the magazine not only appealed to the communalists dreaming of or living on communes, but also to researchers at university labs and defense contractors who had embraced a more project-based work environment that was seen as a challenge to the traditional hierarchical organization. The Vietnam War made it difficult to draw positive lessons from the military, so the *Catalog* rebranded the organizational form as an extension of the counterculture, setting the stage for its members' integration into the corporate world.

The communes were gripped with problems that saw them fail by the early to mid-1970s. Turner ascribed this not only to the lack of political organization, but also to the backward social norms that carried over from the society they purported to want to escape. While the New Left was making room for women in organizational leadership (though it was far from perfect), "many New Communalists recreated the conservative gender, class, and race relations of cold war America."[8] The communalists were "young, white, highly mobile hippies" with good educations and social privilege, and that carried over to the *Catalog*, whose pages made little room for people of color or the poor.

Even though the *Catalog* printed its last issue in 1971, a range of publications and events were built around Whole Earth, with Brand himself as the figure bringing together different ideas and individuals. As the communes collapsed and the communalists started thinking about their futures, Whole Earth's focus shifted from reading material to consumer goods. It embraced the notion that changing the world did not require one to retreat from the structures they opposed, but could be achieved by entering the corporate world and changing it from the inside. As Turner put it, the new world envisioned by Whole Earth and its ideological ancestors would allow "individuals and corporations to negotiate with one another from positions of equality."[9] The relative power of both those players was ignored—no unions were necessary, nor was the size of corporations considered, because once the hierarchy was flattened and new technologies empowered the individual, they would have the power to change the world. The naïveté is astounding, and some critics took notice.

Critical scholars Richard Barbrook and Andy Cameron dubbed the ideology that grew out of this movement, especially as it found common cause with the neoliberal policies of the 1980s, the "Californian Ideology." The way of thinking it embodied "simultaneously reflects the disciplines of market economics and the freedoms of hippie artisanship. This bizarre hybrid is only made possible through a nearly universal belief in technological determinism."[10] The counterculture's aversion to politics was central to the Californian Ideology. Its adherents believed social change would happen by engaging in the market and trusting in the process of technological development to empower not only the individual, but also the wider world. The path to a better world was no longer in retreating from society or simply engaging with corporate America, but faith was also put in technology itself as the means to address social and economic challenges.

Steve Jobs's narrative about the personal computer can be seen as a reflection of the Californian Ideology. By downplaying the role of the state in developing the foundational companies and institutions of Silicon Valley in the first place, Jobs made it seem as though the technologies emerging from the Valley and the economic activity that came along with it were the product of technological progress and its commercialization by private companies. However, this ignored the continued role that government played in fueling the Bay Area's economic miracle.

By the late 1970s, the Soviet threat had waned, but the growth of Japan's electronics industry presented a new challenge for the Bay Area's high-tech companies. Silicon Valley's semiconductor industry had expanded through the 1970s and adopted a strategy of eschewing custom chips in favor of a capital-intensive effort to standardize microprocessors and compete on cost, which required it to consolidate into a few large companies instead of operating as competing start-ups. Yet while innovation slowed in California, the same was not true in Japan, where "a distinctive combination of domestic policies and institutions that promoted investment and innovation in high-volume manufacturing" allowed its semiconductor industry to overtake Silicon Valley by the mid-1980s.[11]

Once again, the government stepped up to the plate to not only support its domestic industries, but also to direct large sums of money into research and development. On the state level, the California Commission on Industrial Innovation decided on an industrial strategy to "pick winners" in 1982, and after mixing "celebrations of free enterprise with pleas for more-aggressive state planning and subsidy,"[12] the Bay Area's high-tech industry was the major beneficiary. The federal government was also not going to let Japan overtake the United States as the world leader in computing and electronics. In 1986, Congress passed the US–Japan Semiconductor Trade Agreement to set a minimum price on Japanese chip exports and require it to buy more American chips, though the semiconductor trade war would continue in the years that followed.

Beyond trade measures, research funding was also increased. Even though Ronald Reagan had come to power on a pledge to cut taxes and government spending, the Pentagon was spared from his austerity plans. Defense spending increased to the benefit of military contractors and university research labs. DARPA, the same agency that was started in 1958 in response to the Sputnik 1 launch but now with "Defense" appended to the beginning of its name, got a boost of new funding with a specific focus on computing and networking. From the mid-1970s to 2000, "federal grants accounted for 70 percent of the money spent on academic research in computer science and electrical engineering."[13] Much of that money came from DARPA, and the research it funded was increasingly focused on commercial deployment.

From the late nineteenth century through much of the twentieth century, it felt like new discoveries were constantly being made, and those developments were disrupting human life around the world. But since the maturation of digital communications technologies, and the internet in particular, a common view has set in that innovation has seemed to slow down. Now there are plenty of new apps and derivative consumer products, but the type of discoveries of the twentieth century seem to have become much rarer.

Venture capitalist Peter Thiel has voiced these concerns many times, and his firm, Founders Fund, once subtitled its manifesto, "We wanted flying cars, instead we got 140 characters," in reference to Twitter. Thiel acknowledged the importance of the state's role in funding basic research in the past, but argued it cannot be replicated in the present. He dreamed of the return of modernist planners like Robert Moses who disregarded how their projects affected the residents of the cities they oversaw, and did not believe the modern political system could deliver technological progress because governments would not "cut health-care spending in order to free up money for biotechnology research" or "make serious cuts to the welfare state in order to free up serious money for major engineering projects."[14]

For Thiel, the successes of the past were not because of expansive spending on major public projects like the New Deal and the Interstate Highway System, but rather in spite of it, and the government no longer has the capacity to direct any such project. The innovation slowdown must be solved by the private sector, where Thiel argued that companies must seek monopoly positions in their industries, even as he criticized tech giants such as Google for losing their innovative edge.

Thiel explained that too many companies are "too drawn to incremental point solutions and very scared of complex operational problems," and that only those with "a fairly inspiring long-term vision at their core" can overcome this problem —a state that he did not think defined many Silicon Valley start-ups.[15]

Thiel's argument is ultimately riddled with contradictions, but there have been more logical explanations for what is considered technological deceleration. The late anthropologist David Graeber argued that the perception that innovation has slowed down is the product of a shift in how research funding was allocated and what kinds of research it is targeted toward. Even though research funding has generally increased over time, especially in the private sector, less of that money has gone to the basic research that often produces the transformative innovations that we associate with the period from the late nineteenth century to the mid-twentieth century or the ambitious moonshot projects that tended to generate unintended technological advancements.

Instead, it became more focused on research that could be more easily commercialized, but also had very different goals than besting a geopolitical foe. Graeber contended that the fading of the Soviet Union allowed the United States to reallocate its research funding in

> directions that could support a campaign of reversing the gains of progressive social movements and achieving a decisive victory in what U.S. elites saw as a global class war. The change of priorities was introduced as a withdrawal of big-government projects and a return to the market, but in fact the change shifted government-directed research away from programs like NASA or alternative energy sources and toward military, information, and medical technologies.[16]

Federal funding for computer science increased rapidly through the 1970s, reaching $250 million annually by 1975, and President Richard Nixon's declaration of a "war on cancer" in 1971 was followed by new funds for medical and biotechnological research.[17]

Rather than seeing the changes in how technological development has progressed as the result of a shift in private priorities, it is much more illustrative to see it as a product of different public goals. Even if Reagan and the subsequent US presidents did not explicitly say their goal was to produce technologies to crush the American working class, that was the product of their policies; and given that a significant degree of research was being done to serve defense purposes before being redeployed for civilian uses, the motivations of the military also played a role in determining which technologies were ultimately developed.

Science fiction author and journalist Tim Maughan has argued that people like Thiel who worry about the slowing of technological innovation miss how technology has been deployed over the past several decades. The space program and other visible projects had slowed down before the recent expansion of the private space industry, but innovation has still been taking place—it has just been outside the realm of what most people see in their day-to-day lives. Thanks to networked technologies, the world has become much more complex as computers have taken over functions that previously had at least some human role. "From social media to the global economy to supply chains," Maughan explained, "our lives rest precariously on systems that have become so complex, and we have yielded so much of it to technologies and autonomous actors that no one totally comprehends it all."[18]

These systems are designed to speed up transactions and interactions in service of efficiency, but, in the process, we have given up a lot of democratic power over them, even as we have failed to equip those systems with "an ability to make ethical decisions and moral judgments."[19] The stock market, where automation has increased both the speed and quantity of trades, is an example of this, but the best one is the system of logistics and global supply chains that has been built out over the past fifty years.

After World War II, the increasing use of standardized containers began to transform the shipping industry, reducing the cost and time of shipping, as well as the power of dockworkers. But the technology did not transform everything on its own. Containerization was essential to allowing the US military to carry out the Vietnam War by making it easier to ship supplies to a distant country, while giving shippers the leverage they needed to break the power of dockworkers and their radical unions. As an example of how the war was integrated into supply chains, ships that left the United States with military equipment for the war would stop to pick up goods from Japan for the return trip. Containers were an essential technology in the creation of the globalized economy we have today, one where unionized jobs in the northern and western parts of the United States were either shifted to non-unionized areas in the south or moved out of the country altogether to emerging markets where labor costs were much lower.

After spending time on container ships, in dockyards, at factories, and at the sites of raw-material extraction in East Asia, Maughan explained that the modern shipping industry that containerization, refrigeration, supply ships, and network technologies have created is beyond the control of any human manager or overseer, and requires the constant rationalization of space, of workers, and of the sea itself. Ship captains get regular updates from the computer system that controls the entire shipping network of a company like Maersk, but are rarely given any reason why they need to take a particular action. When Maughan asked why the ship had to be slowed after one command came down the line, the captain responded with a range of possible scenarios— weather, delays at the port, shipping traffic, changes in the price of oil—but no firm answers. The ship and its crew are just inputs in the system; their agency and power have been removed.

The abundance of cheap goods in the West is predicated on the supply chains that this system has made possible; supply chains where low wages, terrible working conditions, and environmental destruction are not just by-products but are essential to keeping prices low. Commercialized technologies arising from military research funding and the degradation of working rights were central to the ideology being advocated by the newly ascendent tech industry in the 1980s and 1990s, and were embraced by both Bill Clinton's New Democrats and the Republicans under the congressional leadership of Newt Gingrich.

The internet was largely not the product of private enterprise but of military and other public research bodies. In the second half of the twentieth century, many network technologies were deployed toward different ends. In 1962, the US Air Force launched the SAGE air defense system that linked up computers at military bases around the United States. Other countries, including the Soviet Union, built military networks of their own. In the 1970s, IBM, smaller computer manufacturers, and national postal and telecommunications agencies were among the groups trying to set dominant networking protocols, but ultimately it was the ARPANET's TCP/IP protocol that won out. That set the stage for the role it would play in forming the basis for what would become the internet.

Created in the 1960s, the Advanced Research Projects Agency Network (ARPANET) was a network infrastructure to allow researchers at universities around the United States to communicate with one another, and it was funded by ARPA and the US Department of Defense. In 1981, it was expanded further by the National Science Foundation (NSF)—another public research agency—to connect more computer science departments to the network, and in 1985 the NSFNET was established to act as the public backbone connecting universities, government departments, and public agencies at an estimated cost of $200 million. But companies were also getting in on this new means of communication.

By the late 1980s, regional commercial networks had been established, allowing users to send emails, connect to message boards, and share other information through a pre-internet network. They were often established with some public funding, but they were limited by the NSFNET's Acceptable Use Policy that, at least officially, barred commercial traffic from the network. However, companies seeking to cash in on this evolving network infrastructure had influence over NSF decisions and the ears of powerful political figures.

Senator Al Gore was among the prominent members of the group of "Atari Democrats" who believed US high-tech industries would generate economic growth and enhance the country's global influence. When he introduced the National High-Performance Computer Technology Act in 1989, he argued, "The nation which most completely assimilates high-performance computing into its economy will very likely emerge as the dominant intellectual, economic, and technological force in the next century."[20] Gore was not only interested in domestic power, but explicitly positioned the emerging internet as a means to oppose communism while extending US power into the post-Soviet states and encouraging the privatization of telecommunications networks around the world.[21] In service of the goals outlined by Gore, President Clinton's administration moved forward with a plan to transfer control of the internet to private companies because it was "anticipated that the *commercialization* of activity over the Internet would be conditional on first achieving the *privatization* of the infrastructure."[22] By 1995, the NSFNET was decommissioned and sold off to private companies.

Through these decades, there were alternative routes that could have been taken and pushback against the commercialization and enclosure of the technologies we now depend on. For example, in the 1970s and 1980s, the very hackers who are held up by tech libertarians for pushing back against state control were trying to stop software from being covered by corporate licensing agreements. Hackers were used to sharing code and collaboratively building and improving software programs, but the founders of new software companies—Microsoft's Bill Gates being chief among them—wanted to stop that sharing, which they deemed piracy, so they could build a business by requiring anyone who used a piece of software to buy a license. This effort was not just supported by Democrats; there was also a prominent right-wing movement promoting a vision of the internet that lay beyond the reach of the very state that had built it.

In 1987, Brand had successfully used his Whole Earth community to launch a consulting business that created a network of powerful business leaders. Turner explained that through this venture, Brand positioned "the corporation as a site of revolutionary social change and interpersonal and information networks ... as tools and emblems of that change,"[23] a continuation of the message he promoted as the communalists reintegrated into society in the 1970s. The middle-class and even wealthy community that Whole Earth cultivated had already shunned the poor and people of color, and they were primed to buy into the right-wing ideologies of the 1980s and beyond.

John Perry Barlow, co-founder of the Electronic Frontier Foundation (EFF) in 1990—a non-profit that took a libertarian approach to digital rights—believed that government had no authority over what happened on the internet. In 1996, he released an influential essay from Davos, Switzerland, called "A Declaration of the Independence of Cyberspace," in which he positioned governments as the enemy of the public, and especially of the communities and marketplaces being established on the internet, even though the government had funded the creation of the very network that make those interactions possible. Barlow wrote that governments "have no sovereignty where we gather," and declared cyberspace "to be naturally independent of the tyrannies you seek to impose on us."[24] Notably, Barlow did not share the same disdain for the corporations that flocked to the internet and shaped it to serve their bottom lines.

The EFF became influential in the debates about internet legislation through the 1990s, but even more important was *Wired* magazine. Kevin Kelly, its founding executive editor, previously served as editor of the *Whole Earth Review* and imbued the publication with a similar ethos. Louis Rossetto, one of the magazine's founders, "saw the digital revolution as an extension of a long-standing, if not widely acknowledged, American libertarian tradition," and under Kelly's direction, writers "utilized the computational metaphors and universal rhetoric of cybernetics to depict New Right politicians, tele-communications CEOs, information pundits, and members of ... Whole Earth–connected organizations as a single, leading edge of countercultural revolution."[25] As a result, *Wired*'s pages served as a meeting place for the tech industry and the socially conservative Republicans who shared their desire for an internet free of government control or regulation.

After it was founded in 1993, the magazine engaged in "a cycle of mutual legitimation" with the ascendant Christian right wing, placing figures such as Newt Gingrich and anti-evolution telecommunications analyst George Gilder on its cover.[26] As it declared Gingrich a "wired" politician, it also helped to legitimize calls for tax cuts, deregulation, and an embrace of a more "flexible" work culture, while imbuing the so-called "New Right" of the Republican Party with the countercultural ethos. As deindustrialization and globaliza-tion sent more jobs overseas, the push for project-based work that was in line with the long-standing libertarian opposition to the hierarchal corporate management structure continued.

Instead of being an employee with security, benefits, and a union, a worker would be a self-employed agent that joined a company for a particular project, then went back to searching for their next one. This was embraced by Whole Earth's adherents.

Wired, like Whole Earth before it, attracted a well-off, white customer base. After three years, its readership was overwhelmingly made of up men with jobs in management, averaging twenty-seven years of age with salaries over $120,000 a year.[27] Brand's consulting business, the Global Business Network, was promoted to *Wired* readers as a model for the future of work. It echoed the tendency in California's tech industry for workers to frequently take on new jobs and move to new companies, which set it apart from its competing high-tech hub in Massachusetts.

From its privileged position, the tech industry's embrace of right-wing economic policies failed to consider how lower working standards would affect workers who did not share their privilege—the outcomes of which are arguably most visible through the app-based gig work that grew in the aftermath of the 2008 financial crisis and subsequent recession. But, even more than that, the new narratives they embraced about the power of technology to promote economic growth and market-based innovation downplayed the role of government in enabling the development of most of the technologies that they profited from in the first place, and even how many of the businesses that now dominate the Valley received public support.

The internet is a clear example of a technology that originated in the public sector and was consumed by the corporate sector—including the protocols and architecture that make it function. But there is so much more than that. In 1968, Douglas Engelbart showed off the oN-Line System in what has become known as "The Mother of All Demos." Engelbart and his team had developed a number of technologies at

Stanford Research Institute with ARPA funding that went on to define the computing experience: the mouse, the QWERTY keyboard, bitmapped screens, and even the ability of users at multiple sites to edit the same document simultaneously. Think of it like a very rudimentary Google Docs. These technologies, demonstrated more than fifty years ago, still make up the core of the computing experience—even as Apple promotes its products as revolutions for making minor design tweaks and spec bumps every year or two.

The same, however, is true of the smartphone—the device that has come to define not just our online experience, but so much of how we interface with the world. Economist Mariana Mazzucato has outlined how many of the technologies necessary for the iPod, and later the iPhone, were simply the commercialization of research that was done within or funded by public bodies over the course of decades, including everything from touchscreens and gesture control to batteries and displays.[28] Beyond the technologies, the companies themselves also received public support. Apple received funding in 1980 from the Small Business Investment Company, a federal agency designed to support small businesses and entrepreneurs, while the core technology behind Google search was developed at Stanford University with funding from the NSF before it was commercialized. Yahoo! also emerged from Stanford in 1994, and Lycos was a research project at Carnegie Mellon University that was commercialized the same year. Even Elon Musk, who styles himself as a self-made entrepreneur, had benefited from $4.9 billion in government subsidies to support Tesla, SolarCity, and SpaceX by 2015—and they have received much more since then.

When the infrastructure of the internet was privatized in 1995, it did not result in an immediate corporate takeover of everything that happened on the network. There was still a lot of experimentation, including a lot of small communities and rudimentary personal and educational websites, but commercial pressures could be observed from its very early days. In 1994, even before privatization, Carmen Hermosillo published a widely read essay that explained how "many cyber-communities are businesses that rely upon the commodification of human interaction." She explained that early networked services, including the Whole Earth 'Lectronic Link, not only packaged users' interactions as a product, but shaped them to serve the business's commercial ends through censorship and editorial discretion. Pushing back against the narratives of people like Brand and Barlow, Hermosillo criticized those who "write about cyberspace as though it were a '60s utopia," and argued instead that electronic communities benefited from a "trend towards dehumanization in our society: It wants to commodify human interaction, enjoy the spectacle regardless of the human cost."[29]

In 1996, technology historian Jennifer Light also expressed her disagreement with the narratives of "cyberoptimists," comparing their framing of virtual communities to early discourses around the benefits of shopping malls that were not realized. As the automobile was taking over communities in the 1950s and people were spreading far and wide in new suburbs, the mall was positioned as a new public space to replace small-town Main Streets. But planners failed to account for how commercial pressures shaped who could access malls, and what they could do in those spaces. Their mistake, Light wrote, "was projecting an American dream, an historical cultural fantasy, onto a new space without fully evaluating the implications."[30] Yet the same thing was happening in discourse around the internet.

The optimistic language used to "portray cyberspace as a new frontier, a melting pot, and as democratic public space where anyone can talk to anyone else and all are created equal" was inspiring, but it was not accurate. Echoing Hermosillo, Light explained that when virtual communities are under private ownership, "these agora function only in their commercial sense; the sense of the market space as site for civic life is subject to strict controls."[31] These early critical accounts of the nature of digital communities on a privatized network subject to commercial pressures were a warning of what was to come.

After the dot-com crash in the late 1990s, a new vision for the web took hold in the early years of the new millennium. Its adherents called it Web 2.0. Despite libertarian claims about the internet having an inherently decentralized design that guaranteed such positive qualities as openness and democracy, digital services were stored on centralized servers and the web was increasingly enclosed by major corporate players, including many of the tech monopolies we are familiar with today. They sought not only to move online activity from the distributed websites of the early web onto their centralized services and platforms, but to record our actions while we used them and as we browsed websites outside them. In a sense, the web become even more like a shopping mall, as Light had described.

Media scholar Benjamin Peters argued that the early boosters of the internet failed to contend with how power is exerted on networks, explaining that they "do not resemble their designs so much as they take after the organizational collaborations and vices that tried to build them."[32] With its military origins and corporate control, the way the internet has developed is, therefore, hardly a surprise. Peters pointed to the packet-switching protocol as an example of the false promise of focusing on network design: "the protocol once celebrated as solving the problem of hierarchical control has proven the very vehicle for ushering in the current era of private network surveillance."[33] Claims of decentralization did not, for example, stop the vast surveillance apparatuses deployed by Google or the US National Security Agency.

The degree of surveillance, enclosure, and commercialization on the internet was normalized over the course of several decades as narratives about the emancipatory potential of technology and the power of free markets were embraced by powerful interest groups that have no wish to see the status quo disrupted. Silicon Valley capitalists who have benefited from the commercialization of all this public research and the deregulation of the economy are able to influence the public—through tech publications and tech verticals at major media organizations—to think that the digital ecosystem we have today is the natural result of innovation and that technological progress can only take the form that serves their bottom line. Meanwhile, politicians from both major political parties in the United States developed financial ties to the tech industry and fear negative economic impacts from disrupting its monopolies. But this narrow perspective not only affects the way they see the future; it also risks extending these technologies more extensively into physical space as the new dominant industry seeks to reshape the physical environment to suit its interests.

The people at the helm of the tech industry have incredibly narrow worldviews, and that has implications for the types of solutions they present to the perceived challenges that need to be addressed. Those who built the libertarian ideology that dominates its upper echelons, and which subsequently spread throughout society as the industry has grown since the 1990s, came from a privileged background that shaped the way they saw the world. These white men of middle-class and even wealthy backgrounds who were able to reap the benefits of the economic growth in the latter half of the twentieth century did not give much thought as to whether the policies and ideas of progress that worked for them would also deliver for the whole of the working class, particularly women and people of color, who had much higher barriers to gain access to the wealth creation of that period. That continues to be a problem in the present day, with a tech industry that continually fails to diversify and where the women and people of color who do reach higher positions often do not challenge the entrenched worldview that benefits wealthy executives of any background.

Tech critic Evgeny Morozov argued that the approach of these powerful figures creates a quest for technofixes that do not address the real problems we face. He called this "technological solutionism" and defined it as "an unhealthy preoccupation with sexy, monumental, and narrow-minded solutions—the kind of stuff that wows audiences at TED Conferences—to problems that are extremely complex, fluid, and contentious."[34] Part of the problem is that the executives, venture capitalists, and other important figures associated with the tech industry do not take the time to understand the real problems they claim to seek to solve, and instead make assumptions about serious issues and their root causes to legitimize preconceived technological solutions. As Morozov put it:

> what many solutionists presume to be "problems" in need of solving are not problems at all; a deeper investigation into the very nature of these "problems" would reveal that the inefficiency, ambiguity, and opacity—whether in politics or everyday life—that the newly empowered geeks and solutionists are rallying against are not in any sense problematic.[35]

To gain public support, the tech elite frames its solutions in universal terms without taking the time to consider whether the benefits would be broadly distributed. Transit planner Jarrett Walker called this "elite projection," which he described as "the belief, among relatively fortunate and influential people, that what those people find convenient or attractive is good for the society as a whole."[36] This is echoed by Stanford professor Adrian Daub, who wrote, "The tech giants want to make things happen for 'everybody.' But often 'everybody' means 'people like me.'"[37] The problem that these thinkers identify is observable across many different domains, but its effects on the visions that people in tech are putting forward for transportation and the city cannot be ignored.

Rather than address serious problems with existing, auto-oriented transport systems, the solutions promoted by the tech industry—many of which have also been adopted by the automotive industry—are designed to serve the interests of those executives and their companies. The futures they imagine are ones where "technology's benefits are idealized, its applications are universalized, and it becomes detached from its constitutive social and power relations."[38] Proposals for new technological systems to address the problems that have arisen from decades of building cities and transport systems around automobiles too often fail to learn from similar attempts in the past or ignore the new problems that arise from them.

The intervention of tech companies into physical space should not be seen as an altruistic move to improve the lives of urban, suburban, or rural residents. As with the automotive interests of the twentieth century, their primary goal is to remake communities to serve their need for profit and control. Automobiles and the suburban neighborhoods that were built to accommodate them atomized our communities, promoted a more individualistic and consumer-oriented way of life, and made us dependent on a wide range of corporate interests that could continually extract profit from us because we had no other choice than to use the goods and services they provided. Now, the tech industry wants in on that. They have already remade our communications networks so that our interactions are facilitated by hardware and digital platforms that allow them to constantly track us, collect data about us, and place themselves in the middle of a growing number of transactions. Their plan involves remaking our physical environments to benefit themselves in the same ways.

Increasingly, our homes are filled with smart gadgets that constantly report back to the corporations that produce them.

They are sometimes even sold at or below cost because getting the devices into people's homes can earn the companies far more over time than the sale of any single unit of hardware. Tech companies are also partnering with cities to build out smart systems that extend their technologies throughout the urban landscape and transport networks not only to capture data at more points, but also to make us reliant on their systems in more places. This not only makes us dependent on the digital services of tech monopolies, and by extension makes it more difficult for government to take action against those monopolies, but it further entwines our daily lives in the vast supply chains that create all of that technology, from the low-wage sweatshops in Asia where so much of it is produced to the mines that pollute environments and harm communities throughout the Global South and the peripheral areas of the Global North.

In September 2021, Instagram head Adam Mosseri compared social media to automobiles after a damning report in the *Wall Street Journal* about internal Facebook research that found the image-sharing platform was harmful to young people, particularly teenage girls. Responding to the story, Mosseri said, "We know that more people die than would otherwise because of car accidents, but by and large, cars create way more value in the world than they destroy. And I think social media is similar."[39] His comparison served to minimize any potential harm that came of Instagram and social media more broadly by drawing on the example of cars, but in doing so he also narrowly defined that harm as deaths from car crashes. Yet cars have a far greater impact beyond road deaths: there are injuries, deaths from air pollution, and how the technology required structural changes to our built environment and regulatory systems that have had significant consequences of their own.

Social media can be compared to automobility, but not in the way Mosseri chose to frame it. Instead, we should recognize how Facebook, Instagram, and other social media platforms have reshaped our communications networks and how we use them to serve their business interests. The negative consequences generated by that transformation—whether it is the harmful influence on teenagers, broader political questions about the kind of information they choose to amplify, or any number of other concerns that people have—are not mistakes that have arisen in a benevolent campaign to connect the world, but the product of placing growth, profits, and power ahead of the common good. As tech companies seek to extend their footprint into the physical world, those same forces are driving them, and that influences how they believe future cities should look—and, by extension, who they should serve.

3

Greenwashing the Electric Vehicle

I want to describe an electric vehicle company for you. The company in question introduced a vehicle to the market that began to change public perceptions of mobility and induce a shift away from a dirtier form of transportation to a cleaner one. It had its eyes on monopoly, and set up its own offices and charging stations in major cities in the United States and beyond. It imagined it could transform mobility not just through personal ownership of its vehicles, but also through providing on-demand service. Not everything was perfect at this company, though. It fought efforts by its workers to increase their pay and form a union, and its profitability was in serious question, in part because it struggled to work out inefficiencies in its production processes and supply chain. As a result, it engaged in speculative financial activities to fund its operations and expand its footprint to push out competitors—until it finally collapsed.

Can you guess which company I described? Up until the last sentence, you may have thought it was Tesla, the electric vehicle company that Elon Musk took over as chief executive officer in 2008 and which has become synonymous with the billionaire, especially after he pushed out its original founders. Tesla introduced the Roadster in 2009, which is seen as having played an important role in the most recent wave of popularity of the electric vehicle, especially as Musk was hailed as a visionary by media organizations around the world for speaking about the future at a time when the neoliberal political environment seemed to have closed off hope for a better world. It did not matter that his visions were designed to serve his interests above all else.

Tesla set its sights on converting drivers of internal combustion vehicles to its electric cars, and built its own dealership network across the world to sell directly to customers. Its focus has been on selling vehicles, but Musk also talked about creating an on-demand "robotaxi" service. Throughout Tesla's history, it has suffered from production problems resulting in part from an overreliance on automation and a refusal to learn the lessons of other auto manufacturers. As a result, Tesla's factory workers suffer higher rates of injury than the industry standard, and Musk has been vocally anti-union to the extent that the US National Labor Relations Board found he violated labor law for threatening workers with the loss of stock benefits if they unionized.

A combination of these issues meant that Tesla failed to meet both its initial production targets and its revenue targets, and the profits it reported were the result of selling carbon credits, not electric vehicles. But that has not stopped Tesla's share price from soaring far beyond its value on paper, or the value of any other automaker, because of how the stock prices of highly hyped tech companies have become divorced from their earnings after a decade of near-zero interest rates and governments flooding the market with cash through quantitative easing programs. At the time of writing, however, Tesla has not crashed. Investors and Musk's devout followers continue to believe he can deliver all that he promises, and until they lose faith, the company will likely continue to operate.

So, which company have I described if it is not Tesla? While Tesla gets a lot of attention and credit for the growing share of electric vehicle sales in the present—though its shine has diminished in recent years as more automakers have unveiled their own battery-powered options—electric vehicles are not a new invention.

Early work on the technology that made electric vehicles possible began as early as the 1830s, and by the end of the nineteenth century, there were electric vehicles on the roads of Europe and North America. The horseless carriage, as it was originally known, presented a significant improvement over the horse-drawn transportation of the time. As electric power was adopted in streetcars and automobiles, it reduced the street space required for horses and got rid of all the manure they left behind. At the turn of that century, there were three means of propelling the horseless carriage that competed for supremacy: steam power, the internal combustion engine, and the electric battery. For about a decade, the electric vehicle was poised to win.

Formed in 1897, the Electric Vehicle Company (EVC) brought together several electric vehicle manufacturers with the goal of forming a transportation monopoly in major cities. Historian David Kirsch has explained that while it did lease vehicles to customers, its focus was on creating a comprehensive system of transportation that "would have been able to operate electric streetcars where economical, provide electric omnibus service on less traveled routes, and offer individual electric cars where door-to-door-service was required."[1] The company's plan was to own the vehicles, employ the drivers, provide the maintenance, and even generate the electricity through its own power stations. It was a monopoly play that made the EVC the largest auto manufacturer in the United States at its height, but after launching services in major cities like New York, Chicago, Boston, Philadelphia, and Mexico City, things began to unwind by the early 1900s.

The EVC was part of a larger conglomerate, which put it in the crosshairs of government officials who were going after the corporate trusts that dominated the US economy, and in quickly expanding to try to control urban transportation, the EVC engaged in "stock jobbing, financial manipulation, and legal chicanery." In 1899, the various companies within the EVC had issued stock valued at more than $100 million, an almost unheard-of amount at the time, and other vehicle companies were doing the same. It did not last for long. Recognizing that "share prices did not necessarily reflect operational reality," they collapsed near the end of the year, but that was not the end of the EVC's troubles.[2] Its financial issues and even the problems it encountered with battery technology are not the primary reasons why the internal combustion engine won out over battery electric vehicles more than a century ago. Instead, one needs to look at the larger system surrounding the technology.

By 1901, the EVC had abandoned its expansive vision, shut down its regional companies, and reorganized its remaining New York operations into the New York Transportation Company, which continued to operate until 1912. Yet over that time the internal combustion vehicle overtook its electric counterpart. The shady dealings of the EVC and some other electric vehicle companies gave the product a bad name in the eyes of some consumers. *The Horseless Age*, a leading motoring magazine of the time, even engaged in a campaign against electric vehicles for a time, calling them "lead cabs" or "lead wagons" due to their lead-acid batteries, which left other magazine editors wondering if *The Horseless Age* had ulterior motives. But Kirsch has cited two main reasons for the failure of the electric vehicle and its alternative vision for transportation.

The first problem was that the interests that should have backed the electric vehicle failed to do so, or at least not to the degree that was necessary. The electric vehicle was a natural ally for utility companies that were connecting households and promoting new electric products like lights and appliances to increase electricity usage, but they failed to effectively join forces with vehicle makers. The Association of Electric Vehicle Manufacturers was established in 1906, and the Electric Vehicle and Central Station Association finally brought together power producers, vehicle manufacturers, and battery-storage companies in 1909. But even then, few of the central power stations actively promoted the electric vehicle to their customers, and it was arguably too late. Had those ties and organizations been formed a decade earlier, the combined electrical interests could have beaten those behind the internal combustion engine. Their efforts contributed to an uptick in electric vehicle sales, but it paled in comparison to the growing number of vehicles with internal combustion engines, especially once World War I had begun.

The second problem had to do with production. The EVC never produced a standardized vehicle, and none of the other electric vehicle manufacturers succeeded at streamlining their production processes before Henry Ford introduced the gas-powered Model T. As a result, customers could buy an internal combustion vehicle at a much lower price than an electric one, and even though the electric vehicle was quieter, offered a smoother drive, and started more easily (the early internal combustion vehicles needed to be hand cranked), it struggled to compete. The perceived drawbacks of the internal combustion engine also had the effect of making it seem more masculine. The driver of an internal combustion vehicle could go faster, got to show driving skill by switching gears, and even mechanical skill by doing simple maintenance. The electric vehicle, on the other hand, was seen as a vehicle suited to women, who were presumed to have none of these skills.

Electric vehicle manufacturers were unable to overcome these challenges, as they were simply too late in trying to address them as sales of internal combustion vehicles soared and an infrastructure was built to support them. By the 1920s, few electric vehicles were sold outside of commercial trucking. But that did not mean the electric vehicle was permanently dead.

After World War II, automobile sales increased along with postwar prosperity, the expansion of the suburbs, the

construction of more roads and highways, and the dismantling of other transport options. However, like in the 1920s,
the drawbacks of the automobile became apparent, particularly its environmental costs. Los Angeles was the premier
automotive city, but by the 1960s it was beset by heavy smog
produced by the exhaust fumes of all the vehicles zipping
around the expanding communities of the basin. That
prompted the federal government to invest in developing
better electric vehicles, especially after the 1973 oil shock. But,
once again, concepts by General Motors and the American
Motor Company, as well as vehicles that made it into small-
scale production such as Enfield Automotive's two-seater
Enfield 8000, failed to catch on. Not until the 1990s did the
electric car get serious attention from the major automakers, spurring the slow creation of the modern electric vehicle
industry.

In 2006, two groundbreaking environmental documentaries
were released for popular consumption. The first was *An
Inconvenient Truth*, which took a slideshow that former US
vice president Al Gore had been presenting around the world
about the urgency of addressing the climate crisis and turned
it into a feature-length film. It resonated with the public,
was shown in schools around the world, and even won the
Academy Award for Best Documentary Feature. But the documentary, and Gore himself, had a particular message, one that
echoed his work in the 1990s in framing the internet as a tool
to enhance the power of the individual. Citizens could write to
their lawmakers, but they could also change their lightbulbs,
buy a hybrid vehicle, start recycling, or even compost their
leftovers. The narrative seemed empowering, but in focusing
so much on personal action, it helped shift the responsibility
for climate change away from governments and corporations,
and onto individual consumers. Addressing the climate crisis
requires changing systems that most people have no power to

alter, but that was the dominant environmental message for a long time.

A second documentary, *Who Killed the Electric Car?* used a similar narrative, but with a specific focus on electric vehicles. It was a film about General Motors' EV1, the first electric vehicle mass produced by the leading US automobile manufacturer. In the early 1990s, California mandated that automakers had to offer electric options if they wanted to continue selling cars and trucks in the Golden State, and the EV1 was the most visible of the vehicles that came out of the regulation. However, once automakers succeed at getting the mandate revoked, GM ceased production on the EV1 and destroyed the vehicles as their leases expired. This provoked the ire of liberal environmentalists.

Who Killed the Electric Car? even more forcefully pushed the idea that personal consumption decisions—in this case, buying an electric car—were not only essential to addressing climate change, but also to ending US foreign combat operations to secure oil supplies, given the ongoing war in Iraq. As an artifact of liberal environmentalism, the film provided celebrities the opportunity to talk about how much they loved their electric cars, and the filmmaker rejected any argument that called into question the vehicles' environmental bona fides as propaganda from the automotive or oil industries. Some of the claims the film rejected were indeed false, such as industry studies that said electric vehicles had higher emissions than gas-powered vehicles. The truth is that, even if the electricity powering electric vehicles is produced from fossil sources such as coal or natural gas, they still tend to be responsible for fewer greenhouse gas emissions over their lifecycles. But it also dismissed criticisms made by groups concerned about environmental justice that the primary benefits of the shift to electric vehicles would accrue to high-income individuals. One expert interviewed for the film said, "the air doesn't know a boundary between Brentwood and South LA," the former being a predominantly white and more affluent neighborhood, compared to the lower income people of color who live in the latter.

The documentary illustrated how the climate politics of the late 1990s and the first decade of the 2000s—consisting of an environmentalism that prized individual action and consumer choice—aligned itself with electric cars as one of the main solutions to the climate crisis, while ignoring how those vehicles continued to have a significant environmental footprint compared to walking, cycling, or taking public transit. If there are any doubts about the film's politics, one need only look at its 2011 sequel.

Whereas *Who Killed the Electric Car?* was undoubtedly an environmental film, *Revenge of the Electric Car* barely mentioned the environmental benefits of electric vehicles; it was, first and foremost, a car movie. The filmmaker followed four men with different visions for electric automobility: Tesla CEO Elon Musk as the face of the exciting tech upstart, along with his veteran competitor from General Motors, Vice Chairman Bob Lutz; their European-Asian counterpart from Renault-Nissan, Carlos Ghosn; and Greg Abbott, who was trying to launch an independent electric vehicle conversion business in California. Abbott's dream of starting a workshop gets crushed by the end of the movie, illustrating that the transition to electric vehicles is ultimately a fight between corporate actors, and the filmmaker displays a clear preference for the path forward. The documentary served as one of the cultural artifacts that helped build the myth of Elon Musk. It drew comparisons to the inventor of alternating current electricity, Nikola Tesla, and Marvel superhero Tony Stark (who suits up as Iron Man), while making the argument that the future of the auto industry—and the electric car—depended on individuals, not the government.

Just six minutes into the film, *New York Times* columnist Thomas Friedman was on screen saying, "I do not believe this is a problem that is gonna be resolved by regulators and bureaucrats. This is a problem that's gonna be solved by engineers, innovators, and entrepreneurs." But Friedman's statement is not true. Decades of public research funding have been essential to developing alternative fuels, and regulators have historically played an important role in forcing automotive companies to make vehicles safer and more fuel efficient. Government subsidies are also a key part of the ongoing shift to electric vehicles; they incentivize companies to produce them and consumers to buy them.

Stepping back from these documentary films, the narratives around electric vehicles over the past couple of decades leave out important context: the vehicles only appear clean and green because environmental messaging narrowly focuses on tailpipe emissions, ignoring the harm that pervades the supply chain and the unsustainable nature of auto-oriented development. André Gorz's argument that the automobile is a luxury product whose primary harms arise when it is democratized does not just apply to the internal combustion vehicle; it is also the case for the electric vehicle.

Indeed, Kirsch has argued that the focus on the internal combustion engine misses the bigger picture about automobiles:

> there is no such thing as an environmentally friendly automotive technology ... The social, financial, and environmental threats we now face as a result of our reliance on refined petroleum are not the fault of internal combustion technology per se but of the massive expansion of the automobile transport system.[3]

In other words, the problem with automobility is not solely the fuel that powers it, but the way that companies and governments have successfully reoriented our entire lives around automobiles and, in many cases, have decimated more efficient alternatives. Had the transportation system evolved in the same way since the 1920s, but used batteries instead of internal combustion engines, passenger vehicles would still be a source of significant environmental and social harm, in part because they are such an inefficient use of urban space and precious resources.

The truth is that the electric vehicle, whether produced by Tesla, General Motors, or any other company, will not address the fundamental problems with a transportation system built around automobiles. In the same way that the fossil fuel infrastructure that spans the globe has been recognized as a threat to the climate and to human life itself, especially the people who live near the sites where it is extracted and refined, the mining industry has begun a significant expansion to support the mass production of electric vehicles, and it too will create mass suffering and environmental damage unless we address the role of passenger vehicles in our transportation system and prioritize mobility that is more efficient, both in its resource use and in the way it operates.

In December 2019, Tesla was hit with a lawsuit in a US federal court along with Apple, Google, Dell, and Microsoft that was unlike any they had ever had to fight. International Rights Advocates, a human rights organization, sued the companies on behalf of fourteen families from the Democratic Republic of the Congo (DRC) for "aiding and abetting in the death and serious injury of children who they claim were working in cobalt mines in their supply chain."[4]

Cobalt is a key component in lithium-ion batteries, meaning it is not only in most of the technology we use every day, but it is also in the batteries that power virtually every electric car on the road. Demand for the mineral is already soaring, and it is poised to increase far more if the mass conversion of personal vehicles to battery power takes place over the next couple of decades. However, the DRC dominates the global cobalt supply chain, and even though more mines are being constructed in other parts of the world, the level of demand for the mineral means the DRC's central role will not end anytime soon. That means the cobalt powering those electric cars will continue to hurt children and families in nearby communities.

The area of the DRC where much of the mining of copper, nickel, cobalt, and other minerals occurs is among the ten most polluted sites in the world. The water there is contaminated, there is a high rate of birth defects among the local population, and around 40,000 children under fifteen years of age work in artisanal mines.[5] There is ostensibly a line between the industrial mines run by foreign mining companies—where the cobalt in our batteries allegedly comes from—and the artisanal mines that are dug by hand and make use of child labor; but anti-slavery researcher Siddharth Kara, whose work set the stage for the lawsuit against the tech companies, spoke to families who "said their children had been working at sites operated by foreign mining companies for years."[6] Those families described having their children buried alive when tunnels collapsed on them, paralyzed after accidents at the mines, or otherwise injured in ways that forever changed their lives.

British-owned Glencore was one of the two mining companies named in the lawsuit. Its representatives said there was no child labor at its DRC mines, even though the families said their children labored at a mine controlled by the Kamoto Copper Company, which is owned by Glencore. In recent years, Elon Musk has been talking about making cobalt-free batteries, yet Tesla signed a long-term partnership with Glencore in 2020 to supply its new factories in Berlin and Shanghai with the mineral. But this is not just a Tesla problem, or even a Glencore one.

Every technology company and every electric vehicle company uses minerals which have harmful effects on workers, the environment, and the communities surrounding the mines. Multinational mining companies headquartered in the United States, Canada, and Australia have a particularly bad reputation for their extractive activities around the world, and as electrified transportation takes off, greater supplies of many minerals and metals will be necessary to manufacture their batteries. That will have consequences, especially for communities in parts of the Global South and remote and Indigenous communities in the Global North.

The global mining industry has a significant environmental footprint, both in terms of greenhouse gas emissions and the damage it causes to local environments where mines are constructed. For example, 70 percent of the mines controlled by the six largest mining companies are in regions without sufficient water.[7] While electric vehicles are not the only reason that resource demand is increasing, MiningWatch Canada estimated that without significant changes in how we organize transportation networks, "battery storage for electric vehicles is currently projected to be the main driver of additional metals and materials needed for the energy transition."[8]

To that point, the International Energy Agency reported in 2020 that meeting the goals of the Paris Agreement to keep warming well below 2°C will cause total mineral demand to quadruple by 2040, but the distribution of that demand is not uniform across different technologies. Electric vehicles are estimated to account for a significant majority of the increased demand, but most of it—about 80 percent—will be for passenger and light commercial vehicles.[9] While the increased mineral intensity does not mean that electric vehicles generate more emissions than conventional vehicles, the significant proportion of demand coming from passenger vehicles illustrates why we cannot just replace everything that was once powered by fossil fuels with equivalent products powered by batteries. There must be a more fundamental transformation of the systems we interact with every day, including our transportation system, to minimize the quantity of resources that need to be extracted while also reducing, and where possible eliminating, greenhouse gas emissions.

The batteries in electric vehicles require a whole range of metals and minerals, including aluminum, copper, manganese, and a number of rare earth elements, but some of the most important are cobalt, lithium, nickel, and graphite. As part of its aggressive sustainable development scenario, the International Energy Agency estimated that demand for lithium and nickel to make vehicle batteries will increase by over 4,000 percent between 2020 and 2040, compared to over 2,000 percent for cobalt, copper, and graphite, but that assumes the transportation system will continue to prioritize personal vehicles.[10] Researchers at the University of Technology Sydney similarly warned that demand for cobalt to produce batteries could exceed existing reserves— meaning the amount of the resource that can be economically extracted—in the event of a complete electrification of the energy and transportation systems by 2050, and the same could be true for lithium unless there is a significant increase in recycling.[11] Those figures not only present environmental concerns and potential supply problems, but e-waste recycling has traditionally been a very dirty and dangerous industry, with electronics dumped in Global South countries instead of being properly recycled at the end of their lives. No more than a few percent of lithium used today is recycled, and the less that is recycled, the more must be extracted.

Australia is currently the largest producer of lithium, but the countries of the "lithium triangle" in South America— Argentina, Bolivia, and Chile—are expected to overtake it as the major suppliers for the coming boom in global demand. The region is estimated to hold more than half of global lithium reserves,[12] but its extraction requires sucking up vast quantities of salt brine to be evaporated. The process is not only water-intensive, but as the amount of brine is reduced, the water table drops, pulling fresh water from nearby sources and, by extension, the communities that rely on them.[13] Beyond that, the activities of lithium mining companies in South America have polluted local water sources, which affects local wildlife and Indigenous peoples, and the fiscal benefits of mining are often not shared with surrounding communities.

While many of the key minerals for electric vehicles can be extracted from a range of countries around the world, existing production tends to be more geographically concentrated than oil and gas, and new projects can take many years to get started. In the short to medium term, that could create political opportunities or challenges for the countries with existing production or significant reserves. For example, in November 2019, the Organization of American States claimed there were irregularities with vote tallying in the Bolivian election, which helped to pave the way for a coup against left-wing president Evo Morales. Later analyses conclusively showed that no electoral fraud had taken place, and when a new election was held in October 2020, the candidate from Morales's party won an overwhelming victory. This series of events was important for many reasons, but it is relevant because of the role that lithium played in the narratives around it.

Morales claimed the coup had been organized by the United States so it could gain access to the country's vast lithium reserves—an argument that took on steam when Musk responded to a tweet about Morales's allegation, writing, "We will coup whoever we want! Deal with it." It is highly unlikely that the overthrow of Morales was actually a "lithium coup," and even less likely that Musk's tweet was anything other than a brash statement, but it does suggest the potential for such actions in the future as reliance on these resources increases.

In the same way that oil-producing countries created the Organization of the Petroleum Exporting Countries in 1960, which is a cartel that gave its members significant influence over international oil prices, countries with key minerals like lithium could do something similar in future. Yet, over those same decades, the United States and other imperial powers overthrew governments and waged wars to gain and maintain access to fossil fuels. If we shift from an economy based on the extraction of fossil fuels to one based on a vast expansion of the extraction of key metals and minerals, powerful countries could take similar actions to safeguard their mineral supplies—just as they do today with oil, gas, and other crucial commodities.

There is a significant risk that the shift to a "green" economy that relies heavily on increased extraction will continue rather than challenge the long-standing neocolonial relationship between powerful countries in the Global North which extract resources and wealth from the Global South. In recent years, governments in the Global North have made it clear that this is the path they intend to pursue as the pressure for them to appear to be doing something about the climate crisis has grown. But the extractive future they are embracing also has implications for their own populations.

During the 2021 NFL Super Bowl, General Motors shelled out for an expensive ad slot to show its commitment to electric vehicles. In its commercial, Will Ferrell played on Americans' desire to be "number one" at everything by explaining that Norway sells far more electric vehicles per capita and arguing that the United States could not let the Nordic country beat it in the race to electrify the automobile fleet.

After killing the EV1 more than two decades ago, GM wants consumers and governments to believe that this time it is taking electric vehicles seriously. To that end, it committed to releasing thirty new electric vehicles by 2025 and set a goal to end production of gasoline cars by 2035. Other automakers are making similar commitments, such as Ford's promise to sell only electric vehicles in Europe by 2030 and Volkswagen's move to double down on electric vehicles after its emissions scandal. Many of those plans follow legislative measures in countries around the world to phase out the sale of internal combustion vehicles, but given that the batteries for all those vehicles will require significant resource extraction, companies are already trying to head off future controversy.

General Motors announced a plan to source some of the lithium used in its batteries from the United States, promising to produce no tailings and lower emissions than other extraction methods, while Mercedes-Benz promised to buy lithium and cobalt only from certified mining sites. Meanwhile, Volkswagen officials made a trip to Chile's Atacama Desert to show the company's commitment to sustainable lithium extraction, and BMW commissioned a study on sustainable extraction methods. Once again, these actions are examples of an industry-wide trend and, while they sound positive, they do not mean we no longer need to be concerned about the human and environmental effects of mining.

Political scientist Thea Riofrancos has argued that automakers' sustainability commitments are first and foremost about appeasing environmentally conscious consumers and investors who are concerned about companies' environmental, social, and corporate governance.[14] The transition to electric vehicles presents an unprecedented opportunity to increase vehicle sales by converting the automobile fleet to battery power; engaging in what is effectively greenwashing will help to ensure it is realized. But what form that shift ultimately takes will be determined by government policy. Governments are not only providing support to build out the infrastructure for electric vehicles and incentivize consumer adoption, but are promising the necessary minerals will be secured.

With Donald Trump out of office, President Joe Biden and Transportation Secretary Pete Buttigieg put electric vehicles at the center of the Democrats' plan to reduce emissions. Biden spent the presidential campaign talking about the need for "green highways" equipped with vehicle chargers, and made a commitment to develop domestic supply chains for key minerals needed for vehicle batteries and renewable energy. Yet those projects have negative effects not only on local environments, but also on the Indigenous communities that are often located nearby.

Companies are facing considerable opposition as they look to open new mines to supply US automakers' electric vehicle push. Copper mines have been proposed in Minnesota, but they threaten local wilderness and have previously been opposed by members of Biden's cabinet. Native Americans are worried a planned copper mine in Arizona will destroy sacred sites, while a mine in Idaho to extract gold and antimony will poison their fishing grounds. California is looking to extract lithium from the Salton Sea, a large salt lake that is considered one of the state's worst environmental disasters, but nearby Latino communities wonder what it will mean for them, given they already suffer from high rates of asthma and respiratory problems. Yet the most prominent of these contested projects is the planned lithium mine in Nevada's Thacker Pass, where conservationists are worried about the impact on local species and farmers are concerned about the effects of its significant water requirements. A coalition of local Indigenous peoples also protested against the mine and joined a broader lawsuit against the project that includes conservationists, public accountability groups, and a local rancher.[15]

But the United States is also looking to its north for significant mineral imports. A US government source told Reuters that it sees Canada as "a kind of '51st State' for mineral supply purposes,"[16] and, given the continental integration of automotive manufacturing, it is no surprise to see Canada embracing a similar plan. In September 2020, the Canadian government announced its intention to become a world leader in battery manufacturing for electric vehicles by expanding domestic mining operations. That plan was affirmed when Canadian prime minister Justin Trudeau met virtually with President Biden in February 2021 and agreed to work collaboratively "to build the necessary supply chains to make Canada and the

United States global leaders in all aspects of battery development and production."[17]

From cobalt in the Northwest Territories to graphite and lithium in Quebec to rare earths and nickel in Labrador, there are vast mineral resources to be extracted across Canada. Between 2014 and 2018, investment in lithium mining in Quebec surged by 789 percent, and the provincial government is actively trying to build up the industry.[18] But as the pressure to extract grows, communities often bear the consequences. For example, Australian mining company Sayona recently misled the public to try to avoid proper environmental assessments on a lithium mine it wanted to open in northwestern Quebec, even after a nearby mine owned by North American Lithium was responsible for eighty environmental accidents from 2013 to 2018 before it went bankrupt.

Canadian mining projects tend to be responsible for significant environmental harm, and that harm is more likely to affect Indigenous communities than settler Canadians. In recent years, Indigenous peoples in Canada have protested the expansion of the Baffinland iron ore mine in Nunavut, declared a moratorium on development at the Ring of Fire chromite project in Northern Ontario, and halted an open pit gold and copper mine in British Columbia. In the latter case, elected chief of Tl'esqox Francis Laceese said, "the genocide is still here, it hasn't left,"[19] because of how his nation has to constantly fight to have their rights respected by the Canadian state.

The push for domestic mining supply chains is not just a North American phenomenon, however. As the GM ad stated, Europe is leading North America in the adoption of electric vehicles, and it intends for its major automakers to remain dominant players in the shift from internal combustion engines to battery power. In 2020, the European Commission released a strategy on critical raw materials to increase domestic supplies of minerals like lithium and rare earths so it can reduce its reliance on China and other third countries. Yet after decades of closing European mines to outsource the extraction of raw materials and the harm that accompanies it to other parts of the world, that plan is facing pushback. The mines are most likely to be located in the European Union's poorer countries in the east and south, or in remote areas, such as the lands of the Sámi people in northern Europe. In April 2021, Portugal canceled a planned lithium mine after local opposition, but that doesn't mean the push for expansion is over. The country is already the biggest producer of lithium in Europe, and it plans to expand production to reap the benefits of growing demand.

Even when mining "comes home," it needs to be out of sight and mind of the majority of the wealthy consumers whose environmental guilt the electric vehicle is meant to assuage. Yet mining is not the only problem with the mass adoption of electric vehicles, and the Nordic countries, of which Norway is a member, illustrates some of the others.

Unlike Friedman's assertion in *Revenge of the Electric Car*, Norway is beating the United States in per capita electric vehicle sales because the government made adopting them an explicit policy goal. People who bought electric vehicles could save the value added tax on the purchase of their vehicles, avoid road and import taxes, get discounts on parking, drive in bus lanes, and enjoy other perks. Jurisdictions in North America have offered various subsidies to entice people to buy electric vehicles, but none have introduced a system of incentives as comprehensive as that which exists in Norway.

While those benefits do make electric vehicles attractive to buyers, all that public money is disproportionately spent on a relatively well-off share of the population, which is not the most effective way for governments to encourage a reduction in emissions while ensuring an equitable transportation system. When researchers at the University of Sussex and Aarhus University spoke to more than 250 experts in the

Nordic countries about electric mobility, the experts referenced the issue of supply chains, but among their biggest concerns was transport equity in the region. One of the experts told the researchers that "In the beginning, I thought the negative reactions to Teslas was related to envy or jealousy. But after thinking more about it, it's a rational and emotional reaction. Why should we lose a lot of money for rich people getting a cheap, expensive, luxury car?"[20] Since this statement was made, the variety of electric vehicles has grown so Tesla is not the only choice available to people, but they still tend to be more expensive than conventional vehicles.

The researchers outlined how, around the world, electric vehicles tend to be purchased by higher-income individuals— and that means they are the people receiving subsidies and the other privileges of ownership. Americans are even worse off in this regard than Norwegians because the federal tax credit for drivers who purchase electric vehicles is tied to automakers, so once the automaker sells 200,000 plug-in vehicles, the tax credit is reduced and eventually eliminated. Since wealthy people have been at the front of the line to buy expensive electric vehicles, that means they have been the primary beneficiaries of the program, and that presents another problem. The researchers explained that wealthy people do not always buy electric vehicles for the environmental benefits. The electric vehicle will not be their only vehicle and is unlikely to be their primary vehicle. That means the environmental benefit is lessened, as it is not fully replacing all the driving that would have been done with their conventional car or SUV.

With an internal combustion vehicle, most of the environmental impact comes from burning the gas or diesel that powers it, but an electric vehicle is different. There are no tailpipe emissions, and the emissions from grid power depend on the electricity sources that supply it. For example, emissions will be far lower in hydro-powered Norway or nuclear-powered France than Germany, which uses much more coal and gas for its energy needs, but they would all still have a lower environmental impact than filling a tank with gas or diesel fuel. However, the electric vehicle also has emissions from the manufacture of the battery and everything that goes into it, and those emissions can be considerable, especially since they vary based on where the battery is produced. Batteries made in Asia, for example, tend to have a larger environmental footprint than those produced in Europe because the grids that power the factories use dirtier energy sources.

Even though Tesla pitches itself as an automaker that is setting out to save the world by replacing every vehicle on the road with an electric one—already a dubious environmental proposition—its recent actions provide reason to question those environmental commitments. As it shifts production to China with its planned Shanghai Gigafactory, the company's emissions have been rising. But that increase is not simply because it is expanding and producing more vehicles; the production emissions of each individual vehicle are also rising, which means they will need to last even longer to ensure their lifecycle emissions—the total amount they emit from manufacture to when they are retired—are lower than a conventional vehicle.[21]

Tesla's Nevada factory was supposed to derive power from solar panels covering its roof, but the company never finished building the solar array. Further, Tesla vehicles already have a reputation for poor build quality with customers consistently complaining of problems with their vehicles and reports detailing the high quantity of wasted parts in the production process. As the vehicles age, Tesla has been recalling hundreds of thousands of them for everything from drivetrain issues to touchscreen failures. Bear in mind that the company only produced its millionth car in 2020. Tesla even told regulators that its touchscreens were only intended to last for five to six years, far less than the average lifespan of a vehicle. The company may have a great brand image, but its vehicles are not built to last, which should further call into question their "green" reputation.

In recent years, Tesla has also been unveiling larger vehicles, including its Cybertruck concept that takes design cues from dystopian science fiction, and other automakers have followed suit with various electric SUVs, trucks, and even an electric Hummer. These vehicles will not only require larger batteries, which means more extracted material per vehicle, but they could make local air pollution worse.

Electric vehicles may not have tailpipe emissions, but that is not the sole source of the local air pollution that produces smog and causes a range of health problems, including more than 53,000 annual premature deaths in the United States alone.[22] The particulate matter that causes that air pollution also comes from wear to tires, brake pads, and resuspending dust on the roadways. Those particles are incredibly small, and while electric vehicles tend to produce less of the 10 micrometer particles, known as PM10, the heavier electric vehicles that are increasingly being marketed in North America usually produce more of the smaller 2.5 micrometer or PM2.5 variety, which are more harmful to human health.

The particulate matter remains in the vicinity of where the vehicle is driven, but there is a final environmental and social justice concern that accompanies the adoption of electric vehicles. In a similar way to how extraction is outsourced to areas where most drivers will not see it, the emissions for the electricity that powers the vehicles could also be disproportionately shifted to poorer and rural communities where power plants are more likely to be located. That means that wealthier communities that are more likely to adopt electric vehicles will have less pollution from vehicle tailpipes, but the pollution produced from charging their vehicles every night will be breathed in by people who are more likely to be living close to the facilities that generate the power, and when those processes uses fossil fuels, the nearby residents—who are more likely to have lower incomes, be racial minorities, and still be driving vehicles with internal combustion engines—will shoulder the burden of the air pollution.

Ultimately, there are serious implications for environmental and social justice when we consider how to transform our transportation system to reduce emissions and address other challenges that have arisen from the mass adoption of personal automobiles. One of the Nordic experts explained that "the typical, single Tesla Model X owner received subsidies in 2016 worth the same amount you can hand out to provide 30,000 trips on the buses and the subway system of Oslo,"[23] which helps to illustrate the problem: remaining focused on automobiles continues to benefit the elite who have always been the primary beneficiaries of their sale and use. A more equitable, environmentally conscious transportation system will ultimately require reducing the use of automobiles, regardless of what powers them, and embracing other forms of mobility that not only produce fewer emission per person but offer a path to reimagining our communities in a way that does not need to make room for cars.

Over a hundred years ago, there was a decade when it seemed like the electric vehicle might define the future of personal mobility, but those hopes were dashed by a lack of industry coordination and Ford's more efficient manufacturing practices. Now the electric vehicle is back from the dead, and, in the face of the climate crisis, it offers one element of the comprehensive solution that will be needed to address a major part of the problem: reducing emissions from transportation. Yet we cannot allow ourselves to get caught up in the narrow arguments in favor of electric vehicles pushed by industry and liberal environmentalists who ignore the broader consequences of the overhaul they propose.

Any attempt to call attention to the problems with the mass adoption of electric vehicles online is almost guaranteed to draw the attention of Tesla fans or cleantech enthusiasts who consider people concerned about these issues to be shills for the oil industry. But that is not the argument this chapter is making. We must transition away from fossil fuels, and it must be done far more quickly than most governments are proposing if we hope to keep warming below 1.5°C—a goal that, admittedly, seems more unattainable with every passing year of inadequate action. However, we also need to consider the system that is being created in the effort to replace most gas and diesel vehicles with electric ones.

Anyone who sees the transition through a lens of social and environmental justice, instead of just an opportunity to extract economic gains, must recognize that it offers a rare chance to rethink how these systems are organized. As Kirsch has noted, the core problem with the mass adoption of personal vehicles is not that they use fossil fuels, but that they are inherently unsustainable because of the sprawling communities they require and how inefficiently they use resources. We must avoid making the mistake of ignoring the global environmental footprint of building more than a billion electric vehicles to replace all the personal vehicles on the world's roads simply because the serious harms that will be produced by such an endeavor will be out of sight of most consumers.

The problems with fossil fuels do not begin and end at climate change. The extraction, refining, and transport of fossil fuels also cause incredible environmental damage that has been well documented. In Alberta, vast tailings ponds that are left over from bitumen extraction pollute the environment; in the Gulf of Mexico, the effects of the BP oil spill are still being felt more than a decade later; throughout North America, Indigenous groups and activists are constantly trying to stop the construction of pipelines because of the harm and risk they present for their communities; and that does not even consider the harm that has been wrought in the Global South by mining and oil companies. Riofrancos warned that

86

a transport system centered around electric vehicles risks creating a green extractivism that subordinates "human rights and ecosystems to endless extraction in the name of 'solving' climate change," thereby ignoring "the very real harm it inflicts on humans, animals, and ecosystems."[24]

With the interests of tech, automakers, and other influential industries aligning behind electric vehicles, and neoliberal governments seeing them as a means to make it appear as though they are doing something concrete to address climate change while trying to increase employment in manufacturing and resource sectors, there is a clear incentive to downplay environmental harms. Electric vehicles may also fuel a new commodities boom which will create further pressure to quickly open new mines and expand production, instead of taking the time to work with communities to decide where mining should occur, how its impacts can be mitigated, and what support there should be for them if their residents are affected or need to relocate.

Minerals will need to be mined for the electrification of transportation and the construction of renewable energy, but the quantity depends on several factors. Recycling must vastly increase, and leaving the development of recycling techniques to market forces—essentially placing the determination of what gets recycled to questions of whether it can be done profitably—is not good enough.

Instead of trying to have personal electric vehicles match the scale of personal gas or diesel vehicles, the emphasis should instead be on getting people to shift from driving to taking transit and cycling, while building more walkable communities where necessities are closer to home. For example, electric buses and bikes use far fewer minerals per person than personal vehicles, and the size of batteries in buses can be further reduced if there are overhead wires from which they can charge en route, instead of just while parked at the depot.

Continuing to rely on automobiles does not solve how the existing transportation system fuels the climate crisis and the destruction of local environments all around the world. While converting internal combustion vehicles to electric vehicles would reduce the total carbon footprint of the transport system, it would not be sufficient to address transportation's contribution to climate change, nor would it do enough to lessen the other serious social and health problems that result from automobiles and the communities they have created. When we look more broadly at the tech industry's transport solutions, we find that their refusal to contend with the challenges that arise from the dominance of automobiles is a common problem.

4

Uber's Assault on Cities and Labor

In 1914, a new challenger emerged on US streets. The electric vehicle's days were numbered, sales of its internal combustion counterpart were growing every year, and the streetcar remained the most important way for many urban residents to get around. However, due to the recession that year, there were a lot of people left without work who needed to find an alternative income, and they turned to unregulated transportation.

Production of the Ford Model T had begun in 1908, so by 1914 it was possible to find cheaper used models. That was especially the case in Los Angeles, where the automobile was more common than anywhere else in the United States. Even as most people kept using streetcars, which typically cost five cents per ride, some people felt there was room for another service that was not restricted to tracks, could take more liberty with routes, and, naturally, could generate a quick source of income for drivers. These services were called jitneys, and they started in Los Angeles before quickly spreading throughout the western United States and Canada in early 1915, and then to the east coast in the months that followed.

Jitneys were not a traditional taxi service where the driver picks up a passenger and charges a fare based on some combination of mileage, time, and a starting fee. Instead, they typically drove a set route with occasional deviations depending on road conditions and passenger demand, bringing together features of what we would today associate with buses, taxis, and delivery services. They could even be compared to the minibuses that are more common today in the

Global South. While there were multiple vehicle models used by jitney drivers, the most common was a Model T touring car that could seat four or five passengers and could accommodate even more people if they did not mind standing on the running boards. The fare varied and could start as low as five cents, but it could go up to as much as a dollar depending on demand and whether the passenger wanted to be dropped at their doorstep. The highest prices were charged during storms or streetcar strikes.

Jitney drivers rarely belonged to larger companies. There were some groups that operated multiple vehicles, but most drivers were independent and some would only take fares at certain times of the day or to make a bit of extra money on their regular commutes. Seen through the modern libertarian lens that drives thinking among adherents to free market economics and strands of technological utopianism, jitneys may seem like an innovative business undertaken by entrepreneurial individuals to fill a gap in the transportation system of the early twentieth century, but that requires one to ignore many of the effects of these services.

Jitneys were not an equitable transport service. They relied on workers who were struggling as a result of the recession, and were "often yesterday's unemployed locomotive engineer, policeman, bartender, printer, barber, or clerk."[1] Due to the cost of the vehicle, depreciation, and various other costs such as fuel and maintenance, it was unlikely that many jitney drivers were actually making a profit, and as a result there was a high turnover. The real beneficiaries of these drivers' precarity were the customers: businessmen, people "with a high valuation of time," and some younger people; as fares increased at peak times, taking a jitney was largely unaffordable to lower-income residents.[2]

As jitneys pulled riders from streetcars and, in some cities, caused traffic that delayed them, streetcars began losing money. Unlike jitneys, which originally paid little in taxes or fees, the private streetcar companies of the time had significant obligations written into their municipal franchise agreements. Some of those contractual requirements included maintaining the pavement around their tracks, if not to the edge of the street; providing free street lighting; and paying municipal tax of up to 1 or 2 percent of every nickel they brought in. As streetcars cut costs and jobs, there was growing pressure for government action from streetcar companies, organized labor, and even downtown businesses who did not want shopping patterns to be disrupted. But there was another big issue that accelerated the need to do something about jitneys.

For their time, jitneys were fast. They could get a rider to their destination far quicker than a streetcar—that was the main benefit riders were paying for—and speed also allowed the drivers to complete more rides, and so earn more money. However, automobiles and streetcars were not the only vehicles navigating the streets; there were still plenty of people using them, and jitneys created a new hazard. In Los Angeles, collisions had increased 22 percent by March 1915 and jitneys were involved in 26 percent of all traffic accidents.[3] This trend was replicated in every city where jitneys operated. They also had a reputation for being used for abductions, robberies, and rapes.

Through 1915 and 1916, cities across the United States regulated jitneys by requiring them to carry insurance, get proper licensing, pay taxes, and observe other requirements that varied by city. There were estimated to be 62,000 jitneys in service at their peak in 1915, but by October 1918 there were fewer than 5,900 remaining, and their numbers continued to decline. The jitney was dead, but that did not mean the streetcar returned to its dominant position. The popularity of automobiles continued to grow, especially in the aftermath of World War II when state investments explicitly promoted their sale and use. But could history have taken a turn in a different direction?

*   *   *

In 2016, Uber co-founder and then-CEO Travis Kalanick showed up at a TED conference to spin the tale of Uber and impress upon the attendees why his company was essential for the future of urban transportation. But he did not start with his rapidly growing company; he started with the story of the jitney.

In Kalanick's telling, jitneys were an innovative, entrepreneurial service choked out by "the trolley guys, the existing transportation monopoly."[4] He argued that the regulation of jitneys ultimately killed a shared future of mobility in favor of one that centered around personal ownership—which would come to dominate mobility in the twentieth century. But there are problems with Kalanick's framing.

First, the Uber co-founder left out the downsides of jitneys: how they took advantage of precarious labor, caused a surge of traffic accidents, and denied local governments the tax revenue and services they could expect from the streetcars. There were plenty of other reasons for local governments to act in the face of jitneys; the social and fiscal costs of the new service were simply too high and jitneys did not have enough political clout to stop new regulations from being applied.

Second, the dominant means of transportation at the time was not the personal vehicle, but the streetcar. So, with jitneys regulated out of existence, one would have expected streetcars to re-establish their dominance over urban transportation, but that was not exactly what happened. Streetcars enjoyed increased ridership throughout World War I, but people then began to shift away from transit service toward the personal automobile. That was not because a shared option was defeated, but because the interests behind the automobile could reap far more profit from selling a vehicle or two to nearly every family in the United States than they would make from shared jitney services or anything similar, especially at a time when the full implications of a transportation system based around personal ownership of automobiles were not clear to the public.

Kalanick's story was misleading, but it was framed that way for a reason. At the end of his presentation, he told the audience that we missed the chance to have a transport system based on shared automobility, but "technology has given us another opportunity." Kalanick wanted to place Uber within a longer history, to give it a historical precedent that made it seem as though it was attempting to change the transportation system for the better. But like so many of the arguments that have been made about Uber over the years, it was designed to distract from the real outcomes of the company's actions.

Uber is one of many ride-hailing services that have emerged around the world since the 2008 financial crisis, but it is undeniably the most recognizable in Western markets. While the company has expanded into other services in recent years, ride-hailing remains its core business. That essentially means it acts in many ways like a taxi service, but ride requests (and payment) are facilitated by the company's smartphone app instead of through a dispatch service, taxi stand, or simply by waving down a car on the street.

When the service launched in 2011, the goal was not necessarily to take on the taxi industry. Garrett Camp, the co-founder who had the initial idea, wanted a cheaper way to hire a private driver, so Uber started as a method to hail luxury black cars; but it quickly set its ambitions far higher. In 2012, Uber started letting almost anyone sign up to drive on the app with their own vehicle to provide its lower cost UberX service. As part of that effort, Uber unleashed an extensive lobbying operation to rewrite laws in jurisdictions that required longer, more intense fingerprint-based background checks for drivers. In typical "move fast and break things" fashion, it did not ensure it had the proper licensing or regulations from local governments. It just set the service loose regardless of the consequences—and there were plenty.

Kalanick made many bold claims about the benefits that

Uber could bring to cities, but they were as naïve or decep-
tive as his argument that jitneys could have fundamentally
altered the direction of urban mobility. In Kalanick's telling,
the "uberization" of transportation would make taking an
Uber cheaper than owning a car.[5] Unleashing Uber on cities
would reduce personal vehicle ownership, cut traffic congestion, allow parking lots to be converted to other uses, and
complement public transit by providing a "last mile" service.
The service would be better for cities and their residents, and
it would cut emissions by reducing vehicle use.

All these benefits were the product of Uber's innovative
app and its underlying algorithmic trip-planning system, and
that positioning made it a tech company deserving of a sizable
valuation based on the assumption it would achieve the
exponential growth of a software product, not a traditional
transportation company. But to achieve Kalanick's goals, the
"taxi cartel" had to be defeated so it could be stopped from
snuffing out this better future and so avoid a repeat of the
streetcar "monopoly's" strangulation of the jitney.

There is no doubt that the narrative Kalanick wove was an
attractive one. We were taught to believe that technological
solutions alone could address difficult problems, and users
and journalists bought the story Kalanick was selling. In the
years after Uber's launch, and especially its move into competition with the taxi industry, the media adopted the language
of Silicon Valley to echo marketing claims that innovative
new technologies were being developed to disrupt traditional
industries for the better.

Many of the journalists covering the tech beat failed to
dig into the histories of the industries that companies were
claiming to disrupt, and did not do their due diligence on
whether they were really doing what they claimed. Instead,
there was an incentive to break new stories quickly, get in
the good graces of the industry's ascendent firms and founders, and to believe the claims they were making.[6] Years later,

even after a series of scandals among major tech firms kicked off a "techlash" that forced the mainstream press to adopt a slightly more critical perspective on the industry and its claims, companies like Uber could still get away with misrepresenting their earnings and even financial journalists would uncritically repeat them.

The media's representations of Uber and the wider gig economy served to mislead the public, politicians, and regulators about what effects they might have on society. Reporters' uncritical stories gave people permission not to consider the implications of using on-demand services, and that has come with consequences. The promises that ride-hailing services would improve urban mobility have not come to pass, even as the conditions of drivers have steadily worsened. But Uber has also presented a system-wide challenge to regulations and labor laws, the destruction of which serves the interests of Uber and other major corporations, not workers or urban residents—context that was shockingly lacking in mainstream assessments of the company, until it was too late.

Uber executives claimed their service provided an opportunity to take on the cronyism of the taxi industry; in particular, how cities limited taxi numbers, which led to higher prices and slower service. They acted as though this situation was designed to benefit some taxi monopolists over residents and workers. But that narrative ignored the history of the taxi industry, and why those regulations were established in the first place.

After jitneys disappeared from North American streets, it did not actually mean that "shared" mobility was dead. Taxis plied the streets of cities and towns across the United States with little regulation, at least until the Great Depression of the thirties hit. With the unemployment rate soaring, some of the people who found themselves out of work did exactly what the jitney drivers had done a decade and a half earlier: they started driving as "cut rate" taxis. There were 84,000 taxis on US streets before the Depression, but that number almost doubled to 150,000 by 1932.[7] Naturally, that also caused a lot of problems.

In many cities, there was already an oversupply of taxis before the Depression hit. In the framing of modern ride-hailing companies, oversupply is not an issue because it makes the rider's experience more convenient: it becomes easier to find a ride and the price of that ride is lower because there is a lot of competition. But, like with jitneys, the effects were not all positive. As the number of taxis increased, it also made congestion in city centers like Manhattan much worse. Personal vehicles only enter the street for short periods of time to get to their destination, but taxis stay on the road for hours and hours transporting people and looking for their next fare. Yet the more taxi supply there is on the road, the longer the drivers (and their vehicles) need to circle to find the next rider, creating a lot of excess miles driven that make traffic worse and slow down everyone else.

The oversupply of taxis also led to "rate wars" where prices were slashed as taxi operators fought with cut-rate taxis and nickel cabs for passengers. This cannot just be seen through the lens of the rider: as it became harder to find a passenger and those passengers paid less than they used to, the driver's income plummeted. Those factors combined to make the state of the taxi industry unsustainable, forcing local governments to step in by the late 1930s. Their solution was to cap the number of taxis that could operate on city streets, regulate the fare price, and ensure certain safety standards by mandating insurance coverage and vehicle maintenance. As a result, it may have taken a bit more time for a taxi to arrive, but congestion problems were partly addressed and taxi drivers were guaranteed a decent living. Certainly, the industry and the regulations applied to it have fluctuated since that time, but in many cities a regulatory structure similar to that established in the 1930s remained in place—at least until the arrival of ride-hailing services.

As Uber spread in the years following 2012, the streets of cities in the United States and around the world were flooded with ride-hail vehicles and local governments were slow to regulate them. Since the companies claimed they were not taxi services but technology companies—even though they effectively offered the same service—they argued that the existing rules did not apply to them. The only difference, however, was the app-based mediation, which many taxi companies adopted in the years that followed anyway. Even as Kalanick and other ride-hailing executives made bold promises for the future they claimed to be ushering in—one of shared mobility instead of car ownership that would ostensibly solve congestion and many other transport problems—the reality was almost the complete opposite.

San Francisco is the urban core of Silicon Valley, and unsurprisingly one of Uber's largest markets. The tech workers of the Bay Area are among the biggest users of the app-based solutions they create, since they exist to solve what they deem to be problems or hinderances in their own lives. So, if Uber was reducing traffic, we would naturally expect to see less congestion in San Francisco—but that is not what researchers have found.

Between 2010 and 2016, the number of hours that drivers spent stuck in traffic in San Francisco increased by 62 percent, and the average speeds of vehicles on the city's roads dropped by 13 percent. There were many factors that influenced what was happening on San Francisco's roads over that period of time, but the academics who performed the study determined that ride-hailing vehicles "are the biggest factor driving the rapid growth of congestion and deterioration of travel time reliability in San Francisco," and that they exceeded "the combined effects of population growth, employment growth, and network changes."[8] In short, Uber is not reducing traffic congestion in San Francisco; it is making it much worse.

San Francisco's transportation authority backed the academics' findings. In its own research, the agency found that drivers from around the Bay Area drove into San Francisco because they had a better chance to get a passenger in the core of the city. The impact was to add more vehicles on the road and so make the streets of downtown far more congested, even though that is the part of the city where residents or visitors could most easily walk or take transit to get to their destinations.[9] Unfortunately, San Francisco is not unique in experiencing this negative outcome.

In New York City, transport consultant Bruce Schaller examined the effects of ride-hailing services and found that even as the number of taxis on the street and their total mileage dropped, the increase in the number of ride-hailing vehicles and their mileage more than made up for it. Between 2013 and 2017, the combined number of taxis and ride-hailing vehicles increased by 59 percent and their combined mileage jumped by more than one-third.[10] As in San Francisco, the glut of ride-hailing vehicles meant more traffic and slower travel speeds. One of Schaller's most interesting findings was that neither the private ride-hailing services nor the pooled services—where a rider can choose to share their ride with someone else to get a cheaper price—reduced the number of miles driven. He estimated that every mile of a trip completed with a personal vehicle would require 2.8 miles of driving in a private hailed trip or 2.6 miles in a pooled trip—and it makes perfect sense.[11]

If I was driving a vehicle, I would go directly where I needed to go, and the only excess driving might be to find a parking spot. Meanwhile, if I was to open the Uber app and hail a ride, the driver would need to drive from wherever they were waiting to pick me up. After they dropped me off, they would go back to circling until they got another ride, and since Uber avoids the cap on taxi drivers in the vast majority of jurisdictions where it operates, there are more people driving around waiting for a rider to make a request. The Uber model adds vehicles to the road and creates more traffic, especially since the app incentivizes drivers to be active during peak times when traffic is already backed up.

However, the problem is not just due to people switching from driving their own vehicles to hailing rides. Multiple studies have found that Uber not only induces more travel, but encourages people who would otherwise take transit, cycle, or walk to their destination to instead get in a hailed vehicle. In Boston, it was estimated that 54 percent of the trips that users took on ride-hailing services would have been made by taking transit, cycling, or walking if the services had not been available, and 5 percent of trips would not have happened at all.[12]

Meanwhile, a larger survey that covered Boston, Chicago, Los Angeles, New York, San Francisco, Seattle, and Washington, DC similarly found that between 49 and 61 percent of trips on ride-hailing services pulled people from those more efficient transport modes or would not have happened if ride-hailing services had not been available. The researchers also found that people using Uber were very unlikely to get rid of their personal vehicles.[13] This shows that Uber is not reducing congestion or vehicle ownership, and it is also unlikely to reduce transport emissions or to complement traditional public transit.

All the Uber and Lyft vehicles that flooded North American streets also made transit services less reliable and less efficient. Buses get stuck in traffic more often and, naturally, riders then start to look for alternatives. In Toronto, less than half of ride-hailing users had a transit pass, compared to just over one-third in Boston,[14] and a study of twenty-two US cities estimated that the entry of Uber or Lyft reduced the ridership of buses and heavy rail every year they operated.[15] It should go without saying that taking people from transit and putting them in cars not only makes traffic worse, it also increases the environmental footprint of a trip. In fact, an Uber trip is estimated to create 69 percent more pollution when one accounts for the number of trips that would have been made in a more efficient way had the service not been available.[16]

Despite all its big promises, Uber is not improving urban mobility. Ride-hailing services make traffic worse, they increase emissions, and they reduce transit service—but they do benefit some people, and it is not disadvantaged users. By requiring a smartphone and data package, ride-hailing disproportionately excludes poor people and seniors. By increasing prices at peak times through what it calls "surge pricing," it becomes unavailable to low-income residents. And by arguing that the Americans with Disabilities Act does not apply to ride-hailing services by falsely claiming they are tech companies, not transport companies, people using wheelchairs have to wait far longer for a ride—if they can find one at all. It may not be surprising then to learn that ride-hailing customers tend to be young urbanites with a college education and a job that pays above $75,000 per year.[17] That is more than double the US median income in 2019. In Toronto, more than half of Uber users are estimated to earn more than 100,000 Canadian dollars.[18]

What this tells us is that not only is Uber having negative effects on urban mobility and the environment, but it is doing so to serve people who are not struggling to get around. Most of its users are not the people experiencing long waits for the bus to arrive or having to walk long distances because they cannot afford any other options. Instead, they are people who could easily drive, be driven, or hop in a taxi if they did not want to walk, cycle, or take transit. But those options were not cheap or convenient enough, so they had to blow up the existing system and regulatory framework to serve themselves. Yet, like with the jitneys and the taxis of the 1930s, this is not just a story about the customer or the street. There are also drivers involved; if tech workers and their bosses have been the beneficiaries of Uber, it is the people driving them around who have suffered the consequences.

Ride-hailing companies claim their workers are not equivalent to taxi drivers, and so should not be covered by the same rules and regulations even though they provide the same service. Despite strong taxi workers' organizations in cities across the United States, Uber and Lyft have been successful in disrupting the taxi industry and avoiding those regulations that apply to traditional taxis and their drivers. Before digging into how they were able to accomplish that, and the wider implications for workers, what ride-hailing companies have achieved should be placed in historical context.

In a comprehensive article about the history of San Francisco's taxi industry, legal scholar Veena Dubal explained that Uber's successful deregulation of the industry was the culmination of decades of a slow rolling back of taxi workers' rights. Until the 1970s, taxi workers were typically unionized employees with a decent standard of living that included health insurance and access to the rights and benefits that came with employment status. However, that was starting to change. Taxi companies wanted to rid themselves of the unions, even though they had become far less radical since the 1950s. In other US cities, the companies had successfully switched from an employment model to one where taxi workers were independent contractors who leased their vehicles from the taxi companies and were covered by corporate insurance.

By the end of the 1970s, taxi drivers in San Francisco had also succumbed to the leasing model. As one former driver told Dubal, even though they were classified as independent contractors, "there was nothing that changed, except you signed a document. Nothing else changed. Your relationship

with the company didn't change not one iota."[19] The drivers
were still doing the same work, but they were treated as
contractors instead of employees. Yet they still had one tool
available to them.

The decades of union power had left San Francisco and
other cities with a strong regulatory framework that drivers
could use to their advantage. The number of cabs on the street
was regulated, meaning the market could not be flooded to
drive down their wages. Regulations also protected the fares
they could charge. Even though drivers failed to win back
employee status or their unionization rights—independent
contractors are excluded under the US National Labor Relations Act—they did succeed at getting the city to regulate the
price of a daily lease to limit the taxi companies' ability to
squeeze them in 1998. But by then there was another effort to
scale back workers' regulatory protections.

In the 1990s, libertarian think tanks made a big push to
deregulate the US taxi industry, in line with their ideological
bias against regulation and in favor of ostensibly free markets.
Transport consultant Hubert Horan explained that this effort
was not initiated by local residents in cities around the country,
but rather "were entirely organized and financed by external
interests who systematically repeated its key messages across
a range of contexts and publications."[20] The think tanks' push
to deregulate largely failed, but the communications plan they
used was adopted almost wholesale in the early 2010s as Uber
rolled out its service and sought to evade the regulations that
were the last line of defense for taxi workers to protect their
livelihoods.

The Uber model built on the leasing model of the 1970s
by ensuring drivers were independent contractors that the
company had no obligations toward. Only now, instead of
providing vehicles and insurance as taxi companies do under
the leasing model, all those costs and the associated risks were
outsourced to drivers. Even though there is no Uber without

drivers, the company claimed its only role was to facilitate the relationship between drivers and riders through its smartphone app, and most regulators bought it for much of the company's first decade of operation. But that came with severe consequences for drivers, whether they drove ride-hailing vehicles or taxis.

When Uber launched in new cities, it not only sought to flood the market with drivers by allowing virtually anyone with a pulse (and a vehicle) to become an Uber driver, it also offered incentives that were designed to attract existing taxi drivers. The company wanted people to believe that Uber was more convenient than using taxis, had a vision for a better shared transport system, and offered a better deal to drivers. In various campaigns, it claimed that drivers in New York City could earn up to $90,000 per year, while those in San Francisco could earn up to $74,000—much more than many taxi drivers were earning. Unsurprisingly, many within the media were happy cheerleaders for Uber and repeated these claims uncritically, misleading users about how the company was treating drivers and allowing them to believe in the myth that Uber was building out its supposedly technologically innovative approach to mobility.

In 2017, Uber settled charges by the Federal Trade Commission after the agency found its claims about high earnings in New York City, San Francisco, and other major cities were false—but by that time the damage had been done. Uber had already established itself, swept away decades of regulations designed to protect taxi drivers, and decimated the taxi industry by evading the rules that applied to it.

Once Uber had strengthened its market position and riders had become accustomed to turning to its app instead of calling a taxi, the incentives it offered were rolled back and drivers' pay was systematically cut. Simultaneously, Uber told drivers that lower prices would attract more customers, which would allow them to deliver more rides and so make up the difference—but that was rarely how the situation played out in practice. A pay cut was a pay cut, and it made drivers' precarious situations even worse.

Uber drivers had to pay all the costs associated with their vehicles—loan payments, maintenance, fuel, and insurance—and as they worked longer hours to try to make up the difference, many of those costs increased. Despite the company's positive narratives, drivers reported being incredibly stressed, unable to pay their bills or see a doctor, and some even had to resort to sleeping in the very vehicles they ferried their typically well-off users in. Uber's flooding of the market further deteriorated the conditions of workers compared to the taxi drivers' experience under the leasing model by creating an oversupply of drivers and evading the regulation of the fare. Suddenly, Uber was in control, and its drivers were not the only ones to suffer.

Taxi drivers also saw their incomes plummet after Uber arrived, and no matter how much longer they drove, they could not make up the difference. On top of losing customers, taxi drivers had big debts they could no longer pay. The limitations on the number of taxis in cities like New York City and San Francisco were managed through the issuing of medallions, which effectively gave drivers the right to operate in the city, but they came at a high cost as the cities saw an additional revenue source.

In San Francisco, the privatization of taxi medallions took place in March 2009, as the country was still struggling with the effects of the recession. The medallions cost $250,000 and drivers had to scrape together a 5 percent deposit, but the city promised them it was a safe investment. Yet, just a few years after drivers had taken on those large debts, Uber and Lyft entered the market and the city did not hold up its end of the bargain.

Not only did taxi drivers' lives fall apart in the years following the swift transformation of their industry to serve the interests of multinational ride-hailing companies, but some felt there was no getting out of the hole they then found themselves in. A driver in Chicago told NBC News in 2018 that he had colleagues die of heart attacks and strokes after Uber and Lyft left them in dire financial straits. That same year, four taxi drivers, three livery drivers, and an Uber driver committed suicide in New York City.[21]

The most high-profile of those suicides was that of Douglas Schifter. He was a black-car driver who had spent forty-four years driving all manner of vehicles on the streets of the Big Apple. But his livelihood had been decimated. There were few fares anymore and, as he explained in his suicide note, even though he had gone from driving forty to fifty hours per week to up to one hundred and twenty, he was still losing everything. Shifter wrote that his profession had become "the new slavery" as executives "get their bonuses" while drivers were "becoming homeless and hungry."[22] On the morning of February 5, 2018, Shifter published his note to Facebook and parked his black car outside City Hall, where he took his shotgun and pulled the trigger to end his life. He hoped his death would force the city government to finally address the struggles of his colleagues.

In 2013, venture capitalist and Uber investor Shervin Pishevar told *Inc* magazine that Uber was "in the empire-building phase."[23] At the time, Uber had pushed its way into thirty-five cities around the world; it now operates in more than 10,000. From the early days, Kalanick and those around him were not just seeking to capture a large market share in key cities; they wanted to dominate urban transportation by remaking it for their ends and establishing a monopoly that would allow them to extract the enormous profits their investors were expecting.

Uber sought to follow the growth model pioneered by Amazon. Instead of turning a profit as quickly as possible to return value to investors, Amazon CEO Jeff Bezos played the long game. It took his company nearly a decade to turn a profit, and even then it was not a big one. When Amazon made money, it was reinvested to improve existing services and expand into new product categories, and later into whole lines of business. In 1994, Amazon was an online bookseller operating out of Bellevue, Washington, but less than three decades later it is the leading ecommerce platform and cloud computing provider in the United States, with its hands in film production, game streaming, pharmaceuticals, grocery, and much more. Uber wanted to build its own monopoly, but the central element of Amazon's success did not translate to transportation.

As Amazon grew, it took advantage of economies of scale to ensure that as its business expanded it was able to make its fulfillment and logistics operations more efficient and reduce the costs of picking, packing, and delivering an order. But Uber cannot replicate those cost savings through growth. As Horan explained, about 85 percent of the cost of an urban car service comes from drivers, vehicles, and fuel, and they are not costs that fall as a company grows, especially when Uber requires each driver to maintain their own vehicle instead of managing a vehicle fleet.[24] The shocking thing about Uber is that, despite the narrative of the efficiency offered by its ride-matching algorithms, it actually provides a less efficient service than a traditional taxi company. That helps to explain how, after a decade, it is still losing money hand over fist.

In 2020, Uber lost $6.77 billion on its global operations—that, however, is not an anomaly caused by the global pandemic; it was actually an improvement on its 2019 loss of $8.5 billion. In fact, given that Uber continues to lose money on most of its rides, the fewer it delivers, the better it may be for its financials. The persistence of these significant losses, even after going public, tells us something about the company's business model and the potential motivation of those who keep stringing it along.

There is no question that Uber's app made hailing a ride more convenient than having to call a taxi, but it also felt like the future: users were tapping a button on their smartphones, they could see where their driver was on the virtual map, and payment was handled automatically once the ride was complete. Yet the technology was not why Uber exploded in the way it did; it was because it underpriced its service in comparison to its competitors.

Taxi companies not only had regulated fares in many cities, but drivers also had to cover their costs so they could pay their bills. There was nowhere else they could turn for money to sustain themselves if they set a price that was below the cost of operation. But that was not the case for Uber. Ride-hailing companies around the world got billions of dollars from investors with the goal of driving traditional competitors out of business. Evading regulations certainly helped, but the key was predatory pricing.

When Uber entered a new city, it not only offered incentives to entice drivers; it also ensured prices were lower than comparable services. In 2016, Horan estimated that Uber users were only paying 41 percent of the total cost of their ride; the rest was being covered by the company.[25] Naturally, there was no way taxis could compete even though their cost structures were more efficient. A traditional taxi company has drivers, vehicles, and the dispatching operation to cover, but Uber had many more expenses that cost the company a small fortune.

Uber's executives were paid millions of dollars a year, and that was before their stock options. Uber had to maintain expensive headquarters in cities around the world and staff them with highly paid engineers to work on the technical side of its business. It also had a research and development operation through which it burned hundreds of millions of dollars a year on autonomous vehicles, flying cars, and other pie-in-the-sky ideas that brought no returns. In short, Uber not only missed out on the efficiencies of having a vehicle fleet and in-house insurance, it had many costs that taxi companies did not, which made its service more expensive to deliver, despite its claims to the contrary.

As activity picked up in the summer of 2021 with the rollout of Covid-19 vaccines in the United States, users got a taste of what ride-hailing services will look like as the companies try to turn a profit. Users complained of higher fares, especially for trips to the airport, and much longer waits. There was a common recognition that the days of subsidized rides were coming to an end, and some users even reported turning back to taxis or bicycles for more of their trips.

Uber could not fulfill its promises to reduce congestion and solve other urban problems, nor could it give drivers a good living with a stable income. And even after breaking those promises, it still could not turn a profit. The question then is how it is still able to operate such a service despite the heavy losses and little sign of any public benefit. The answer is that the interests that have coalesced around it may have a bigger goal in mind.

Let us return to the story of the jitney: the cut-rate taxis that arose in 1914, but were quickly regulated in 1915 and 1916, and had effectively disappeared a couple of years later. Not only were they intruders on streets that were still seen as shared spaces where pedestrians could roam freely, but they also got in the way of the dominant streetcars whose operators did not want jitneys disrupting existing transport patterns. Local governments heard the concerns of streetcar operators and pedestrians, but also realized how jitneys threatened the revenues and services provided by streetcars. The regulations they brought in were designed to ensure jitneys provided public benefit and did not curtail other road users' rights. But because many of the services were barely profitable, if they made any money at all, the individual drivers and small franchises could not cope with the regulatory burden and gave way to other forms of mobility.

Jitneys sought to carve out their own space, separate from the existing transport options—but failed. They were disorganized drivers with limited support among the establishment of the time, and while they did form an organization to represent their interests, it was not nearly as powerful as the dominant players. But with ride-hailing services, things were different. Drivers worked for one of a small number of large companies, and those corporations fought to ensure the regulatory system and transport network served their business goals.

Uber was able to take advantage of the large pool of precarious labor that lingered after the 2008 recession, promising it would create employment—a message that can reliably be counted on to win politicians' support. Furthermore, the post-recession years were a time of incredible technological optimism. People wanted to believe that Silicon Valley and its rapidly growing tech companies would save the economy, so much of the media and the political class bought into the narratives of innovation that permeated the culture and the new services that benefited white-collar workers while exploiting those that had been left behind by the economic crash. But it was more than just a collective vibe; there were powerful forces at work behind the scenes.

Uber not only had the support of powerful players in Silicon Valley, including Google executives and influential venture capitalists, but given that it was replaying the deregulatory agenda of the 1990s, albeit with a tech twist, it also had the support of the network of conservative and libertarian think tanks that had been built in the preceding decades by right-wing billionaires such as the Koch brothers. By operating on a national and then a global scale, Uber could draw on many more resources in its fight against the taxi companies and drivers who operated in just a single city or region.

When Uber perceived the threat of regulation on the local level, where taxis were typically regulated, it would bring its massive lobbying operation to state lawmakers and get them to preempt local laws with more lax, state-wide regulations that codified ride-hailing services as separate from taxis. Naturally, this happened first in California. The state's Public Utilities Commission (PUC) created the classification of "Transportation Network Company" in 2013 to cover ride-hailing companies, which had the effect of taking regulatory authority away from San Francisco and other cities in the state.

At the time, the San Francisco Cab Drivers Association argued that the PUC's actions effectively deregulated the industry. In a statement, a spokesperson for the organization said, "any additional class of transportation provider, which offers the same on-call/on-demand passenger transportation service without the same regulatory standards, renders existing regulations meaningless."[26] They deemed it unfair competition because ride-hailing companies and their drivers would not have to follow the same rules as taxi drivers. Yet, even then, Uber still developed tools to evade enforcement.

In 2017, *New York Times* journalist Mike Isaac reported that Uber had been using a tool called Greyball since 2014 that identified authorities using their app and gave them a special designation. The authorities were then shown a different interface where attempts to hail a ride failed and the map was filled with fake cars so they could not easily identify ride-hail vehicles. Greyball was used in cities across the United States, Europe, and beyond to evade regulatory enforcement as it broke local laws in order to operate. Isaac explained that in Portland, Oregon, Uber had launched without permission of the city before getting banned, but it used Greyball to keep operating and stifle the authorities' ability to shut it down.

While the service was eventually normalized on a regulatory level in cities around the world, drivers did not stop organizing to win back the rights they had lost in Uber's industry deregulation. The most notable of these campaigns was, once again, in California.

As Uber grew, there was always debate about whether its drivers were really contractors or whether they should have been recognized as employees. Arguably, they were misclassified from the beginning, and in 2018, a California Supreme Court ruling made that much easier to affirm. In the *Dynamex* decision, the judicial body altered how it determined which workers were contractors or employees. The new standard assumed all workers were employees, unless the employer could prove otherwise under strict new guidelines. In September 2019, the decision was codified into law when California's state legislature passed Assembly Bill 5, which set a deadline of January 1, 2020, for employers to reclassify their workers—and the emphasis was placed on companies in the gig economy, including Uber and Lyft.

January 1 came and went without gig workers' status changing, but they kept pushing lawmakers to ensure the law was observed. In May 2020, California's attorney general and the city attorneys for San Francisco, Los Angeles, and San Diego took Uber and Lyft to court for misclassifying their workers, and the following month the PUC ruled that drivers for Uber and Lyft were employees, not contractors. On August 10, a judge ruled that the companies had ten days to reclassify their workers as employees, but at the last minute the ruling was delayed until after the election on November 3. As these challenges were playing out, the gig companies had another plan to evade reclassification.

Uber and Lyft had joined forces with other companies in the gig economy like DoorDash and Instacart to prepare a ballot measure to be considered by California voters that would cement their workers' status as independent contractors. Proposition 22, as it was named, also promised those workers a minimum wage and some benefits, but the wage guarantee was only for the time when a worker had a passenger or was completing a delivery order, meaning it effectively came to an estimated $5.64 per hour.[27] The benefits were similarly restricted, so few workers would actually be able to access them.

The companies put more than $200 million behind the campaign. They flooded users and drivers with pro–Proposition 22 notifications; paid off prominent figures to support the ballot measure, including the leader of the California branch of the National Association for the Advancement of Colored People, who later resigned over conflicts of interest; and sent out fake mailers making it seem as though Proposition 22 was supported by progressive groups associated with Senator Bernie Sanders. As a result, the initiative passed with more than 58 percent support—but in the weeks that followed, many voters said they were misled into believing it would help drivers, not deny them employment rights. Within a few months of the vote, the companies had raised their prices, despite claiming they would not have to do so if Proposition 22 passed, and workers said their pay had actually fallen.

After deregulating the industry, the gig companies had effectively rewritten the state's labor law to serve their interests. But in doing so, they also opened the door for other companies to reclassify their workers as contractors in the future. Dubal called Proposition 22 "the most radical undoing of labor legislation since Taft-Hartley in 1947,"[28] a federal bill that restricted the activities and power of unions, and its full effects remain to be seen.

The story of Uber demonstrates the continued relevance of the Californian Ideology. The company's faith in the market and new technologies to transform the taxi industry was unwavering, and at least presented the outward justification of improving the world. To that end, Uber ignored rules and regulations that impeded its rapid expansion and engaged with the political system only to stifle any attempts to enforce them. But despite all the bold claims about its transformative potential, Uber ultimately served an insidious agenda that harmed workers and the public while increasing corporate power.

When Kalanick said that Uber would crush the taxi cartel, he was not talking about the taxi companies, though they were certainly swept up in it; rather, he was talking about the last vestiges of taxi drivers' power over the conditions of their industry. This campaign was not undertaken to benefit the public as a whole, and it certainly did not benefit drivers. Instead, the fruits of deregulation accrued to the white-collar workers who escaped annihilation in the recession and to those young professionals in industries like tech and finance who prospered in the decade that followed at the expense of those who were wiped out by the crash together with the poor, immigrant, and workers of color who had never made it out of precarity to begin with.

Sadly, that is not just Uber's story, but the reality of so many of the tech industry's ideas for the future of transportation and cities. More technology and regulatory rollbacks do not solve fundamentally political problems; they just allow wealthy, powerful people to impose their will on everyone else. In Uber's case, at least the technology worked, but that is not always the case. And since the faith in technology can exceed its capabilities, rolling it out onto public streets before it is ready can have deadly consequences.

5

Self-Driving Cars Did Not Deliver

Google was an essential tool of the early web, but as the company grew to become one of the largest in the world thanks to the profits it derived from its search engine monopoly, it also gained the power to assert itself in industries outside of its main competency. In the early part of the 2010s, the company and its founders took a particular interest in the future of transportation, and naturally influenced how the entire industry—and much of the public—thought about how we should move in the years and decades ahead.

Sergey Brin, one of the company's co-founders, had been trying to turn himself into a technological visionary by running the experimental Google X division and hyping several of the technologies it had under development, with mixed success. Brin pitched a set of ugly smart glasses called Google Glass as the next big consumer tech product in 2012, but they were a flop. However, his vision for an urban future where self-driving cars would take over streets around the world initially seemed like it might avoid the same fate.

In September 2012, then California governor Jerry Brown appeared alongside Brin at Google's headquarters in Silicon Valley to sign a law aimed at accelerating the testing of autonomous vehicles. At the event, Brin told reporters that he believed "self-driving cars are going to be far safer than human-driven cars."[1] On top of that, the vehicles would reduce traffic congestion, improve fuel efficiency, be prepared for any eventuality that could arise, and better serve those "underserved by the current transportation system."

It was a bold vision; one that not only seemed to address many of the key issues created by the mass adoption of automobiles through the second half of the twentieth century, but that would rely on technology to solve those problems rather than government or regulators. Most importantly, this magical future of technological automobility was not far away. "You can count on one hand the number of years until ordinary people can experience this," Brin told reporters, as he assured them that while the company's goals were ambitious, he did not feel he was overpromising.[2] But that naïveté about the difficulties that would arise in development and whether the bold futures on offer would ever be achievable might end up being the definitive story of the autonomous vehicle.

The idea was that Google and other companies working on self-driving cars would place a number of sensors on a fleet of vehicles so they could "see" their surroundings, then their teams of engineers would train an artificial intelligence system, or AI, through simulations and real-world driving to be able to maneuver the vehicle in any road condition. People like Brin had such faith in the power of technology that they believed it would quickly be able to navigate public roads much better than a human driver, making us effectively obsolete.

Brin's vision of the mobility system that autonomous vehicles would usher in was very similar to the promises of ride-hailing companies, which were, not coincidentally, taking off in Silicon Valley at the same time. UberX, the lower-cost version of Uber's service that was specifically designed to take on the taxi business, launched in July 2012, just months before Brin appeared alongside Governor Brown. It too promised to solve congestion, serve the underserved, reduce emissions, and usher in a transport system that no longer relied on ownership. Whenever you wanted to go anywhere, you would request a ride and a vehicle would show up to shuttle you to your destination.

In the next two years, the hype around self-driving cars started to grow. Elon Musk told reporters that he was exploring an Autopilot system for Tesla vehicles in 2013, before beginning to build rudimentary hardware to operate such a system into new vehicles by September 2014. Toyota, Nissan, and other automakers also engaged with the question of driver automation, though they expected it to take more time than Brin proposed. At the Code Conference in May 2014, Uber CEO Travis Kalanick jumped on the self-driving bandwagon, telling the conference's co-founder Kara Swisher that "the reason Uber could be expensive is you're paying for the other dude in the car," and while automation would not happen overnight, it was his intention to automate the human drivers who were essential to delivering Uber's core product.[3] At the same time as Kalanick was making those statements, Uber was in a public relations battle over reports of drivers' incredibly low pay; and in the same way that the shine was coming off Uber, there were also troubles behind the scenes of Google's self-driving project.

The day before Kalanick had taken the stage, Brin had made his own appearance at the conference and autonomous vehicles were, once again, at the forefront of his mind. He described how Google X was working on projects to "transform the world," and showed off a prototype vehicle that was later dubbed the Firefly.[4] The vehicle looked more like a pod than a traditional sedan or coupe, and it had no steering wheel or pedals. The idea was that it would be driven by the self-driving system and human passengers would never need to worry about taking over. The utopian vision of autonomous vehicles was contained within the design of the vehicle itself: that the engineers at Google could develop a system that could drive in any road condition, any weather event, no matter what was happening around it, and at any time of the day or year. Brin repeated the vision he had laid out two years earlier of reducing congestion, parking spaces, and vehicle deaths and

collisions, and still believed the company would have autonomous vehicles giving rides to regular people within its original
five-year timeframe—so it had two or three years left to go.

Notably, the event also gave a glimpse of the role that tech
media played in legitimizing self-driving cars and the other big
ideas coming from influential figures in the industry. Swisher,
who was also the co-founder of tech news website Recode,
appeared in a short promotional video for the Firefly where
she called it delightful and cool, and affirmed it was "concep-
tually where things are going." Later in the interview, she said
she believed "the self-driving car is critically important."[5]

As a result, Brin was allowed to make his case for why
autonomous vehicles would give the company "the ability to
change the world and the community around you" without
much pushback, including the claim that there had been
no crashes in the vehicles. But despite safety being the core
argument in favor of getting rid of human drivers, there had
already been issues with the team's safety record. Prioritizing
the technology's development over safety would become a
problem as more companies sought to compete in the race for
the illusive self-driving car.

By the mid-2010s, Silicon Valley and many of the major
automakers had successfully led a significant segment of the
media and, by extension, the public to believe that the future
of ubiquitous autonomous vehicles was only a few years
away. They were going to transform the world, reshape our
communities, and solve all the long-standing problems with
mass automobile use, if only we could be patient and trust
the brilliant engineering minds at these companies to deliver
their groundbreaking products to market. There was no way
it would not happen; we just needed to have faith in the power
of technology. But this was hardly the first time that we had
been told that autonomous vehicles were going to revolution-
ize automotive mobility.

As vehicles were swamping urban streets and racking up a high death toll through the 1920s and 1930s, demonstrations of "phantom autos" were stunning audiences across the United States. A newspaper in Ohio remarked in 1932 that, "it is true that the driverless car will travel about the city through the heaviest traffic—starting, stopping, sounding its horn, turning right or left, making U-turns and circles, and proceeding thus as though there were an invisible driver at the wheel."[6] They were "one of the most amazing products of modern science," piloted not by a computer system, but by remote control. They were driverless in the sense that they did not have a driver behind the steering wheel and so hid the human labor for spectacle, which is not as distant from what is happening today as it may seem.

Self-driving cars became a common feature of the pulp science fiction of the time, and even made their way into seemingly more realistic visions of the future. General Motors' Futurama exhibition at the 1939 World's Fair in New York not only imagined millions more automobiles on the road and elevated pedestrian walkways to separate people and cars, but automated highways where vehicles were guided with radio control. The idea was that all these innovations would be in place by 1960, and, while the suburbs and expressways became more common in the following two decades, the technologically enhanced highways did not.

The Radio Corporation of America, better known as RCA, started testing a system of wires buried in the pavement to guide vehicles along highways in the 1950s. The "electronic chauffeurs" were designed to eliminate accidents and make the roads safer. When the system was demonstrated for journalists in 1960 using GM vehicles with coils in their front ends to pick up the electromagnetic fields, the *Press-Courier* declared that RCA had "put the driverless car on the road" and that riding in one "tends to be scary as the ghost, until you get used to it. But someday we may have to live with it."[7]

Sixty years later, we still do not have to live with any such thing, but development on the self-driving car continued in the United States and abroad.

In 1977, Tsukuba Mechanical showed off its own autonomous vehicle in Japan that improved upon earlier experiments by using two cameras that could detect street markings with a maximum speed of twenty miles per hour. A decade later, German engineer Ernst Dickmanns showed off VaMoRs, a vehicle equipped with cameras on the front and back. Using microprocessing units, it had a "dynamic vision" that could detect relevant objects on the road, allowing it to drive at speeds of up to sixty miles per hour on the Autobahn.[8] But despite those advancements, the autonomous vehicle remained an experiment.

The US government was also interested in the prospect of autonomous driving, both for military and civilian uses. In the 1980s, the DARPA Strategic Computing Initiative funded the Autonomous Land Vehicle project as part of its efforts to "bring new technologies to the battlefield."[9] The project made significant advances in the use of laser imaging and computer vision for autonomous navigation. One of the beneficiaries of that funding was Carnegie Mellon University, which used the money from DARPA to create its first Navlab autonomous vehicle. The experiment served as a foundation for future research aimed at civilian uses.

To that end, the Intermodal Surface Transportation Efficiency Act of 1991 mandated the Department of Transportation (DOT) to "develop an automated highway and vehicle prototype from which future fully automated intelligent vehicle-highway systems can be developed."[10] To achieve its aims by 1997, it handed out nearly $100 million to partners in the private sector and university research centers, including the same team at Carnegie Mellon. By 1995, the fifth Navlab made a semi-autonomous cross-country trip during which the computer controlled the steering wheel and a human driver did everything else. The DOT terminated the program in 1997, but that was not the end of government involvement.

Military funding continued into the 2000s with specific programs aimed at improving the capabilities of autonomous driving systems for battlefield uses, but it did not only fund its various contractors. DARPA also set up a series of challenges that were open to teams from around the world with monetary prizes if they could successfully engineer an autonomous vehicle that could navigate a designated obstacle course. The Grand Challenge featured an off-road course that no team was able to complete in 2004, so a second round was organized for 2005 where the group from Stanford University narrowly beat their colleagues from Carnegie Mellon, claiming the million-dollar prize.

In 2007, the Urban Challenge was held featuring a course in a mock urban environment where vehicles had to navigate interactions with pedestrians and other vehicles instead of uneven terrain. This time, DARPA gave eleven teams a million dollars each to aid in the development of their respective driving systems. The team from Carnegie Mellon took the two-million-dollar prize for first place, while the Stanford team won a million dollars for coming in second. Much of the experimentation for those challenges took place in universities and private companies, but it also corresponded with the rise of Silicon Valley and the growth of several of its key companies into economic juggernauts on the lookout for technological solutions beyond their core businesses. Unsurprisingly, those companies took notice of what these teams were up to.

Among the people working on vehicles to compete in the first Grand Challenge was Anthony Levandowski, an engineering student at University of California, Berkeley. He had relocated to California from Belgium in the mid-1990s before starting at UC Berkeley in 1998, but his role as team lead of a Grand Challenge group paved his way to join Google X and work on

SELF-DRIVING CARS DID NOT DELIVER

Street View in 2007. Street View allowed people using Google Maps to see what neighborhoods and businesses looked like at street level, but that required capturing images of all the streets in cities throughout the United States, then across the world.

Around the same time as he was hired by Google, Levandowski co-founded 510 Systems, which developed the box of sensors that sat on top of all the Google Maps cars to capture all those photos, which he sold to his employer. In 2008, he also founded Anthony's Robots to put together an autonomous Toyota Prius for a television show on Discovery Channel. By the next year, Brin and co-founder Larry Page had approved a driverless car project led by Sebastian Thrun, who led the Stanford team that competed in the DARPA challenges, with Levandowski working on hardware. Problems arose almost immediately.

Levandowski developed a reputation for being "an asshole," as one former co-worker put it to *New Yorker* journalist Charles Duhigg,[11] and his team felt he was more focused on elevating himself than advancing the project. To accelerate development, Google made use of some of the technology Levandowski had already developed through 510 Systems, but he was shopping it around to competitors at the same time as it was becoming a key component of Google's driverless vehicle project. When his actions became known, his team thought he would be fired, but the opposite happened. Page thought the company needed people like Levandowski because innovation on its core products was slowing down, so his authority was expanded despite resistance from Thrun and his colleagues. Google also acquired 510 Systems and Anthony's Robots, and structured the deal so Levandowski earned a significant payout because Page knew getting rich was one of his driving motivations. But being rewarded for his actions only intensified Levandowski's worst qualities.

In the early 2010s, as Brin was making the rounds talking up the wonderful future that autonomous vehicles would enable, Levandowski was on the development side and the approach he took embodied the "move fast and break things" mentality that considered safety a secondary goal to hitting the market before competitors. The software that the vehicles were using was limited to particular routes that the team believed it would be safe to operate on, but Google executive Isaac Taylor discovered that while he was on parental leave in 2011, Levandowski had disabled the safety protocol so he could use the vehicle wherever he wanted.

In an attempt to show that what he was doing was safe, Levandowski took Taylor out for a ride. But when the Prius he was using encountered a Toyota Camry trying to enter the freeway, it demonstrated the exact opposite. As Duhigg explained:

> A human driver could easily have handled the situation by slowing down and letting the Camry merge into traffic, but Google's software wasn't prepared for this scenario. The cars continued speeding down the freeway side by side. The Camry's driver jerked his car onto the right shoulder. Then, apparently trying to avoid a guardrail, he veered to the left; the Camry pinwheeled across the freeway and into the median.[12]

When Levandowski took over from the automated system, he had to maneuver so hard that Taylor sustained a spinal injury that later required several surgeries. Neither Levandowski nor Taylor reported their involvement to authorities or informed them that an autonomous vehicle was involved in the crash.

Afterward, Levandowski was unrepentant, defending the incident as "an invaluable source of data" as he sent around a video of the incident to his colleagues. He was not disciplined, and in fact continued driving on routes that were not part of the software. Former Google executives told Duhigg that there had been more than a dozen crashes in the early years of the project, and that at least three were serious, but that did not stop Brin from talking about how safe the vehicles would be.

Duhigg's report appeared in the *New Yorker* in 2018, at a time when the shine was already coming off the dream of autonomous vehicles and the hype machine was in free fall. But had that information been in the public domain years earlier when Brin was building the hype in the first place, the perception of autonomous vehicles and their capabilities could have been very different. Instead, we were treated to years of news cycles that helped create the myth that ubiquitous self-driving vehicles would solve all our transport problems, to such a degree that libertarian groups funded by the billionaire Koch brothers used the promise of autonomous vehicles to attack plans to expand public transit systems in the United States.

As with ride-hailing services, criticism of public transit became one of the defining narratives of the autonomous future. There were some who pushed the idea of automating bus drivers while maintaining a form of collective mobility, even as those proposals ignored the value of those workers beyond just driving the bus. But many advocates did not even pretend to want to maintain transit services. No longer would riders have to share space with other people—as Musk once said, a fellow transit passenger could be a serial killer!—or walk to a transit stop. Instead, a self-driving car would pick them up from any location and take them wherever they wanted to go—the perfect solution to the last-mile dilemma that assumed away any spatial problems with the dream of everyone having their own autonomous pod. Yet for all the hype, there are numerous problems built into the grand vision of our future of self-driving mobility, and getting people to accept them will require changing how they think about the streets once again.

In the early years of the automobile, it was believed that this new form of mobility would find a way to coexist with the existing multimodal street arrangement where horse-drawn carriages, street vendors, pedestrians, streetcars, and bicyclists shared the same space. Their low travel speeds and ability to see one another without a tinted windshield made it possible to navigate the busy streets, but as automobile speeds accelerated, they went from being just another one of those transport modes to an intruder that presented a lethal threat to other road users.

The desire for speed eventually sent the competing interests into their separate camps to fight for their respective visions of the street: those who favored the existing arrangement and those who wanted the automobile to dominate. As we know, the automotive interests came out on top, but the process of remaking streets and cities for the automobile was not a quick one, nor an easy one. As Peter Norton has explained, it required not just a physical reconstruction but also a social reconstruction so people would accept the new norms of the street.[13]

From the 1910s through to the 1930s, there were campaigns that slowly increased in intensity in cities around the United States to change the way people perceived the street and how it could be used. In schools, children were instructed to be careful around the street and only to cross at designated places. Even though they had a right to use the street, it was effectively lost because the speed of automobiles put them in such great danger. Newspapers also got in on the campaign, especially as the advertising dollars they received from automotive companies increased. They shifted their coverage of car crashes to place greater emphasis on the victim instead of the driver, which shaped public sentiment over time. This practice is still common today in the United States, with deaths and injuries more often attributed to the vehicle instead of the person behind the wheel.[14]

But one of the most consequential shifts was to smear pedestrians who walked into the street as "jaywalkers." The term was popularized in the 1920s and it implied that people who did not cross at designated spots were the equivalent of hicks or rednecks—people who did not understand the norms of city life. However, the "jaywalker" was not a concept that urban residents came up with themselves. Rather it was the product of the automotive industry, which designed it to shame pedestrians into surrendering their right to the street by altering the way that residents thought about themselves—and it was successful. Pedestrians were pushed off the streets, and those streets were physically and legally remade for automobiles. Roads were paved with smooth asphalt, lines were drawn to direct the flow of traffic, new lighting systems were developed for use at intersections, and the system of automobility grew from there.

Over the course of several decades, the automobile went from a pleasure vehicle for the rich that fit within the prevailing streetscape, even if imperfectly, to utterly dominating it with severe consequences for the environment, urban life, and the health and safety of anyone at street level—pedestrian and driver alike. The visions for how the autonomous vehicle will fit into existing street dynamics are similarly naïve, if not outright dishonest, assuming a whole range of benefits and failing to consider or even dismissing any drawbacks.

When the automobile rolled onto city streets, automakers did not tell Americans about the millions of people who would be killed by it in the United States alone, nor that it would be a driving force in the warming of the planet—but these things still happened, and many of the benefits promised by the auto industry were not realized. Similarly, instead of accepting the autonomous vehicle utopia that companies and their executives have tried to sell us, we should be more critical of what is likely to come of this new transportation technology. In the same way that automobiles required a social reconstruction in addition to a physical reconstruction, so too will autonomous vehicles—and some people involved with them have already admitted it.

As the date when autonomous vehicles were supposed to arrive came and went, and the challenges facing the technology became apparent both to those in the industry who were trying to make progress with their driving systems and to the public who began to see a growing number of stories about autonomous vehicles crashing in troubling ways, some experts started to discuss how more than just a smart AI would be necessary to bring their fantasies to life. In 2018, the *Verge* reported that Andrew Ng, one of the co-founders of the Google Brain deep-learning AI team, said, "the problem is less about building a perfect driving system than training bystanders to anticipate self-driving behavior." He added, "we should partner with the government to ask people to be lawful and considerate. Safety isn't just about the quality of the AI technology."[15]

What Ng described was a far cry from what people like Brin or Musk were saying autonomous vehicles would do. Instead of detecting anything around them, Ng's response suggested that social norms and pedestrian behavior would once again have to be altered to make way for autonomous vehicles. The police will be necessary to ensure that people follow the new rules, reflecting how enforcing regulations on automobiles vastly expanded the powers of the police in the twentieth century. In the aftermath, there were autonomous vehicle advocates who rejected Ng's comments, but his admission is a more realistic assessment of what will be required to make self-driving cars "work" in any meaningful way than the much more common utopian visions.

In the years that followed, there were other worrying statements about what changes a world for autonomous vehicles could usher in. In 2019, the *New York Times* published an article that echoed fears that "jaywalkers" could hold up the rollout of autonomous vehicles. "If pedestrians know they'll never be run over," the article stated, "jaywalking could explode, grinding traffic to a halt."[16] An unnamed official from the automotive industry suggested that "gates at each corner, which would periodically open to allow pedestrians to cross," could be a solution to the problem, and even though the article brushed off that specific suggestion, it recognized that "it's an example of the thinking by those who worry about planning for the future."[17] In short, there are a lot of people who think autonomous vehicles are coming and pedestrians will have to be further restricted for them to function properly on a large scale.

Researchers at Princeton University, for example, figured that if autonomous vehicles are going to need constant connection to navigate the streets, why not also connect pedestrians? They suggested that everyone be required to wear radar reflectors so the vehicles' sensors would be able to pick them up in bad visibility,[18] but the notion that everyone should have to wear a sensor to avoid being run down by a self-driving car naturally struck many readers as ridiculous—at least until a similar measure was included in the Infrastructure Investment and Jobs Act that was signed into law by President Joe Biden in November 2021. If such beacons are necessary for the vehicles to function safely, why should they be on public roads at all?

But shaping behavior can go beyond changing how pedestrians act. In the early twentieth century, planners altered their approach from one that sought to shape how the roads were used in the public interest to one that responded to perceived demand, thereby vastly increasing the supply of roads and, by extension, incentivizing people to drive automobiles. Continuing such an approach with autonomous vehicles could have unforeseen consequences for how we get around and plan our communities.

The assumption of many autonomous vehicle boosters is that they will reduce the number of necessary parking spaces, which will free up space for development, increase urban density, and reduce suburban sprawl—but that is not guaranteed. Depending on how autonomous vehicles are priced, they could incentivize longer commutes, especially if riders see them as more comfortable because they will not have to drive, allowing them to use their phones, watch videos, sleep, or do any number of other things. For a company like Google, whose primary source of revenue is advertising, having a large captive audience to which it can serve ads throughout their journeys could be an attractive expansion of that segment of its business. But other capitalist dynamics may also push people farther out from the urban core rather than bringing them in.

The financialization of land and property has caused housing prices in major cities to soar, even after the 2008 housing crash. Housing has become a speculative investment that wealthy people buy up even if they have no intention of living in their properties, because it is seen as a safe investment with high returns—and as billionaires saw their net worth soar through the Covid-19 pandemic in 2020, they have more money than ever to sink into speculative assets.

With property already at unaffordable levels for a growing segment of the population, autonomous vehicles (in the form that is promised by tech executives) could act as a relief valve that makes it feasible for more people to move even farther from the city center in search of homes and rental units that do not eat up the majority of their incomes because the commute will be more tolerable. This is exactly the experience of the automobile: once it allowed communities to sprout in areas away from streetcar stops, they did; and they continued to expand as automotive and real estate interests got the government to spend public dollars to support that form of development. Many of those same policy measures and tax incentives remain in place, and with Musk promoting a future of green suburbia that I will detail further in Chapter 8, it is possible that the "green" automakers who still want to sell a lot of vehicles will not wish to see them overturned.

We must be able to imagine better ways of organizing mobility; but in the process, we also need to consider the regulatory systems those visions will require and how existing measures will need to be altered to make way for them. This is one of the problems with tech elites: by seeking to evade politics, they ignore how existing structures will constrain their ability to achieve the very outcomes that justify their solutions. Given the technological nature of their ideas, they also require the construction of vast new infrastructures, and that is a crucial aspect of the vision of autonomous vehicles that is too often hidden in the concept art and public pronouncements. However, such infrastructures and the algorithms that organize the autonomously driven mobility system could create a range of new challenges of their own.

In his debut novel *Infinite Detail*, Tim Maughan imagined a future where the internet has gone down, along with all the connected systems that we do not think about as we go about our daily lives. In his view, society would be irreparably changed by such an event, yet we are consciously building vulnerabilities that could lead to a similar outcome into the systems we rely on every single day. For example, in the event of a sustained internet outage or even a virus that successfully severs the link between cargo ships and their computer brain, as happened to Maersk with the NotPetya malware in 2017, the supply chains we rely on could grind to a halt, causing economic chaos and cutting people off from the essential goods they need for basic survival. Autonomous vehicles would build similar vulnerabilities into transportation networks.

In 2019, Thomas Sedran, Volkswagen's head of commercial vehicles, came clean about the challenges that remained for the mass rollout of autonomous vehicles that the public had been led to believe would already have arrived by then. Sedran compared the complexity of developing an autonomous driving system that could function in any condition as being "like a manned mission to Mars," and estimated it would never work on a global scale. In his view, at least five more years of development would be necessary, but that was not all.

> You need latest-generation mobile infrastructure everywhere, as well as high-definition digital maps that are constantly updated. And you still need near-perfect road markings. This will only be the case in very few cities. And even then, the technology will only work in ideal weather conditions. If there are large puddles on the road in heavy rain, that's already a factor forcing a driver to intervene.[19]

Sedran described what has become apparent to many of the people working on and paying attention to the development of autonomous vehicles. They will not only require a level of road maintenance and adherence to driving rules that does not exist in many cities, but they also need an expanded and even more reliable technical infrastructure to deliver and coordinate all the rides happening through this new mobility system.

This is not to say that there are not computerized planning systems in other modes of transportation. Bus and subway networks are planned and monitored through technical systems operated by transit agencies, but there are redundancies built in: if the network goes down, the bus can keep running its route. Yet if the network coordinating a distributed fleet of autonomous vehicles goes down or the maps it has for a particular area are not current, that is another story. There would be no driver that could simply take over, especially if vehicles no longer have steering wheels and pedals like Google's Firefly or the novelty self-driving shuttles in use in cities like Las Vegas, or if passengers no longer learn to drive because they assume the computer will do it for them.

The fifth-generation wireless networks that telecom companies are in the process of constructing are said to be the silver bullet to enable autonomous vehicles and a whole slew of new ways for algorithms to manage aspects of urban life. Yet there are already warnings that our technological overlords may be overpromising what those networks will be able to deliver. As 5G has been rolling out in the United States, its limitations have become much clearer. The range of the signal is very short, meaning a lot of base stations are required; the speed boost has so far been marginal; and it struggles to go through common objects like window glass. Making such a system work will require a massive investment, but it also has important implications.

Building a new, complex infrastructure that takes control out of the hands of the public and the people hired by our elected governments to act in our interests will be a challenging one with its own environmental dilemmas. Autonomous vehicles are promoted as saving energy and reducing emissions, but they will require significant computing power to operate, and each vehicle will collect immense quantities of data that will be sent back to data centers. The vehicles themselves may require more energy than conventional ones—whether powered by fossil fuels or batteries—and the data centers they rely on are quickly becoming significant sources of new emissions which already rival the airline industry.

Further, placing so much of the transportation system under the control of algorithmic planners creates risks similar to those that exist in shipping networks: not only can everything be tracked, but they are also vulnerable to cyberattack and other means of failure. The argument for autonomous vehicles suggests that the only way to rectify the serious problems that exist in transportation systems is to heavily digitize their operation and ensure every aspect is constantly tracked and managed—yet that does not guarantee that any of the problems we are grappling with will be effectively addressed. Over many decades, racist and discriminatory policies have shaped cities and their social fabrics, and automated driving systems could simply entrench those patterns.

The truth is that the problems with automobility do not require a vast new technical infrastructure, consisting of both hardware and software, to be fixed; that is simply the direction most appealing to people in Silicon Valley who not only believe that digital technology can solve virtually any problem, but who also have a financial incentive to build such systems into every aspect of society. The problems that autonomous vehicles claim to solve—traffic congestion and road safety foremost among them—can be effectively addressed through low-tech means, but that will require engaging with the politics of transportation and the distribution of benefits and harms that arise from both the existing system and the proposals for the future.

Part of Silicon Valley's promise is that its solutions are apolitical and do not involve digging into these difficult political questions, even though the seemingly apolitical nature of autonomous vehicles hides how they maintain and reinforce the existing unequal dynamics that already define transportation networks. In short, their promise is a lie.

On the evening of March 18, 2018, the hype bubble around self-driving cars burst. A forty-four-year-old safety operator named Rafaela Vasquez was on her second shift of the week testing Uber's autonomous vehicles on the public roads of Tempe, Arizona. Not long after she had enabled the autonomous driving system (ADS) and it started doing its loop, a woman stepped into the roadway with her bicycle to make her way to the other side, but Vasquez did not notice because she had looked away from the road six seconds before impact.

The ADS struggled to classify the woman in the road. It cycled between considering her a vehicle, a bicycle, and not knowing what she was, but the whole time it assumed they would not collide because it could not predict her path. When she finally moved into the same lane as the vehicle, the system realized it would hit her with just 1.2 seconds to slow down, but it did not take any action. The engineers had built in a one-second delay, so it did not start slowing until two milliseconds before it collided with the woman. By that time, Vasquez had looked up. She saw what was about to happen but could not stop the vehicle from plowing into the woman at nearly forty miles an hour. The bicyclist died at the hospital sometime later. Her name was Elaine Herzberg, and she was the first pedestrian reported to be killed by an autonomous vehicle.

It is easy for a society conditioned to do so to place the blame for the crash on Herzberg. There was no crosswalk where she stepped out, a test found drugs in her system, and she is no longer around to defend herself. But that does not change the fact that she was a pedestrian. She was not in a large metal cage moving at a deadly speed.

Vasquez could also be blamed. She was performing her job of monitoring the vehicle irresponsibly by taking her attention off the road—there is no denying that. But this situation is different. The company overseeing the experiment is a multibillion-dollar corporation, and decisions that were made by its executive leadership and the management of Uber's Advanced Technologies Group (ATG), the division responsible for the ADS, had a material impact on the outcome of the crash and the events leading up to it.

Even before March 18, it was well known that ATG's self-driving efforts were failing to keep pace with its competitors. When an operator takes over for the ADS, it is called an "intervention." In the days after the crash, the *New York Times* reported that Uber's team was struggling to meet its goal of thirteen miles per intervention in Arizona, while competitor Waymo, a sister company of Google, was getting 5,600 miles per intervention in California. The documents obtained by the paper also revealed that ATG was under immense pressure to deliver a "glitch-free ride" before CEO Dara Khosrowshahi visited in April so they could show off the technology and seek regulatory approval for a driverless service in Arizona in December. That pressure pushed the team to cut corners on safety.

In October 2017, just a few months after Khosrowshahi took over as CEO, ATG shook up its operations. It effectively shut down the trial passenger service it was running to focus on collecting more data with the goal of improving the system as quickly as possible. In the process, it cut the number of safety drivers per vehicle from two to one so it could have more vehicles on the road. Uber claimed this change had no impact on safety, but the *New York Times* found that some employees did bring up safety concerns with their managers, specifically that "going solo would make it harder to remain alert during hours of monotonous driving."[20]

In its final report on the incident, the National Transportation Safety Board (NTSB) further excoriated Uber's safety record. ATG had neither a safety division, a dedicated safety manager, nor even a safety plan at the time the fatal crash had occurred. The NTSB also backed up the concern of the operators that taking away their co-pilot "removed a layer of safety redundancy," and concluded that the operator's distraction was "a typical effect of automation complacency" that ATG did not develop countermeasures to prevent.[21] These findings are damning on their own, and illustrate how the company's actions created additional risks that could have been avoided, but there were also problems with the vehicle and ADS themselves that put pedestrians in danger.

In 2016, Uber replaced its fleet of Ford Fusion test vehicles with Volvo XC90 SUVs. Both vehicles were equipped with cameras, radar, and lidar sensors—the latter being lasers to detect the vehicle's surroundings. However, in the switch, the number of lidar sensors was reduced from seven placed on top and around the Ford Fusion to just one 360-degree sensor placed on top of the Volvo XC90. The single sensor had a narrower vertical range that made it more difficult to detect objects close to the ground, including people. Further, the NTSB found that the design of the ADS "did not include consideration for jaywalking pedestrians."[22] Pedestrians detected at a crosswalk would be assumed to be crossing the street, but if they were detected outside a crosswalk, they were "not assigned an explicit goal," which explained why the system struggled to determine Herzberg's path.

These details may make it seem as though Herzberg's death was unavoidable, but she could still be alive today if it was not for another decision made by the ATG team. The Volvo XC90 had its own automatic braking system, but it had been disabled to give full control to Uber's ADS. Based on the NTSB's findings, had it been enabled, "the SUV was predicted to avoid a collision with the pedestrian in 17 out of 20 variations of pedestrian movement,"[23] and even if it had hit her, it would have slowed down enough to almost guarantee she would have survived.

In its finding for cause, the NTSB placed primary blame on Vasquez for being distracted and failing to monitor the vehicle and its surroundings. In the days after the crash, a video circulated which purported to show Vasquez watching an episode of *The Voice* on her phone, but at time of writing, that version of events is being challenged. Vasquez was indicted on a charge of negligent homicide over the incident, but her defense team argues that key information about Uber's culpability was not presented to the grand jury in the case and that Tempe police did not follow up with a whistleblower who contacted them with further information about Uber's safety practices. The lawyers are also challenging the narrative about Vasquez's phone use, arguing the full recording shows her removing an Uber-provided phone from her bag, not her personal phone, and that she was monitoring the display screen of the ADS, not watching *The Voice*.

While the NTSB placed secondary blame on Uber for its lack of safety and driver monitoring, as well as on Herzberg herself for being impaired, and on the Arizona Department of Transportation for its ineffective oversight of autonomous vehicles, it is clear that the company wanted to avoid a precedent-setting judgment that could have left the developers of autonomous vehicles with liability when they get into accidents. The agency's decision was not a surprise, but placing blame on an individual misses the bigger picture, both in a technological sense and an urban planning sense.

The actions of Uber executives and engineers are in line with the "move fast and break things" culture that is promoted in Silicon Valley, one which is motivated first and foremost by beating competitors to market by launching a minimum viable product and capturing market share as quickly as possible in the pursuit of monopoly. Not only did Uber's hardware and software decisions not properly consider the safety of pedestrians, but the area where the crash took place was hostile to pedestrians—as are so many areas in North American cities. The collision happened next to an elevated freeway and the area was designed at the scale of the automobile with long distances between everything. There were bike lanes painted onto the road going in each direction, but there was no actual protection from the automobiles zooming past. Meanwhile, the median between the northbound and southbound lanes had a feature that looked like a walking path, even though there were no crosswalks.

While the area is described in the NTSB's report, the agency did not consider the larger urban landscape where the crash occurred—and that is a problem. As this event illustrates, technologies developed within the context of a transportation system designed to serve automobiles before pedestrians will replicate the problems with those systems; they will not solve them. Anyone hoping to fix the problems with the existing transportation system and the broader urban landscape that has evolved out of it must dig deeper into the roots of those problems instead of mistakenly believing that adding new technological solutions will address them.

*   *   *

In the years following the death of Elaine Herzberg, there have also been concerns about the safety of Tesla's Autopilot system. It was pitched as a fully self-driving system by Musk, but it is more of an assortment of assisted driving technologies like those that are present in many other vehicles, especially high-end cars and SUVs. As a result, a court in Munich ruled that Tesla could not even call the system "Autopilot" in Germany because it misled consumers about its real capabilities. There have been a growing number of incidents involving Autopilot— some of which, tragically, have even taken lives—and instead of addressing the concerns with the system or taking additional safety precautions, Musk has pushed forward, even allowing Tesla drivers to use beta software versions on public roads, placing other drivers and pedestrians at risk.

In a sensible world, regulators would have acted to put the brakes on Tesla's deployment of a driving system that is not ready to be used by the public. But only now, after years of crashes and vocal demands for action by a growing chorus of people, including safety advocate Ralph Nader, does it appear that the technology will finally undergo regulatory scrutiny.

As of April 2021, the National Highway Traffic Safety Administration (NHTSA) had opened twenty-eight investigations into Tesla vehicle crashes—twenty-four of which were still active—and the NTSB had opened nine investigations of its own.[24] In those crashes, Autopilot-enabled Tesla vehicles slammed into transport trucks, fire engines, police cars, trees, medians, and more, killing and injuring their passengers in the process. In June 2021, the NHTSA began requiring automakers to report any collisions involving partially and fully automated driving systems to the agency within one day— a rule that was perceived to specifically target Tesla—and it opened a formal safety probe into Tesla's Autopilot system two months later.

These developments could finally produce regulatory action to ensure that assisted and automated driving systems deliver the benefits they claim, instead of trusting automakers and technology companies that have incentives to oversell their capabilities for corporate gain, at least in the short term. Yet, even as that process moves forward, parts of the industry itself have admitted that the bold visions put forward by Silicon Valley boosters are not coming.

Six months after the Uber crash in 2018, Waymo CEO John Krafcik told attendees at a *Wall Street Journal* event that "autonomy always will have some constraints." He explained that there will always be some conditions that autonomous vehicles will never be able to drive in, and that the timeline for their ubiquity would not be measured in years, but decades.[25] The following year, Ford CEO Jim Hackett made similar comments. At a Detroit Economic Club event, he said the company had "overestimated the arrival of autonomous vehicles," and that when the technology is eventually ready, "its applications will be narrow, what we call geo-fenced, because the problem is so complex."[26] By 2021, Waymo had even dropped the term "self-driving," after feeling Tesla had too greatly tainted it by misleading customers over the capabilities of its "Full Self-Driving" version of Autopilot.

The dream of ubiquitous autonomous vehicles that we were sold in the early and mid-2010s is not coming. Musk is one of the only prominent people who still pushes it, and some people in the industry believe he is giving the technology a bad name and could even scuttle the more limited functions it could serve. But despite Musk's public claims, Tesla admitted in an April 2021 filing with the Securities and Exchange Commission that it may never be able to deliver the self-driving capabilities it has long promised.[27]

Autonomous vehicles presented the dream that we could all step back and let the tech sector solve the problems that have built up over the past century of bad political decisions about transportation—decisions that have cost millions of lives, trillions of dollars, and utterly devastated our communities by spreading people so far apart.

The reality is that autonomous vehicles—even if they worked as Brin, Kalanick, Musk, and many others have promised over the years—are not the solution to the problems created by automobiles, because they themselves are *still* automobiles. They still take up too much space in our communities; they would continue auto-oriented development patterns; and they bring a whole range of new vulnerabilities that city governments are not well-equipped to address, especially after decades of having their budgets squeezed through tax cuts and austerity measures.

The failure of the grand project of autonomous vehicles should be a signal that we will have to contend with the politics of transportation and begin reconstructing our neighborhoods around more egalitarian forms of mobility if we are to truly solve these problems, stitch our communities back together, and find a more sustainable way of living. Yet many powerful people have not learned that lesson, and have instead dreamed up even more outlandish transportation solutions that have no chance of mass success.

6

Making New Roads for Cars

At the turn of the millennium, Houston had a problem. The section of Interstate 10 that ran for about thirty miles from downtown through to the growing suburbs on its western edge was blocked with traffic. One of the interchanges on the Katy Freeway, as it was called, was even given the distinction of being the second most congested in the entire country in 2004.[1] Given how much transport planning is still driven by the idea that agencies need to respond to demand, especially when it seems that drivers are in need of more roads, the state drew up a plan to significantly expand the highway. If cars were backed up, the thinking went, then giving them more space would allow them to drive more freely to their destinations.

The state of Texas poured nearly $3 billion into its expansion of the Katy Freeway, taking it from eight lanes to twenty-three. When it was completed in 2011, it was among the widest highways in the world—but the benefits did not materialize. There was an initial improvement to travel times on the freeway, but within the few years that followed they got substantially worse, to the degree that 85 percent of commuters had a longer commute after the expansion.[2] Desperate not to learn from its mistakes, Texas is planning to move forward with another major widening of Interstate 45 that is estimated to cost the state at least $7 billion. But Texas is hardly the only state making bad planning decisions when it comes to transportation infrastructure.

In the minds of many US liberals, California is not just a

more progressive state than Texas, but one that makes better public policy because it is solidly under the control of the Democratic Party. Certainly, in recent years Los Angeles has been putting a lot of money into improvements to its transit system, but it has also been expanding its road infrastructure through a similar logic to that which prevails in Texas.

Los Angeles's Interstate 405 is notoriously congested, so between 2009 and 2014, $1.6 billion was spent to add a ten-mile carpool lane on a particularly bad segment of the highway through Sepulveda Pass. Yet, once again, traffic got worse despite the additional road space. Months after construction was completed, travel times were already found to be a minute longer than the year before, and between 2015 and 2019, they increased by another 50 percent.[3] Taxpayers' money was wasted expanding road infrastructure with no real benefit.

It would be easy for me to cherry-pick two examples that support my argument, but the experiences in Houston and Los Angeles are part of a much wider trend that has been getting increased attention in the past couple of decades. A 1998 study by the Surface Transportation Policy Project that looked at seventy metropolitan areas over fifteen years found those that "invested heavily in road capacity expansion fared no better in easing congestion than metro areas that did not."[4] This may seem difficult to comprehend. Like the planners in Houston and Los Angeles, one would assume that adding road space would allow vehicles to spread out and so reach their destinations more quickly. But that fails to consider the additional incentives created when new roads are built.

In 2011, economists Gilles Duranton and Matthew Turner published a study that compared the amount of new roads and highways built in US cities to the amount of new miles of driving that took place between 1983 and 2003.[5] They found a causal relationship between the two that they called "the fundamental law of road congestion": when the amount of highways or roads in a city increased, the amount of driving tended to increase by a proportional amount on highways and a slightly lower amount on major urban roads. So, as new road capacity was made available, people were incentivized to drive more, including by moving farther from the urban core and making longer commutes. In transport planning, this concept has another name: induced demand.

The decision to move from seeing the roads as a public space where city officials chose which means of travel to incentivize in service of maximizing the public good to one that responded to perceived transport demand set the stage for the expansion of automobile use. As more space was made for cars on existing streets, new roads built for them, and eventually freeway systems that cemented their supremacy, each of those actions was not just responding to demand but inducing greater demand for automobiles and places to drive them. As traffic got worse, those demands increased, and the additional roads built as a result only served to make the problem worse again: not only were people incentivized to drive more, but communities were constructed with the assumption that everyone would drive, thereby closing off access to alternatives.

As we have seen in the previous two chapters, traffic is at the center of the tech industry's interest in transportation. It is one of the few drawbacks of the automotive system that the industry's executives cannot easily escape. Sure, there are toll roads in some areas where they can pay for privileged road access to speed past everyone else, but in general if anyone is stuck in traffic, the rich drivers will be stuck alongside the poor drivers—and if anyone feels their time is valuable and cannot be wasted in such profligate ways, it is people with a lot of money. Naturally, that means when they think about transportation, they think about the time they are losing in traffic and how they might opt out. The problem is that they are typically not transport experts, so, as Jarrett Walker has observed, when they think of solutions, they tend to believe that narrowly focused ideas that serve their exclusive interests can be deployed at scale for everyone.

The last time that happened, when the automobile went from a luxury object to one that was owned and used by nearly everyone, it started creating the very problems that tech executives interested in transportation claim to be trying to solve. Recalling what André Gorz and John Urry wrote about the automobile as an object of individualism—one that makes the individual user feel powerful and as though they are in control of their own destiny, even as it increases their dependence—the wealthy are not willing to give up their private, enclosed means of transportation to sit alongside the plebs on the bus or subway. That means their transport futures are constrained by their attachment to the automobile, and that sets those futures up for failure from the very outset.

On December 17, 2016, Elon Musk pulled out his iPhone from wherever he happened to be—presumably, stuck in traffic—and sent a declaration to his millions of followers: "Traffic is driving me nuts. Am going to build a tunnel boring machine and just start digging." For those who did not believe the billionaire automaker, he followed it up several hours later with, "I am actually going to do this."

Certainly, there was plenty of reason to be skeptical. Tesla had experienced a rough year between its "production hell" caused, in part, by the failure of Musk's plan to automate the intricate final assembly of its vehicles, and its acquisition of SolarCity, a solar panel company founded by Musk's cousins whose terrible financials Musk hid from Tesla's board to ensure the deal went through. Meanwhile, several years earlier he had also announced a visionary intercity transportation system called Hyperloop that he had no intention of pursuing and which he later admitted was unveiled with the goal of killing the high-speed rail line being built in California.[6] Musk did not want the government to build a state-of-the-art train system; instead, he wanted to distract people with a technology that would not be feasible for at least several decades while keeping people reliant on personal vehicles. And that same trickery was at the center of what came to be called the Boring Company.

By 2017, Musk was building a test tunnel on SpaceX's property in Hawthorne, an area in southwest Los Angeles, and he was already pumping up the expectations for how his tunnel-boring company and the transport system it was purportedly planning to create would transform the way we move.

Initially, he claimed he was planning to build between ten and thirty layers of tunnels beneath the streets of Los Angeles; by 2018, that had grown to one hundred, or even more as they were needed. As the initial tweet suggested, Musk was motivated by traffic, and that was backed up by his later statements that traffic was "soul-destroying." He went so far as to say the traffic in Los Angeles had gone from "seventh level of hell to like eighth level of hell" since he had moved there.[7] Musk's motivation for the Boring Company was to alleviate this traffic, but he proposed an incredibly inefficient—even unworkable—means of achieving it, and that became more apparent the more he tried to make his underground transportation system a reality.

In Musk's mind, the problem with transportation was that it existed only on the surface. As he described it:

> the inherent problem with the way cities are constructed is that you've got all these tall buildings that are in 3D and then a road network in 2D, and then everyone wants to go in and out of the 3D building at the same time. Necessarily, this will result in traffic … You have to make transport 3D.[8]

Some people live in apartment or condo buildings, or work in office buildings, and when they all try to move at the same time, there can be congestion, whether that is of people in personal vehicles, on buses or subways, riding bicycles, or even walking to a destination in a busy part of the urban center at peak times of the day. But Musk was only thinking about what congestion meant for drivers like him.

Even though many cities, including Los Angeles, already have "three dimensional" transportation in the form of subway or metro systems that can very effectively move a lot of people if cities and incentives are designed in a way that make them feasible and attractive to use, Musk considered them only as "two-dimensional" because there were not enough layers of subway tunnels. In 2017, Musk said that transit was "a pain in the ass" where "there's like a bunch of random strangers, one of who might be a serial killer,"[9] which provided a good indication of how he felt about any form of collective mobility, reflecting his affinity for the individuality of the automobile, desire to avoid being around people he is not familiar with, and assumption that everyone else must feel the same way.

Instead of solving this transportation problem through improving bus services and expanding subway systems, Musk instead displayed a preference for "individualized transport, that goes where you want, when you want." He planned for the Boring Company to "increase the happiness of both drivers and mass transit users by reducing traffic and creating an efficient and affordable public transportation system,"[10] but there is no evidence his planned transportation system would be able to achieve anything of the sort. Moving people in cars will always take up far more space than moving people on transit, bicycles, or by foot, and the best way to reduce congestion is to get people out of their cars and moving in those other ways. But by showing a clear preference for "individualized transport," Musk was firmly closing off those possibilities, and by extension making his claims to solve urban congestion through tunnels impossible to believe.

* * *

The Boring Company's transport system is called the Loop. In Musk's original plan, it was supposed to be a series of tunnels designed to take the rider where they wanted to go. Vehicles would enter by driving onto platforms called "skates" that would guide them into the tunnel system and take them to their destinations at up to 130 miles per hour. On arrival, the vehicles would drive off their platforms and continue on their way. It sounded straightforward, but making the frictionless vision work in the real world did not turn out to be so easy.

The entry points to the Loop, at least in the initial plan, were to be located under on-street parking spaces that would operate like elevators into the tunnel system. Yet the Boring Company never explained how it would stop other cars from driving into the gaping holes on the side of the street that were left as the platforms descended. None of their concept art or videos featured any kind of cage or fence to stop such a thing from occurring. Unsurprisingly, this was not the only aspect of the project that disappeared through the course of multiple tweaks and redesigns.

After Musk detailed the project, it was heavily criticized for being yet another transportation system trying to move cars instead of people. Critics said that the plan might have made sense if he was making tunnels for trains, but the capacity would be far too low to make a difference if they were for cars. In response, Musk slightly moderated his tone on transit, saying at one of the company's events that, "we're not opposed to mass transit; mass transit is fine. Let's try every solution possible, but the thing about tunnels is that you can go 3D underground," once again ignoring the existence of subway systems.[11]

To address the criticism, he placed greater emphasis on another type of skate. Instead of a platform to transport cars, the concept vehicle was covered in a glass dome large enough to carry eight to sixteen pedestrians or cyclists. It was not clear how a pedestrian would access one of these skates, or how long they would have to wait for one, but the system did not even exist so it seemed that it may have been improving on paper.

In December 2018, Musk pulled back the curtain on the prototype tunnel that the Boring Company had been building in Hawthorne. It was supposed to be the big event that showed the Loop was real and could be turned into something bigger, but instead it generated even more questions about its feasibility. Musk had promised speeds of up to 130 miles per hour, but when *Los Angeles Times* journalist Laura Nelson took a test ride, it topped out at fifty-three miles per hour and was "so uneven in places that it felt like riding on a dirt road."[12] Instead of waiting until it was done properly, the tunnel felt rushed and unfinished, which is not the feeling you want from critical transportation infrastructure. But beyond that, there were no skates.

At the event, Musk explained that the skates were gone—for cars and pedestrians—and instead only electric vehicles that had autonomous driving capabilities and specially equipped guide wheels that deployed on entry would be allowed in the tunnels. Naturally, that meant the tunnels not only privileged people who owned their own vehicles, but more explicitly people who owned a Tesla. Rollercoaster enthusiasts later pointed out that the Boring Company's guide wheel system had been in use for well over a century in side-friction rollercoasters. It was a technology "so outmoded that only a handful of vintage amusement parks worldwide still have one," yet for some reason it was being used in a supposedly futuristic transportation system.[13]

To make up for the lack of pedestrian skates, Musk said there would be "continuously operating cars" in the Loop for anyone who did not have their own. Once again, not only was it not clear how those vehicles would be accessed, but the change brought the capacity from eight to sixteen people back to a maximum four or five per vehicle while creating new safety concerns. There were no drivers or station attendants, limited space to spread out, and no stops where someone else might get on or the rider could get off if they thought they might be in danger. The bold vision of layer upon layer of car tunnels to take a driver wherever they wanted to go was already being reined in, but when Musk finally got the chance to build the system, it was even further simplified, showing just how much of a gimmick it really was.

Musk tried to get multiple Boring Company projects off the ground. In 2018, the company was going to build a Loop system from downtown Chicago to O'Hare Airport that would run along almost the exact same route as the Blue Line subway, while carrying far fewer people. After a local election, it was canceled. Later, Musk pitched the Loop to connect the Red Line subway in Los Angeles to Dodger Stadium. At a public event, nine people spoke up in favor of the plan, but afterward journalists discovered that at least three of them had ties to SpaceX, Musk's aerospace company. The project did not move forward.

In Las Vegas, Musk finally got his chance. Instead of the city-wide transport system he started with in Los Angeles, the company was hired to build a 1.7-mile tunnel to connect one end of the Las Vegas Convention Center to the other. At the groundbreaking event in November 2019, President of the Convention and Visitors Authority Steve Hill said, "I think that ten, fifteen, twenty years from now, we'll look back at this as a Kitty Hawk–type moment."[14] After setting the target so high, he had to have been disappointed with the result.

When the tunnel opened on April 8, 2021, the main talking point in the media was about the colorful lights installed in the tunnel as it was the only way to distract from how severely underwhelming it was. After all the big promises Musk had made about the Loop, the cars in the tunnel went a maximum of thirty-five miles per hour, and they were not even autonomous; each vehicle had a human driver. After all the bold statements and futuristic concept art, it felt like little more than a Tesla-branded children's ride you might find at Disney World. The company tried to distract from how pathetic their final product was by emphasizing plans for a larger system to go all the way to the airport, but there was really no hiding the fact that, once again, Musk had over-promised and vastly underdelivered.

In December 2019, Musk tweeted a poll asking his followers whether he should build "super safe, Earthquake-proof tunnels under cities to solve traffic," but one user replied with a link to a Wikipedia article on induced demand and asked him to read it. In response, Musk, who has no training in transport planning, dismissed the concept, writing, "Induced demand is one of the most irrational theories I've ever heard. Correlation is not causation. If the transport system exceeds public travel needs, there will be very little traffic. I support anything that improves traffic, as this negatively affects almost everyone." Yet Musk's efforts were putting more cars on the road and proposing narrow tunnels that would not solve the problem. It was therefore not surprising to read that he was dismissive of induced demand and wanted to preserve suburban community planning.

When pitching the Boring Company's transport system, Musk made a particularly illuminating argument about how it would fit within existing neighborhoods. In 2018, he explained that:

> you can weave the Boring system tunnel network into the fabric of the city without changing the character of the city. The city will still feel the same; you're not going to get in anyone's way; you're not going to obstruct anyone's view ... You will have this revolutionary transport system and your city will still feel like your city.[15]

The language Musk used mirrors the concerns of a particular type of anti-development organization that has gained notable leverage and attention in California and is typically made up of white, financially stable homeowners who do not wish to see denser housing built near their homes. They are commonly known as "not in my backyard" or NIMBY groups, and Musk's specific appeal to them reflects his own vision of sustainability that encompasses electric cars, suburban homes with solar panels, and presumably narrow tunnels for cars to avoid the gridlocked freeway.

After a few years of slowly deflating hype, the Boring Company's Loop turned out to be little more than a narrow tunnel for luxury cars—and it is unlikely to amount to much more. Adding some tunnels for cars in major cities will not alleviate traffic congestion, and Musk's plan failed to account for how few passengers the system would be able to accommodate because it was designed for cars instead of people. Beyond that, the initial design of the Loop had innumerable flaws. If it was really going to be a mass transportation system, the on-street entry elevators would have been a significant bottleneck, constantly backing up nearby traffic. Meanwhile, the speeds Musk was promising—up to 130 miles per hour—were completely unrealistic unless the system was only moving people in straight lines.

After reviewing how the system developed, it is impossible to conclude anything other than its plan was never to solve congestion for everyone, but for one person in particular: Elon Musk. The Boring Company was yet another case of elite projection, where Musk framed a tunnel that would be personally convenient as something that could work for everyone. In fact, the first tunnel that Musk proposed was supposed to run along Interstate 405—the same one that Los Angeles had widened to try to reduce traffic congestion—from an area near Musk's then-residence in Bel Air to SpaceX headquarters in Hawthorne where he usually worked. It was a tunnel to allow him to evade traffic on his daily commute that he built a larger vision around—one that allowed him to sell it not just to the public and the media, but to the lawmakers whose approvals he would need to make it a reality.

If one needs further proof of Musk's bad judgment on transportation, they need only look to the solutions he backed to solve congestion before he started touting tunnels. In 2013, Musk was advocating double-decker highways and even offered money to speed up the widening of Interstate 405 so he would not spend so much time in traffic.[16] Yet we know it did not fix the problem.

Once again, big promises about a proposed transportation system turned out to be about entrenching the privilege of a man who already has much greater access to mobility than virtually anyone else on the face of the planet. But the Boring Company is not the only solution specifically targeted at congestion to have been boosted with grand visions that should have never been taken seriously. While Musk wanted to send cars underground, the revival of a vision of ubiquitous flying cars instead imagined carving out new roads in the skies above our heads. Its greatest proponents even built on Musk's justifications to claim for themselves some of the credibility that had been granted to his tunnel system—but it too was doomed to fail from the start.

The dream of flying cars is not at all new. In the mid-twentieth century, people were predicting we would all be flying around by the year 2000—not to mention taking commercial trips to space or even living on other planets. The first article about flying cars in *Popular Science* was written all the way back in July 1924, and it estimated that flying cars would be ready in twenty years. That forecast, writer E.V. Rickenbacker assured readers, was "more than pure fancy. It is founded on present progress in automobile and airplane design."[17] As modern snake-oil salesmen predict transportation revolutions that are only a few years away, the decades-long timelines of those in the 1920s are refreshing, even if they were still wrong. To compare, after the modern flying car frenzy began to take hold in 2018, the *Guardian* published an article that stated, "It's probably a matter of when, not if, road-based travel becomes obsolete."[18] It's baffling that such a statement made it past an editor, but it is also a product of the blind adherence that tech companies have cultivated in some circles.

The modern take on the flying car is, in truth, not a flying car at all. The vertical takeoff and landing vehicle, also known as a VTOL or an eVTOL for the electric version, is more akin to a helicopter, but instead of the large rotor on top, it typically has several smaller rotors positioned along the craft. These vehicles will never be seen cruising down the highway, then taking off into the air, and like a car or a helicopter, they are not going to carry very many passengers. Companies around the world are working on improving these flying craft as another means of air travel, primarily designed to operate within a metro area. They include such traditional aerospace companies as Airbus and Boeing, as well as much newer ones like Volocopter in Germany and EHang in China that were founded specifically to stake a claim in the VTOL market. While some of these companies certainly hoped VTOLs would become a mass-market product, such a vision was popularized not by either category of aircraft maker, but rather unsurprisingly by a company anointed with the "tech" label.

In 2016, after launching its ride-hailing service in cities around the world and announcing its intention to automate its drivers, Uber was on the lookout for new ways to appear to be on the cutting edge of future transportation. It was losing vast sums of money and had to pull out of China, selling its operations to Chinese ride-hailing giant Didi Chuxing. The company needed a new distraction from the growing issues with its core business, and it turned to eVTOLs. In October of that year, its Uber Elevate division released a white paper laying out its vision of the future of on-demand urban air transportation. After allowing users to hail a car and driver, the Uber Air service would allow them to hail a flying car in some cities by 2023. Instead of being stuck in surface traffic, they would go into a "third dimension."

Reflecting similar statements made by Musk, Uber's Head of Elevate Eric Allison said at the 2019 Elevate Summit that "the transportation grid ... is in two dimensions, its cities live in three dimensions, and when we live in three dimensions we have to take our transportation into three dimensions as well."[19] Like Musk, Uber also ignored the existence of subway systems; but rather than building "3D" tunnels of its own, it decided to look to the vast open space above us. Allison said Uber wanted to make cities into "smarter, better, more efficient places to live and to work," yet that is impossible to believe without being brainwashed by the company's slick marketing operation.

A smarter, better, more efficient transportation system would not look to unproven eVTOL technology to become a new form of mass mobility when the streets below are already clogged with low-capacity vehicles, especially when the very company proposing we use flying cars is partially responsible. Uber Air was a direct response to the traffic congestion that Uber itself made worse, and in the same way that its ride-hailing service failed to address the problems with a transport system oriented around personal vehicles, its imagined urban air service continued to ignore them. That is not a smart approach to mobility, nor is it efficient.

Unlike a car that can drive around on roads that were built and maintained with public funds and pull to the side to pick up a passenger, an eVTOL service would require a whole new infrastructure of landing pads and storage facilities. Beyond that, it would require an entirely new air traffic control system to ensure the eVTOLs buzzing around future cities do not crash into one another or some other object in the sky, such as a commercial, consumer, or police drone. Yet, in the visions of Uber and its partners for the design of these sites, the automobile continues to exert its dominance.

The first promotional video released to show off Uber Air in 2017 was a perfect example of the larger vision of the urban system within which it would exist.[20] It followed a woman as she left work and boarded a VTOL to get home, and it had three features that stood out. First, the woman was not traveling from one part of a dense urban area to another. She appeared to depart from a car-oriented commercial area and arrived in a low-density suburban area where an Uber SUV ferried her from the landing area to her single-family home. The urban form imagined in Uber's future remained largely dependent on automobiles. Second, the VTOL itself only held the woman, three other passengers, and the pilot. For a mass transportation system, there would need to be a lot of them flying around in the skies to make any significant dent in congestion, a claim that was further called into question by the third aspect that is worth noting. During the woman's journey, she passed over an overlapping section of road and freeway where cars remained gridlocked in traffic, showing that congestion had not been solved in Uber's future of urban air mobility. The woman was simply able to pay for access to Uber Air to escape it. The depiction in the promotional video was a much more accurate reflection of what the service would do than what Uber was trying to make people believe in its public statements.

In later conceptual renderings of Skyport terminals that were planned to serve as the hubs for the service, the same problems were present. Only two of the fifteen unique concept drawings shared on the Uber Elevate website were in urban areas, and both were surrounded by wide roads with no visible public transit. One of the urban concepts even had a highway running through it, which was surprisingly not an uncommon trait—but none was more outlandish than a design produced by architecture firm Humphreys & Partners.

The building they proposed was a wide cylinder covered in holes. Trees and other forms of greenery poked out of them, alongside landing pads that jutted out from the structure's sides. The Skyport appeared to be a busy connection point: pedestrians were crowding the entrance and walking to it from outside the frame of the image, there were plenty of vehicles (and even a couple of minibuses) out front, a highway running underneath it with roads on every side, a Hyperloop tube emerging out of it, and even a light-rail line along the route of the highway. In every way, it seemed like a transport hub, but it was not clear why anyone would be using it. On one side of the building was a forest, and on the other there were parking lots and some low-density buildings. It was a veritable Skyport to nowhere.

Uber saw the urban air service as a partnership between itself and a number of other firms that could, for example, design Skyports, produce VTOLs, and manage the air traffic service. But ultimately, it was setting the terms and shaping the vision. The concept art and videos it released suggest, like with its ride-hailing service, that it had little intention of significantly altering existing auto-oriented city and transport environments. They would continue to exist as they already did, with all their associated problems, and Uber Air would be layered on top. That clearly limited its ability to solve any real problems, but unlike with its ride-hailing service, the company had a harder time fooling people with its VTOL plans.

In 2019, Uber announced a service called Uber Copter that would ferry passengers between Manhattan and John F. Kennedy International Airport. While it used a helicopter instead of a VTOL, the company positioned it as the first step in its plan for urban air mobility. Yet it immediately showed the problems inherent in the company's larger vision. Even though Manhattan is a dense urban area, users' only option to get to the landing pad was having an Uber vehicle pick them up; they could not choose to take transit. As far back as the 2016 white paper, Uber admitted it expected to "see a larger share of multi-modal itineraries containing automobile legs, rather than walking," even in major cities.[21] But the bigger problem was that for the vast majority of people, it was a terrible deal.

Some journalists tried the new service and found that only someone with a lot of disposable income could be impressed by it. Reporters for the *New York Post* found they reached the airport three minutes faster than Uber Copter by taking transit, while another group with CNBC found Uber Copter arrived fourteen minutes faster, but cost an extra $213.07.[22] Despite being pitched as an accessible option, the service was targeted at wealthier Uber users, recalling how its ride-hailing service is far more likely to be used by people with incomes over $75,000. But there was something even more insulting about Uber's sales pitch.

When it came to its ride-hailing service, Uber argued it was not a transportation company, but a technology company, and as a result it refused to abide by the Americans with Disabilities Act. That meant it did not need to ensure wheelchair access in its services in the same way a taxi company would, so when people in wheelchairs tried to hail a ride on Uber, it would take much longer than for the average user, if there was an accessible vehicle available at all. Yet, when it came to Uber Air, a service that would clearly be far more expensive than the ride-hailing service, Uber made a targeted pitch to people in wheelchairs—people who have lower than average incomes because of the systematic discrimination they face, which Uber's own actions are an example of.

Justin Erlich, the Head of Policy of Autonomous Vehicles and Urban Aviation, stated that Uber wanted to be "thoughtful long-term about where the routings are to make sure that we're serving underserved communities in transit, and to make sure that this technology is made available to everybody."[23] But there was no way that was realistically going to happen. It was nothing more than a public relations exercise that took advantage of vulnerable people for positive press.

As with the Boring Company, Uber Air is yet another example where executives used attractive talking points to make people believe that a service designed to cater to an elite would benefit the masses. Urban air mobility would take a similar role in consumer transportation today as the helicopter. In short, primarily for the wealthy, and maybe tourists who are willing to splurge. But it is not and will never be a mass transportation option, and it certainly will never make any difference to traffic congestion on city streets.

In 2017, Musk made a dig at VTOLs while defending his tunnels as the superior form of "three dimensional" transportation. In a TED interview, he said, "if there are a whole bunch of flying cars going all over the place, that is not an anxiety-reducing situation ... You're thinking, 'Did they service their hubcap, or is it going to come down and guillotine me?'"[24] If only he could extend the same critical thinking to his own farfetched ideas.

In 1973, as André Gorz wrote about the automobile as a luxury object, he also observed that it "has made the big city uninhabitable."

> It has made it stinking, noisy, suffocating, dusty, so congested that nobody wants to go out in the evening anymore. Thus, since cars have killed the city, we need faster cars to escape on superhighways to suburbs that are even farther away. What an impeccable circular argument: give us more cars so that we can escape the destruction caused by cars.[25]

Gorz identified how purported solutions that maintain the supremacy of automobiles will never address the problems that are endangering our lives, damaging the environment, and reducing our quality of life. In the same way that expanding highways did not reduce congestion, adding narrow tunnels for cars or creating new roads in the skies above will similarly not solve the problem for anyone other than the wealthy few.

Sociologist Mimi Sheller argued that many of the supposedly bold visions for urban change "only accrue benefits to the kinetic elite and often directly harm the mobility poor," and that can be seen by focusing on who has to wait for transportation. She provided the example of road pricing, which allows quicker access to the city center for those who can pay, while those who cannot they must either wait in traffic or are "relegated to long pre-dawn commutes on multiple slow bus lines, or in meandering informal shared taxis ... or exposed to dust and danger on the back of motorcycle taxis," depending where in the world they live. The ability to drive faster than other road users, and to have infrastructure designed for that purpose, is an elite luxury that is not widely distributed. "Having to wait," she wrote, "while others 'speed' past, is a form of power, for instance, experienced daily by car drivers who jump into the electronically tolled EZ-Pass 'fast lane' in the USA," but the same could be said for visions of Boring Company tunnels or on-demand VTOL services.[26]

These new infrastructures promoted by Musk and Uber executives use egalitarian language to gain public support for a vision of mobility where the urban form and transport systems effectively stay the same, but wealthy people have new ways of paying to opt out of the problems that other residents have to experience every single day. What is particularly concerning is how many people and media organizations took the marketing claims of the Boring Company and Uber at face value, even though what they would have accomplished was light years away from what they claimed to want to achieve.

In these cases, the visions quickly unraveled. The Boring Company has been reduced to a few car tunnels in Las Vegas that act mainly as free advertising for Tesla vehicles, and although some city officials still claim they are interested in what Musk is selling, they are likely just trying to get close to the billionaire himself.

Meanwhile, we can erect a headstone for Uber's grand flying car visions. In December 2020, it had to pay another company to take its Uber Elevate division, including Uber Air, off its hands in an effort to improve its bottom line.

The span of time between the initial bold claims of prominent tech figures and the general realization that they are fraudulent appears to be shrinking, but that does not mean new narrow-minded solutions to transportation problems are not emerging from the tech industry every year. While the Boring Company and Uber Air sought to create new automotive space above and below the surface, other companies' visions depend on taking over our dwindling public space. The threat they pose is even greater than gimmicky tunnels and redesigned helicopters.

7

The Coming Fight for the Sidewalk

Before the automobile transformed urban mobility, another mode of transportation had its own revolutionary effect on the way people moved about. In 1885, John Kemp Starley invented the Rover: a safety bicycle with two wheels of similar size that was much easier to ride than the models that had come before it. When it was fitted with pneumatic tires a few years later, allowing it to ride more smoothly and move at faster speeds, it began to take off in Europe, North America, and beyond. Within a decade, the Stanley Bicycle Show in London featured more than two hundred bicycle makers showcasing 3,000 different models.

The bicycle boom of the 1890s challenged the social norms of the era. Streetcars had become more common, but as bicycle prices plummeted, they were no longer just another tool for well-off men. The middle and working classes embraced them for recreation and utility, young people found it easier to socialize where their parents would not see them, and they provided particular benefits to women who gained more freedom over their mobility and their lives.

In 1896, women's rights activist Susan B. Anthony told the *New York Sunday World*, "I think bicycling has done more to emancipate women than anything else in the world." That same year, a writer for *Munsey's Magazine* explained, "To men, the bicycle in the beginning was merely a new toy, another machine added to the long list of devices they knew in their work and play. To women, it was a steed upon which they rode into a new world."[1] Yet, while the bicycle improved the mobility of women, it was not without its detractors.

The freedom that women derived from the bicycle created a backlash from some men who did not like to see their personal power over women, nor their dominant position in society, challenged by women who could move around more freely. The popularity of the bicycle also had unexpected consequences like altering women's fashions, since it was difficult to ride one in a heavy dress or skirt. As a result, bloomers, pants, and other garments that made it easier to engage in physical activity became more common, but they were derided by traditionalists who felt they made women look more masculine.

Some doctors warned that medical conditions affecting women could arise from bicycle use. "Bicycle face," for example, was based on the idea that riding at the high speeds made possible by bicycles—high for the time, at least—would alter a woman's face, with the implication that she should avoid riding altogether. There were others who cautioned that riding bicycles could make women more vulnerable to a whole host of diseases, while certain groups were concerned with the more moral questions of whether the seat of the bicycle would teach women how to masturbate.

Over time, of course, bicycle campaigners effectively pushed back against these unfounded maladies and worries. They formed bicycle clubs to demand road improvements so they could ride faster and more smoothly, and some cities even built dedicated bike lanes and paths. In 1892, an article imagined how with the bicycle "the development of cities will be nothing short of revolutionary," making residents healthier, cities calmer, and enabling even more social interaction.[2] While it may not seem so today, US cities were just as caught up with the bicycle as those in Europe, but the boom started to slow in the early 1900s, leaving the grand plans for the cycling city on the drawing board.

In 1901, Kemp died at the age of forty-six. But in the years that followed, his bicycle company started putting internal combustion engines on bikes to make them go faster, eventually creating some of the first motorcycles. It later moved into making automobiles, the very vehicles that forced bicyclists to move out of the way and claimed the paved streets for themselves.

Throughout the twentieth century, there have been several bicycle resurgences, mostly notably in the 1970s when the price of oil soared and created enough pressure to shift some European cities toward a more bicycle-oriented development path. In recent years, as interest in bicycles has grown once again, there has been a new push for infrastructure to encourage bicycle use. Unsurprisingly, the tech industry has sought to insert itself into that movement as some people within it perceived a new market that they could capture and shape to suit their purposes.

On March 28, 2018, residents of San Francisco woke up to a new service that had not so much taken over their streets, but their sidewalks. Bird was one of the first Western entries in a new wave of mobility companies emulating the app-based rental model for bikes that had originated in China a few years earlier. Instead of going to a dock and unlocking a bike, these dockless services left bikes, e-bikes, and electric kick scooters (or e-scooters) around the city that required a smartphone, the company's app, and a method of payment to activate.

Bird positioned itself in a similar vein to Uber; it was a tech company disrupting the mobility landscape, but instead of decimating the livelihoods of taxi workers, it was providing a way for people to avoid using a car. In typical "move fast and break things" style, it also did not seek permits or permission from the city to launch its service; San Franciscans just woke up one day to find e-scooters branded with the company's logo and rentable via its app littered throughout the city.

On the day it launched, the *San Francisco Chronicle*, the largest newspaper in the city, ran a story that described the scooters as an "electrified version of the kind little kids ride."[3] The journalist acknowledged there were questions about the service and whether it had the proper permits, but positioned the scooters as fun and neutral, if not a positive addition to the city. But it did not take long for the coverage to turn. Two days later, the story was that scooters had "descend[ed]" onto city streets, blocking the sidewalks and "making a big push to make money from sidewalks to the detriment of pedestrians," which the San Francisco Municipal Transportation Agency said would not be tolerated.[4]

By April 1, the idea that scooters were toys for grown-ups was gone. The *Chronicle* reported that the sidewalks had been "invaded" and become "dumping grounds" for dockless scooters.[5] Pedestrians tripped over them and people in wheelchairs suddenly faced new obstacles in navigating the city—something that was not easy at the best of times. Complaints rolled in as the city attorney said he was "examining all legal options" to protect the city's more than a million pedestrians.

There was undoubtedly positive coverage of dockless scooters as they arrived in more cities across the country, but the reaction—and coverage of it—in San Francisco was particularly negative. These were the people on the front lines of "disruption," and after suffering through the effects of Uber on their streets, the gentrification of their neighborhoods as housing prices skyrocketed with the influx of tech workers, and all the new technological solutions being trialed by the start-ups constantly trying to find the next big idea, it seemed like residents had finally had enough.

Early on, they recognized that these new companies offering dockless bike and e-scooter options, which collectively became known as micromobility, were not simply trying to get people to adopt a new service, but were staking a claim to some of the little remaining public space in the city, and residents were not going to let it go without a fight.

The response of San Franciscans to the incursion of scooters can be seen in two ways. First, it could be framed as just another example of a group of people overreacting to the presence of a new technology, similar to the traditionalists, moralists, and those who did not want to see prevailing power and gender dynamics overturned as the bicycle empowered women in the 1890s. Given the strong belief in technological determinism among the powerful people pushing these ideas for the future of mobility, it is no surprise that this was one of the prominent responses, especially since it fit into an existing narrative.

In recent years, there has been a lot of discussion about "not in my backyard," or NIMBY, sentiment in California. These are people who, according to their pro-development, "yes in my backyard" opponents, oppose any changes to their neighborhoods—whether it is the construction of denser housing, the addition of bike lanes, or any other initiative that could alter the area they live in. The criticism of these people is not entirely undeserved, since there is a vocal group that is vehemently against any attempt to change environments designed for single-family homes and automobiles, but that also does not mean that every time a resident opposes a change to their community it is simply for aesthetic reasons or to protect perceived property values.

The problem with framing the negative response to micromobility as a typical reaction by people who do not know better or simply oppose any and all change is that it ignores the power dynamics at play in the rollout of these services. Residents' anger at the littering of scooters throughout their communities should instead be seen through the lens of the opposition to the automobile in the 1920s, as outlined in Chapter 1, because of the power relations involved. When bicycles were originally introduced, it was the mobility freedom of people with lower incomes and from groups with relatively little power that was enhanced, while people who held significant social power attempted to continue restricting it.

But when automobiles were becoming more common several decades later, there was a real revocation of public space that residents opposed, and it affected women and children most of all. They had less freedom to move around the city because the street had become a dangerous place and they were far less likely to be able to drive. They were relegated to the sidewalk, and while it is much more common for women to drive today, pedestrians never regained their rights to the street, even as the automobile took over more and more space and, in many places, sidewalks were not properly maintained.

That lens provides a second way to understand the opposition to scooters, and it is far more accurate than simply seeing it as a backward response that rejects a notion of progress as defined by the tech industry. With their space already so limited, people reacted to the imposition of micromobility services that staked a claim to the thin strips of pedestrian space that remained at the edge of the street. While they may not have had the historical context, they perceived that a powerful industry was trying to take over a public space, and the benefits of that enclosure would primarily accrue to a small number of executives, investors, and some early employees with stock options—not to the public at large.

San Franciscans know more than anyone else why the territorial expansion of tech must be opposed as soon as it begins, because once their services become normalized, it is nearly impossible to get rid of them, regardless of their actual impacts. They have experienced the downsides of ubiquitous services designed to serve a narrow class of tech worker but which are promoted as though they will benefit the wider public to get the initial buy-in.

Residents did not want to walk out their door every day and step over scooters to get where they were going, if they could do that at all. For people in wheelchairs, the scattering of scooters on sidewalks was an even more serious limitation on their mobility, and the experiences of vulnerable and marginalized road (or sidewalk) users are the least likely to be considered by most of the people in the start-up world. This also forces the question of whether these dockless services should be on sidewalks in the first place, and since that contradicts the ideology of Silicon Valley, many of its adherents naturally chose to see it another way.

Micromobility services, as well as the autonomous delivery robots that are also being deployed on sidewalks, are not designed to place accessibility and affordability at the fore; rather, while forcing their way onto sidewalks, they are also seeking to entrench rentier business models that ensure they take a cut every time people access them. The services are designed to benefit the company, and what is best for users and the broader society is much further down the list of priorities.

Less than two weeks after Bird's scooters hit the streets of San Francisco, Uber also joined the micromobility race by acquiring Jump. The company had already been operating a dockless bikeshare service in San Francisco since January 2018, but unlike Bird's scooters, which could be discarded almost anywhere when riders were done, Jump's bikes had to be locked to a bike rack or pole at the end of the ride. That allowed the company to avoid the worst of the sidewalk blockages that the newly arrived scooters were causing, and, by extension, the public backlash. But that did not mean it was set up for success. Jump's history and, in particular, how its operations changed during its time under Uber illustrate how the ethos of Silicon Valley is not about best serving urban residents—it's about dominating in service of corporate ends.

When Jump started in 2010, it was called Social Bicycles, or SoBi, and sought to expand easy access to bicycles through bikeshare systems commissioned by city governments. As *Vice* journalist Aaron W. Gordon described after speaking with former Jump employees, the company's initial business model involved responding to formal requests by governments for bikeshare systems, after which they engaged in a process that took around two years and involved "a deep partnership with the city that would minimize long-term uncertainty or community outrage over bike rack locations."[6] During that time, SoBi employed urban planners to design bike racks and work with communities to ensure the system not only met their needs, but avoided backlash once it began operating. The company kept operating costs low and valued its relationships—until the venture capital–backed micromobility model swept in.

Instead of going through the proper processes, working with communities, and building a reliable product that did not block sidewalks, the micromobility services—first from Chinese companies using dockless bikes, then Western companies with dockless e-scooters and e-bikes—had very different motivations. They either spent heavily to get permits without going through consultations or ignored them altogether, then flooded the sidewalks with bikes and scooters to capture the market. They usually bought cheap products that were not designed to hold up to frequent usage, and the lack of locks led to immediate problems with accessibility. As one former employee told Gordon, not having to lock the bikes and scooters at the end of the ride "turns the vehicles into trash and blocks the sidewalk, which is both bad for business and bad for cities."[7]

As communities were flooded by highly capitalized micromobility companies that were dropping vehicles on sidewalks and losing millions of dollars in the process, SoBi lost business because many cash-strapped cities went with the easier option, especially as the companies made big promises about accessibility and affordability without knowing whether they could actually be realized. This change was also seen within SoBi.

After it rebranded as Jump and was purchased by Uber, things changed very quickly. Rather than being frugal, employees told Gordon the company became flush with cash and Uber applied "a software business mentality to bikeshare."[8] They hired so many people that they quickly became overstaffed, moved into new markets as quickly as possible, burned through millions of dollars in the process, and the problems they faced only escalated. There were not enough parts to fix the bikes when they broke, and after Uber switched the sturdy lock on their e-bikes to a flimsy cable lock, theft soared. While the company kept trying to put out fires, it was ultimately not able to recover from Uber's changes. In May 2020, Uber invested $85 million in Lime (another micromobility company) in exchange for taking Jump off its hands and, more importantly, its balance sheet. Jump had been losing $60 million a quarter.

Weeks later, Jump's e-bikes were being crushed at disposal sites around the United States even as there was a bicycle shortage in the early months of the Covid-19 pandemic. The perception that bikes and scooters were so disposable they should just be trashed instead of repainted and deployed into Lime's fleet, or donated to charities, or even sold to people who might want to ride them illustrated the flawed model that the micromobility industry is designed around.

The appearance of bikes and e-scooters on the sidewalks of cities around the world undoubtedly kicked off conversations about public space and the distribution of street space—with mixed results. In 2019, *Wired* reported that cycling activists had been joining companies like Uber and Lyft as they moved into micromobility to try to advocate for better cycling infrastructure,[9] though as the story of SoBi showed, it is not clear that selling out was ultimately a good strategy to achieve those goals.

As the services rolled out, venture capitalists jumped in, seeing them as a new tech-adjacent service through which they could attempt to capture a mode of transportation and later extract monopoly profits. Micromobility companies like Bird and Lime were looking to do for bikes and scooters what Uber promised (and failed) to do with car ownership. Instead of people owning their own or having inexpensive access to a docked, city-approved bikeshare system, they would be reliant on the extractive app-based rental model. Yet, in the same way that venture capitalists wanted to see faster progress in micromobility than they had in ride-hailing, the problems with the model also became apparent more quickly.

The issue that Uber found with Jump's bikes tending to have a short lifespan once it removed their sturdy locks was an industry-wide problem. In Louisville, Kentucky, Bird's dockless scooters lasted an average of a mere 28.8 days between August and December 2018 before having to be replaced,[10] and just 126 days in Los Angeles between January and April 2019. In Los Angeles, the company's newer, more rugged model had an even shorter lifespan than its older models.[11] Meanwhile, Lime was running into major maintenance problems with its scooters, and a dockless bikeshare pilot project in Washington, DC, found the bikes lasted an average of only seventy days before being replaced, compared to 1,614 days for the city's docked bikeshare system.[12]

For all the claims of sustainability by these companies, treating bikes and scooters as disposable products did not align with those goals. After assessing the lifespan, manufacturing information, and charging frequency of dockless e-scooters, along with how riders were using them, researchers at North Carolina State University estimated their lifecycle emissions were 65 percent higher than the transport modes they were replacing.[13] Another detailed lifecycle assessment by Anne de Bortoli at University Paris-East was published in April 2021 and found that dockless micromobility services had a significantly higher carbon footprint per mile traveled than a privately owned bicycle. She also calculated that e-scooters specifically could have higher carbon footprints per passenger mile than some forms of public transit.[14]

On top of the unsustainable nature of the services, they were also not particularly equitable. The companies running the services lost money, as Silicon Valley's rapid growth model requires, but the prices were often significantly higher than docked bikeshare services, and even transit tickets. As the Washington, DC, pilot found, the services had few regular users, often consisting of tourists or people trying them out, and many of the trips were in the center of the city.[15] With high prices and low ridership, it is not surprising that surveys found that the services' users were overwhelmingly young men with higher than average incomes, which was not only similar to ride-hailing users, but reinforced the demographics of existing cyclists instead of expanding it to groups that are less likely to make their trips on a bike.

Due to the way the services rolled out—trying to quickly establish a foothold in as many cities as possible to maximize market share—some communities were left underserved when it became clear the companies had expanded too quickly and there was not enough demand to keep running such an inefficient service. In the United Kingdom, when the original Chinese dockless bike companies started pulling out, some cities were left without bikeshare services altogether.

Sheffield, for example, had a docked bikeshare system before the arrival of the dockless services, but shut it down when Chinese company Ofo rolled out its dockless bike service because the existing system was no longer financially viable. Officials assumed that if the company was rolling out a service, it would stick around to serve the community, but they were wrong. After about six months, Ofo pulled out of Sheffield and the docked service was not re-established, leaving residents with fewer options. Chinese micromobility companies are not the only ones that have abandoned communities on short notice.

For all their promises about changing urban mobility patterns for the better, micromobility services did little such thing. They challenged existing docked bikeshare services with a less sustainable, more expensive alternative and tried to shape the use of bicycles and scooters so users would have to pay every time they wanted to use one. While the companies claimed to support efforts to establish more bike lanes and other infrastructure, they seemed to do little to change the existing mobility calculus and instead relied much more on effectively taking sidewalk space for themselves without permission. In San Francisco, the city even seized improperly parked scooters for a time.

The ineffectiveness of micromobility companies was put on full display after the initial wave of the Covid-19 pandemic. With cities in various stages of lockdown and people needing to socially distance from one another, many cities closed streets or converted on-street parking to sidewalk extensions. As the summer of 2020 approached, there were bicycle shortages around the world as the number of cyclists soared and many cities added temporary bike lanes that gave way to permanent changes.

New York City built more than twenty-eight miles of protected bike lanes and another thirty-five miles of conventional bike lanes in 2020—a record amount for a single year. Boston announced it was expediting its bike lane plan, Austin made some of its pop-up bike lanes permanent, and other actions were taken in cities across the United States. Meanwhile, just to provide a few examples, Paris announced plans for 400 miles of new bike lanes, Montreal planned 75 miles of additional permanent bike infrastructure, and cities across Latin America made a push for more bike lanes.

As all this was happening, micromobility services were being pulled off the streets in many cities. Instead of a relatively expensive shared service, people rightfully recognized that if they were going to get around without a vehicle or transit, it was best to own their own bicycle, e-bike, or e-scooter. After all, if they used the micromobility services with any regularity, the price would quickly add up. Not only was it more environmentally friendly to buy their own bike, but it was also cheaper, especially as many cities offered incentives to promote the purchase of bikes and e-bikes. France even provided subsidies for people to get their existing bikes repaired.

For all the hype about micromobility services, their exponential growth, and inflated valuations, when it comes to something like bikes and scooters, it makes far more sense for people to own their own and for cities to build the proper infrastructure to enable them to do so. That includes bike lanes, of course, but also safe bike parking facilities, especially near key transit hubs. But micromobility services were the most visible part of a broader campaign to seize the sidewalk in service of unproven tech businesses without a clear public benefit.

As dockless bikes and scooters were hitting sidewalks around the world, other start-ups were looking to those stretches of concrete as a public infrastructure that could enable their ventures. In 2018, Starship Technologies began making deliveries in Milton Keynes, not far outside London, with autonomous robots designed to roll along the sidewalks. The following year, it expanded its service to universities across the United States, but it was still a very niche product.

In 2017, another sidewalk delivery robot company called Marble had partnered with DoorDash and Yelp to deliver orders from various restaurants in select cities across the United States. Meanwhile, Nuro, which has a larger delivery robot designed to drive on the street, has piloted its service with CVS pharmacies, Kroger's for groceries, and Domino's Pizza.

During the Covid-19 pandemic, there was renewed attention on autonomous delivery companies as contactless delivery became an important means through which to stop the spread of the virus while allowing non-essential workers to stay at home. But some of those companies also saw it as an opportunity to assert their place on the sidewalk at the same time as many people had vacated it.

The transportation solutions from the tech industry have long been hostile to walking, whether it was through their focus on individualized, door-to-door services like ride-hailing and autonomous vehicles, or even micromobility services that operated with the assumption that even walking short distances was next to unimaginable. They claimed to be driven, in part, by finding a "last mile" solution, without considering whether most people needed one or why some distances were so long in the first place.

Naturally, a worldview that provides little consideration for people's desire to walk on sidewalks makes it easy for start-up founders interested in transportation and delivery to see them as an empty space to claim for a new business venture. Matt Delaney, a Marble co-founder, was quoted by the *Guardian* in 2017 as saying, "the sidewalk is an infrastructure that is barely used."[16] A spokesperson for Starship Technologies similarly told *Mercury News* in 2016 that they envisioned "thousands and thousands of robots in thousands of cities around the world doing on-demand deliveries."[17] Yet there seemed to be little consideration of what those thousands of delivery bots would mean for pedestrians.

The companies claimed that their robots would not impede people using the sidewalk, but even the small number of robots they had deployed created problems. In 2019, University of Pittsburgh student Emily Ackerman described her harrowing experience after encountering one of them. Ackerman uses a wheelchair, and as she was crossing at an intersection a Starship delivery robot was waiting on the other side. It positioned itself directly in the middle of the curb cut that Ackerman needed to use to get on the sidewalk. "I found myself sitting in the street as the traffic light turned green," she wrote, "blocked by a non-sentient being incapable of understanding the consequences of its actions."[18]

Beyond that encounter, Ackerman made a larger point about the rollout of new technologies into physical space and how little consideration their designers have for marginalized groups.

> The advancement of robotics, AI, and other "futuristic" technologies has ushered in a new era in the ongoing struggle for representation of people with disabilities in large-scale decision-making settings. These technologies come with their own set of ethical design challenges, with more unknown consequences than ever before. And we have yet to have an honest, critical conversation about it.[19]

As outlined in previous chapters, ride-hailing companies refused to observe the Americans with Disabilities Act (ADA), and companies like Uber have even used people in wheelchairs and other marginalized groups as public relations tools to justify services like flying vehicles that are clearly not designed for them. Sidewalk delivery robots are replicating that playbook, and their case is especially egregious: they rely on the curb cuts at intersections that only exist in the United States because the ADA required them on all sidewalks when it was passed in 1990.

Six months after Ackerman's experience, Haben Girma, a deaf-blind person with full mobility, encountered a Starship robot with her guide dog. While her life was not endangered by the robot, it still blocked her way and did not move to allow her to pass. Her guide dog sat down in front of it because it was not trained on how to react to a delivery robot. Ultimately, she had to maneuver around it so she could continue on her way. Girma wrote that when it comes to these new technologies, "In my experience, the word 'everyone' means everyone except disabled people."[20] In truth, its definition is much narrower than that.

Once again, despite claims that delivery services would benefit disabled people, Girma found that the Starship app did not work with VoiceOver, the gesture-based screen reader on iPhones designed for people who cannot see the screen, making it inaccessible to her and other blind people. "During a pandemic disproportionately extinguishing disabled lives," she explained, "the last thing we need is cities adopting tech that excludes blind people and endangers pedestrians with mobility disabilities."[21] Sadly, many cities have shown that they are far more interested in appearing innovative and attracting the attention of the tech industry than considering who its solutions actually work for.

In March 2021, Pennsylvania joined many other states in legalizing sidewalk delivery robots, and its legislation was seen as among the least restrictive in the country. The regulations legally classified the robots as pedestrians, allowing them to weigh up to 550 pounds and move at speeds of up to twelve miles per hour on the sidewalk, which is much faster than a pedestrian, and up to twenty-five miles per hour in a bike lane. The state law also ensured local governments could not set stricter regulations in their own jurisdictions. It was a repeat of what had happened in some states with ride-hailing services.

The *Pittsburgh City Paper* noted that pedestrian and accessibility advocates, along with labor unions, were opposed to the rules.[22] The National Association of City Transportation Officials warned that the robots could increase noise pollution and the companies could "flood sidewalks with bots, making walking increasingly difficult and unpleasant."[23] The group called for severe restrictions on their use, if not an outright ban, but that did not stop lawmakers from opening the floodgates and placing pedestrian space at risk.

The excitement around these robots ignores how ill-equipped any kind of mass delivery service would be for many real-world environments. Delivery robots require well-maintained sidewalks or roads, depending on which they are using, and for those areas not to have high levels of traffic so the robots' paths are not frequently interrupted. That is precisely why Starship has been establishing itself at universities because the paths and roads are usually well-maintained, campuses have less internal vehicle traffic, and outside peak times they will not encounter many disruptions on walkways.

Suburbs might also seem like ideal areas for these robots since they experience far less foot traffic than urban areas, but distances can be excessive given that businesses are often located far from suburban homes. In addition, as tax revenue has shrunk over time, communities in cities and suburbs have struggled to maintain their roads and sidewalks, which can cause obstacles for delivery robots. Even though they would not need to travel as far in urban neighborhoods, there are usually more people using the roads and sidewalks that could get in their way, or vice versa. The frictionless delivery experience promised by the companies operating delivery robots is easily disrupted by the friction of human life.

There is also the question of how people react to the robots. If a delivery person is not waiting at the customer's door with the order, how long will they let the robot sit outside before they retrieve it? *Ars Technica* found the Starship robot would not move until its lid was fully closed,[24] showing that people will need to be taught how to properly use them. There is also a general concern about vandalism, and whether people will try to steal orders or simply trash the robots if they come across them. The companies' solution to that problem is to equip the robots with the ability to call the police and record their attackers. Given the trigger-happy nature of US law enforcement, that could have deadly consequences.

The final issue of note with this delivery "solution" is its approach to labor. One of its selling points is the automation of app-based delivery workers that companies have been exploiting for the past decade, not coincidentally at the very moment that workers in some countries are making progress in gaining employment recognition and other rights and benefits after years of organizing. The robots present the fiction that there is no human labor involved in their operation, even though, as is the case with many purportedly autonomous driving technologies, the delivery companies rely on low-paid remote drivers as far away as Colombia and the Philippines to take over when the robots cannot navigate a particular situation. It should not come as a surprise that those workers are not employees in the United States or Europe, continuing the process of using technology to deskill and outsource labor.

Micromobility and autonomous delivery companies sought to capitalize on the pandemic. Even though dockless bike and scooter services missed out on the closed streets in the spring of 2020, they began escalating their services again in 2021. Yet the pandemic showed that true progress in getting people to switch to bikes and scooters came not from app-based services, but from public policy promoting bicycle use and ownership.

Similarly, the more delivery robots are deployed, the more they will get in the way of pedestrians and cyclists who already have to fight for what little space they have. The focus so far has been on sidewalks simply because they are everywhere, but the same problems will face cyclists as companies seek to take over bike lanes. Ultimately, if there is ever a mass rollout of delivery robots, the backlash is likely to echo San Francisco's response to micromobility services. When they take up more sidewalk space, it will become clear to a broader subsection of residents that they are premised on colonizing the bit of public space that is left on the edge of dangerous roadways.

Too often, governments stand back and allow the tech industry to roll out whatever ideas its executives and engineers can dream up. There is an assumption that whatever tech companies want is inevitable—it is the future—and that neither governments, traditional companies, nor even the public should stand in their way. But after more than a decade of their push into urban space, we need to reset our assumptions. Their ideas of the future are not the only path forward, and they often benefit people like themselves at the expense of low-income and marginalized residents. That is not the way to create more equitable communities; instead it allows the tech sector to shape our existence to serve their narrow interests.

Recalling the public outrage of San Franciscans at dockless scooters being littered in their streets, their local government also provided an example of a somewhat positive approach to these services. In 2017, San Francisco Supervisor Norman Yee initially proposed a ban on sidewalk robots after a coalition of residents demanded action, but he instead settled on a series of restrictive measures to significantly limit the number of robots on the street and require them to have a human chaperone at all times, effectively making them pointless.

Yee boldly stated that "not every innovation is all that great for society,"[25] and unlike with ride-hailing services, the city acted quickly instead of waiting for the state government to preempt its regulatory power. Less than a year after the restrictions on sidewalk robots, the city also implemented a temporary ban on dockless e-scooters, forcing them all off the sidewalks as it established regulations and a permitting process to control the number of dockless bikes and e-scooters on the street. A similar process was created for sidewalk delivery robots.

While San Francisco's Board of Supervisors allowed the technologies back onto the sidewalks after a time out, it is worth noting that the city on the front line of disruption has turned into the one that will occasionally take some of the most restrictive approaches to its newest innovations. While the city arguably did not go far enough, such as forcing the companies to prove they were actually providing the benefits they claimed and assessing whether the realized benefits justified the services' presence, it does show that the services can be resisted, and governments should use that power far more often.

The technologies unleashed by Silicon Valley are not neutral. They contain within them the worldviews of the people who develop them; and when they go unquestioned, we allow those very people to make important decisions about how and for whom our society should operate without any democratic deliberation. When we assume that technology can only develop in one way, we accept the power of the people who control that process, but there is no guarantee that their ideal world is one that truly works for everyone.

They champion ideas that would ensure that automobiles continue to dominate our transportation system, that active mobility becomes a rentier service as its adoption grows, and that sidewalks are converted into a space for robots instead of people. Such a future would be hostile to the goal of more egalitarian cities and would make us more dependent on commercial interests rather than trying to free us from their control. The futures suggested by the technologies profiled so far are not the kind of world we should be striving toward.

8

The Real Futures That Tech Is Building

In the aftermath of the 2008 financial crisis, the tech industry grew substantially and claimed a dominant position not just in the United States, but across the global economy. The internet was firmly established by that point, and it began moving from the desk to the palm of people's hands as smartphone adoption soared through the 2010s. Cloud computing and other software products made it much cheaper than in the past to launch a start-up and compete for a piece of the rapidly growing industry. Meanwhile, financing was abundant, not just because decades of inequality had caused more wealth to flow to those at the top, but also due to policy choices taken to combat the recession.

The trillions of dollars printed by the Federal Reserve and other central banks through quantitative easing and the low interest rates that persisted throughout the 2010s created an environment that boosted the stock market even as most workers' prospects continued to stagnate, which benefited venture capitalists and made it much easier for new companies in the tech sector to access capital. Such a dynamic granted investors, influential founders, and executives at the dominant companies in the industry a significant degree of power in shaping what the post-recession economy looked like—and who it served.

By 2010, today's tech giants were continuing their rapid growth, but they were not yet the juggernauts they would become a decade later. Google had a number of popular services in addition to Search, but many people still believed its "do no evil" slogan. Amazon's positions in ecommerce and cloud computing were growing, but it was not yet seen as such an existential threat to brick-and-mortar retail. Apple was reinventing itself with the iPhone, but it was far from being one of the largest publicly traded companies in the world. Yet, as they expanded, other companies made use of smartphone access, new digital tools, and the excitement around the tech economy to make their own splash.

Airbnb was founded in 2008, Uber in 2009, and WeWork in 2010. They were part of a business trend that further extended the reach of the tech industry into the physical world. These companies operated under the assumption that taking the mindset of tech into a traditional industry would not only modernize and transform it but would generate previously unrealizable returns. Many of them also promoted the idea that smartphone apps would allow people to work and monetize their assets in ways that increased their freedom and prosperity, while making consumption more convenient. Yet what they were really doing was taking advantage of—and cementing—the precarity of the post-recession years.

Eric Levitz, an associate editor at *New York Magazine*, argued that venture capitalists, especially in this period, acted as the United States' central planners.[1] While the political right criticized government decisions to provide support to particular companies and sectors, they ignored how a powerful group of wealthy men educated at Ivy League institutions were in control of multibillion-dollar funds that they used to cherry-pick companies that could corner particular market segments and finance them while they recorded substantial losses over the course of many years, driving out competition. In the process, they created elaborate public relations campaigns about the broad-based benefits their "disruption" would produce, even as the real gains from those services typically accrued to the same class of well-off men who created them in the first place. Not only is this an extension of the elite

projection that Jarrett Walker wrote about, as these founders and venture capitalists backed projects that worked for
them but assumed—or at least claimed—they would work for
everyone, but it is also a continuation of the history discussed
in Chapter 2.

In the aftermath of the recession, the same ideas that had
been born in the 1970s and 1980s were once again at work;
the same ideas that had created the techno-deterministic, free
market ideology of Silicon Valley by men who held countercultural ideals but used them to justify their participation in
the capitalist system. Even as the tech industry became a powerful force in the US economy and spread its influence around
the world while people became dependent on hardware and
software produced by American companies, the titans of the
industry continued to see themselves as scrappy upstarts; the
Davids fighting some increasingly abstract Goliath. University
of California researchers Martin Kenney and John Zysman
argued that the dynamic these venture capitalists created had
social and economic consequences, and they were not positive. Rather, they funded "a drive toward disruption without
social benefit" that not only distorted market fundamentals
by pursuing a predatory growth strategy, but actively attacked
regulatory structures designed to protect workers and the
public.[2]

In his article about this phenomenon, Levitz used the
example of WeWork because it was a high-profile case where
the model failed. WeWork offered co-working spaces around
the world, but instead of positioning itself as a company that
rented office space, it claimed it was a tech company, which
came with a different set of expectations. While a traditional
company would seek sustainable growth and expansion to
provide a return on investment within the first few years of
operation, a tech company—even one operating in a traditional industry—is expected to deliver the kind of exponential
growth that one would expect from digital services, while

significantly reducing the marginal cost of expansion. That works well for software products, cloud platforms, and logistics companies, but it does not translate to office space, for-hire vehicles, and many of the other conventional businesses that the post-2008 crop of so-called tech companies sought to disrupt.

In the case of WeWork, its success was less the product of offering superior co-working spaces than it was in the undercutting of its competitors and offering of a slew of perks to members while losing millions of dollars a day. Investors went along with it because, at least for a while, they bought into the vision of CEO Adam Neumann even as he used the company to finance a lavish lifestyle for himself and his family—engaging in self-dealing by personally buying real estate then having WeWork rent it from him—and created a work environment with the misogyny and "bro" culture that is a major problem in the industry.

The bold claims of founders like Neumann, even if they have no grounding in reality, are central to the inflated valuations of these companies, along with the hope that they will one day monopolize and produce large returns, as Amazon succeeded in doing. Yet, in the case of WeWork, it became increasingly clear that the monopoly would never arrive, so investors tried to keep up the ruse until the company went public. But as the date of its initial public offering (IPO) approached, scandalous stories about Neumann in the press and documents produced by the company that showed his cult-like influence caused potential investors to lose confidence. Instead of cashing out, the IPO was canceled, Neumann was forced out, and there were mass layoffs as employees' stock options went to zero.

WeWork may have failed, but it was hardly the only company pursuing a model that, in reality, is unlikely to ever succeed. Many of the companies seeking to transform mobility that have been the focus of this book fall within that same category—these companies lose millions, if not billions, of dollars every year as they bid to transform the transportation system in line with how their founders and investors believe it should function, with little to no regard for public benefit, or indeed public need.

Uber is a prime example. Between 2016 and 2020, it lost approximately $25 billion—an eye-watering amount when compared with Amazon—the company held up as the example to emulate—which lost $2.8 billion dollars in its first seventeen quarters, before turning itself into the dominant force it is today. In 2018, a decade after its founding, Uber was still losing an average of fifty-eight cents on every ride it delivered,[3] and its prospects have not significantly improved.

Uber promised to transform the taxi industry by bringing prices down, increasing convenience, and improving the lot of drivers (as outlined in Chapter 4). The first was achieved by subsidizing the cost of the rides with billions of investor dollars; the second by flooding the streets with cars that had the impact of worsening traffic. But they came at the expense of drivers who saw their wages fall at the same time as they were compelled to shoulder more of the risk by using their own cars and buying their own insurance, all while having no control over their work.

After it became a major force, Uber cycled through several bold visions to keep investor money flowing as it failed to profitably deliver its ride-hailing service. It promised to automate drivers. It promised to reduce car use through micromobility and reduce congestion with flying cars. It promised to become the "Amazon for transportation," making its app the go-to destination for urban mobility. But all these efforts failed, to the degree that in 2020 Uber divested of its autonomous vehicle, micromobility, and flying car divisions. It effectively had to pay other companies to take its failed bets off its balance sheet.

At the beginning of 2021, Uber promised to refocus on its ride-hailing and food delivery services as its path to profitability, even though Uber Eats had even worse margins than ride-hailing. Uber was able to lose billions of dollars for more than a decade, and while it made it to the IPO stage, its share price plummeted after it went public. But that does not mean it has produced no benefits for the capitalists who funded it.

Over its more than a decade in business, Uber has decimated the taxi industry, the regulations that governed it, and the labor protections of its workers. Even if Uber eventually dies, it spent 2020 fighting to roll back the employment rights of workers in California's gig economy and committed to fight for similar laws across the United States, Canada, and Europe. If it does not produce a profit, investors will have still been able to recoup some of their investment after it went public, and they may yet cement a third category of labor that restricts workers' protections and bargaining rights that other companies can exploit in the future. That could be a far bigger win in the long term if it is not reversed by government action.

There is no denying that the vast wealth captured by the tech industry is being successfully deployed to transform the society in which we live. But whether one benefits often depends on if they lucked into working in one of the shrinking number of industries that still allow workers to be financially stable. The futures imagined by those in tech are promoted as though they will benefit everyone, but that group is as narrowly defined as their worldview. The truth is that when we look at the world that is actually being created by the tech industry's interventions, we find that the bold promises are in fact a cover for a society that is both more unequal and one where that inequality is even more fundamentally built into the infrastructure and services we interact with every single day.

After the ascendence of the tech industry, its captains are remaking the physical environment—in the same way they have the digital environment—to benefit themselves. They do not market their ideas that way, as that would generate a backlash that could delay their plans; but in the same way that the automotive industry and other sectors that were tied to it promoted a different vision for the city in the early and mid-twentieth century that immensely benefited their interests, the tech industry is now doing the same. The expansion of automobility was paired with the language of freedom, even as it killed millions of people, made communities almost impossible to traverse without a car, and forced drivers to be dependent on a whole range of products and services needed to function in the world of the automobile. There is no reason to believe that the positive language of the tech industry will not give way to another set of inequitable, and even harmful, outcomes.

We can already see this very clearly with many of the companies and visions outlined in this book. Uber promised to reduce congestion, cut car ownership, and benefit drivers; it did none of those things, while pulling people from transit and increasing emissions. Google said it would have radically altered urban transportation by now, but instead its Waymo division runs a small service in a suburb of Phoenix, Arizona, and is slowly establishing limited services in other cities. Elon Musk promised to build a massive network of underground car tunnels to solve traffic congestion, but instead delivered an unimpressive conference attraction and continues to promote the fiction that electrifying automobiles is the solution to climate change, all the while downplaying the environmental damage caused by their production. These ideas not only overestimated the capabilities of the technologies they relied on, but they also ignored the politics and social relations that are key to our mobility.

The founders, executives, and venture capitalists that back these initiatives for the future of transportation have a very narrow experience of the city. Their proposed solutions respond to the problems of urban life as they experience them—not as most residents do. That leads to grand plans that are not only naïve, but which fail to address the real challenges that people face in getting around their communities, accessing jobs and services, and visiting family and friends. Cities were not ideal living environments before the automobile. There were problems with sanitation, mobility, access to housing, and other aspects of life—and while suburbanization and the automobile solved some of those problems for certain residents, they also created many other challenges that have been entrenched over the course of many decades and that must be addressed today.

Yet, in the vision of the "frictionless" city that is held by many in tech, where virtually every city service, human interaction, and consumer experience is to be mediated by an app or digital service that not only cuts out the need to deal directly with another human but places technology at the heart of those interactions, there is no serious attempt to deal with deeply entrenched problems—at least outside of rhetorical flourishes. The decisions of venture capitalists to fund companies that are transforming the way we move, consume, and conduct our daily lives should not be perceived as neutral actions. Rather, they are pushing particular visions of the future that benefit themselves by funding the years-long efforts of companies to monopolize their sectors and lobby to alter regulatory structures in their favor. Furthermore, rather than challenging the dominance of the automobile, their ideas almost always seek to extend it.

After more than a decade of being flooded with idealized visions of technologically enhanced futures whose benefits have not been shared in the ways their promoters promised, we should instead consider what kinds of futures they are far more likely to create. In the pages that follow, I will outline three future scenarios that are far more realistic and illustrate the world that is being created: first, it is even more segregated based on income; second, it is even more hostile to

pedestrians; and third, it wants to use unaccountable technological systems to control even more aspects of our lives.

The Gated Greenwashed City

If we were to believe Elon Musk, the vision he promotes for
a green future is one that will address the climate crisis, along
with many other urban and mobility issues. However, there
is another way to see what he is doing when we look beyond
Musk's elite projection.

There are three main aspects to the future vision being laid
out by Musk—setting aside his plans for space colonization.
The first is electric personal vehicles. Musk believes in "individualized transport," which effectively means that automobiles
should continue to be the primary means of mobility and most
of the problems that accompany an auto-oriented transportation system should be ignored. However, his vision is more
than a simple preference for personal vehicles, and luxury
ones in particular. In 2019, Musk unveiled the Cybertruck,
an unusual vehicle not because Tesla had never made a truck
but because it took styling cues from dystopian science fiction
and was designed to withstand brute force attack. The vehicle
has panels that cannot be dented with a sledgehammer and
windows that are supposed to be bulletproof. While the latter
did not work in Musk's public demonstration, the decision to
build such features into an incredibly large vehicle likely says
something about the personal fears that undergird Musk's
ideas for the future.

The second element of Musk's vision is the use of solar
panels, particularly those affixed to suburban homes.
Following the purchase of SolarCity, Musk championed the
idea of homeowners generating their own electricity through
solar roofs and arrays that could be used to charge their
electric cars, fill up their in-home batteries, and potentially

even earn them a profit by feeding into the grid. The third and final piece of the puzzle is the Boring Company's imagined system of tunnels that turned out to be little more than narrow underground roads for expensive vehicles with autonomous driving systems—if they are ever truly realized. These two aspects also display Musk's preference for sprawling suburbs of single-family homes over dense, transit-oriented development.

Putting these three elements together and considering them alongside the current trajectory of our capitalist society reveals a different kind of urban future than the one Musk wants us to believe will solve our problems. Without altering the underlying social relations, these technologies are likely to reinforce the trends of growing tech billionaire wealth and their desire to close themselves off from the rest of society.

Recall that the first of Musk's proposed tunnels was designed to make it easier for him to get from home to work and back without getting stuck in traffic with everyone else. Rather than a network of tunnels for the masses, such a system could be redeployed as one designed by and for the wealthy. The tunnels would exist not to relieve traffic congestion but to serve as roads for the rich that are inaccessible to the public and connect the places that they frequent: their gated communities, private airport terminals, and other exclusive areas of the city.

For the times when they are beyond the walls of their gated communities and need to drive (or be driven) outside of their exclusive tunnel systems, the Cybertruck will provide protection from the unruly mob that is the general public. With inequality in the United States having risen to higher levels than any time since the Great Depression and the accelerating effects of climate change creating the potential for hundreds of millions of climate refugees, the wealthy are making additional preparations for the moment when the public finally turns against them—hence the walls, tunnels, and armored vehicles.

Indeed, the wealthy have already been building bunkers and buying property in countries like New Zealand to prepare for such an eventuality.[4]

While the world outside their gated communities becomes more hostile and the effects of the climate crisis change life for virtually everyone, distributed renewable energy generation and the battery backups being sold by Tesla as a mass solution will work perfectly as a means to make gated communities as self-sufficient as possible. Such a use of renewable energy should be seen as a form of "resource-intensive solar separatism for the rich and the geographically lucky" who can retreat into "affluent enclaves,"[5] and it is an outcome that is not so difficult to imagine.

Neill Blomkamp's 2013 science fiction film *Elysium* presented a world divided between a climate-ravaged Los Angeles where residents were poor, struggled to find work, found it almost impossible to receive healthcare, and were kept in line by oppressive technological systems and robotic police. Meanwhile, floating in the sky above was the Elysium space colony, the world that the rich escaped to when life on the surface turned against them. While the narrative is compelling and the situation is quite believable, the reality is that the rich will never retreat to space; they will segregate themselves to an even greater degree than they already have.

There is no doubt that electric vehicles, renewable technologies, and transport tunnels (for transit, not for cars) will be integral to the creation of a more sustainable way of life that is necessary to avoid runaway climate change. But the way they are conceived of in the minds of people like Musk—as part of a green capitalism that exists first and foremost to maintain the privileges of elites and derive profit for their benefit— precludes their socially emancipatory uses in favor of continuing a pattern of inequitable development that defines the system of automobility. In short, Elon Musk's future cities and transport networks are not for us.

The City without Pedestrians

Silicon Valley hates walking. For the past decade, their interventions into mobility have been obsessed with finding the "last-mile solution" that will get people directly to their door without having to walk more than a few steps. This is the preoccupation of a group of people that are wealthy enough that they not only never have to consider walking anywhere, but increasingly do not want to be in public for fear of being recognized, asked questions, heckled, or worse. Given that they want to close themselves off, and certainly cannot imagine taking public transit, they project that desire onto much of the rest of society, under the assumption that few other people living in major cities will walk for a few minutes to reach their destinations.

Yet that is simply not a reality of urban life. People who take transit walk to and from the bus or subway stop every single day, while other residents walk to and from the bikeshare station. Many drivers have to park and walk some distance to where they are going. And there are also people who, either by choice or circumstance, complete many of their trips by walking alone. Walking is a normal part of living in a city, even for those who primarily rely on automobiles; but tech companies want to replace even this very rudimental form of mobility with app-based services.

Instead of walking, Silicon Valley would prefer that people hail a ride from Uber or Lyft to take them straight to the door; rent a dockless bike or scooter that they can drop in front of their destination; or, in the future, take some form of autonomous mobility that will achieve the same outcome. Either way, people are expected to use a service mediated by an application that benefits one or more tech companies not only by producing a transaction but by creating data that can be fed into an automated system or resold to other companies who can derive value from it. This is a vision of mobility that is hostile to pedestrians in a different way than early automotive concepts like General Motors' Futurama with its wide highways. Instead, even the sidewalk is imagined to be reoriented for other uses.

At the same time as tech has been aggressively trying to get us to stop walking, it has also been creating a service economy designed to deliver whatever it is people want to their doorsteps as quickly as possible. This takes the form of on-demand apps where gig workers with terrible pay and no protections hastily try to fulfill as many orders as possible so they can eke out a living, and ecommerce services—particularly orders made through Amazon—where the expectations for delivery have fallen to a couple of days, if not hours. This also has consequences for urban living.

Rapid delivery services create a greater incentive for people to stay at home and have everything brought to them. They were undoubtedly very convenient for some people during the Covid-19 pandemic—though certainly not for the workers doing the deliveries and packing the orders—but they have the potential to further erode urban social interactions and community in the medium to long term. The shift toward ecommerce presents a threat to the sustainability of brick-and-mortar retail if that transition is not handled properly, while the growth of food delivery apps presents a threat to restaurants by charging high fees while creating a network of "ghost kitchens" that cannot be visited and only make food for delivery.

In addition, all these deliveries take up space on the street. In recent years, the increase in delivery vans and trucks on urban roads has been an important contributor to traffic congestion, while blocking bike lanes and sidewalks. Since some delivery drivers are under pressure to meet unachievable targets, they drive fast and cut corners, putting themselves and the people around them at risk. One of the proposed solutions to this problem, as discussed in Chapter 7, is to take over the sidewalks with delivery robots that are driven partly by autonomous software and partly by virtual drivers located in countries where they can be paid low wages.

These visions of convenient delivery paired with ubiquitous mobility are part of the broader notion of the frictionless society: where technology mediates transactions and interactions to remove anything that would stifle convenience. But frictionlessness works best when humans are taken out of the equation: whether it is to remove the human interaction from purchases, or to stop humans from getting in the way of fulfillment. Automobiles pushed pedestrians off the streets in the twentieth century because they created friction that slowed the vehicles down, so they were limited to the sidewalk. But as people get in the way of deliveries, there is a new desire to get anyone or anything that could slow them down out of their path—whether on the road or the sidewalk.

In an article for *Real Life* magazine on how ecommerce is transforming logistics and fulfillment in the United Kingdom, Charlie Jarvis made an important observation.

> For all its complexity, contemporary logistics aspires to purge commerce of the kinds of connection that reveal our interdependencies, that make a political understanding of our situation in the world possible. Where goods move freely, the spaces in which we can move without friction shrink.[6]

In the same way that the urban landscape was sanitized to make way for the automobile, a similar process will be necessary to make way for the frictionless world of technologically mediated consumption that tech companies desire to usher in. There are benefits to some forms of on-demand services and ecommerce, but the way they are designed and implemented under capitalism does not enrich communities, nor make them more equitable. Rather, they take away the human elements that are perceived as friction and hollow out our social existence.

The City of Algorithmic Control

Through the 2010s, there was a concerted push for us to conduct more of our lives through our smartphones. People took rides through Uber instead of taxis or transit. They booked vacation rentals through Airbnb instead of hotel chains. They found people to walk their dogs, clean their homes, fix their pipes, and fulfill other needs through a new cluster of gig services, then found new ways to consume through subscription services and ecommerce sites with free shipping. Digital services are preferable to their traditional counterparts, even when they are worse for the task—and that has consequences.

As discussed in the previous scenario, we are sold the convenience of digital consumption and communication through the virtue of frictionlessness. Tech companies promise to use technology to take any concerns or obstacles out of the way, so all we need to do is press a button or use an app, and they will handle everything else. This promise ignores how the technology can create new forms of friction of its own—but the friction created by technology is not considered to be friction. It is normalized, while human interactions or engagement with analog systems must be purged.

Consider the grocery store. First there was the self-checkout machine. Instead of having to deal with a human cashier, a customer could check themselves out; but anyone who has ever used one knows the machines are notorious for making mistakes or being unable to properly detect the weights of products. Users will be familiar with having to wait for a human attendant to come and resolve a problem, if not be instructed to use a different machine. Instead of giving up, Amazon introduced the Amazon Go and Fresh stores with the promise that customers could walk in, pick up what they want, and walk out—all without going to the checkout. But the trade-off is that every part of the store is watched to ensure the system knows which items customers pick up.

The Amazon store experience, while presented as frictionless, contains a lot of friction—so much so that many people are excluded from entry. On top of the complex surveillance system, every customer needs to have a smartphone, have downloaded the Amazon app, logged into an Amazon account, and connected a means of payment. When an Amazon Fresh store opened in West London in March 2021, a journalist observed an old man trying to go in to pick up some groceries, but he gave up when he was told all the steps he would have to take just to enter. "Oh f*** that, no, no, no—can't be bothered," he said, then kept walking to reach a normal grocery store.[7] But in the future he may run into similar issues at even more stores as countries like Sweden pioneer a cashless economy and the Amazon model inevitably spreads.

The extension of inequities, and even the creation of new ones, is a key part of the frictionless society that gets hidden by the digital services that claim to increase convenience and reduce the barriers to consumption. Researcher Chris Gilliard coined the term "digital redlining" to describe the series of technologies, regulatory decisions that enable them, and investments that allow them to scale as actions that "enforce class boundaries and discriminate against specific groups."[8] In the same way that biases in artificial intelligence systems were long ignored, if not purposefully hidden, to protect the business interests of various companies, these frictionless tools also claim they will eliminate inequities, even as Gilliard argued that "the feedback loops of algorithmic systems will work to reinforce these often flawed and discriminatory assumptions. The presupposed problem of difference will become even more entrenched, the chasms between people will widen."[9]

It is hard to believe any different when the larger social context is considered, as was discussed in the first scenario. There is already a growing economic divide that produces and reinforces social and geographic divides. This is not an assumption; it is observable in the development of the app-based economy to date, as well as the proposals for how these frictionless systems will work.

In 2015, journalist Lauren Smiley described the growing on-demand, app-based economy as the shut-in economy, where "you're either pampered, isolated royalty—or you're a 21st century servant."[10] Smiley observed that San Francisco was increasingly divided into two groups. On one side were the tech workers and a broader group of "knowledge" workers who earned high salaries, worked long hours, and used the gig apps to get everything from food delivery and laundry services to house cleaning, dog walking, and childcare. On the other was the contract labor force that delivered those services with few protections, no benefits, and precariously low pay. But the apps allowed the served to ignore the conditions of their app-based servants. They could even avoid seeing them altogether.

These frictionless digital services provide a technological curtain to hide the worker exploitation that makes possible the convenience that companies are selling and customers are buying. As Amazon promises ever-faster delivery, its ware-houses are dystopian environments with lower than industry average pay and double the industry standard injury rate, while its delivery drivers are under such high pressure they have to resort to peeing in bottles and even defecating in bags. Uber's drivers have been reported to sleep in their cars, and many of the purportedly self-driving mobility systems rely on virtual human drivers located in the Global South to take over in the regular instances that the technology cannot navigate its environment. This even extends to the smart city with its constant promises of more efficient urban systems which hide the humans that are required to maintain them.

The shut-in economy is a further example of the desire to keep people at home and work, where they can be delivered everything they need instead of going out to get it themselves, thus keeping the streets clear for autonomous delivery bots, cars, and other forms of mobility, as outlined in the second scenario. Yet the potential implications of the frictionless society for urban life and the design of cities go far beyond being encouraged to stay at home. Mediating so much of our society through apps and digital systems can also create technological barriers to the access of physical places.

Researcher David A. Banks described the kind of society that these services are creating as "the subscriber city." Similar to digital redlining, it is made up of "a set of technological, legal, financial, and marketing techniques that manage segregation for the purposes of capital accumulation and resource management."[11] For many years, tech companies' power was largely limited to what we did on the internet. Our online interactions were captured by a small number of dominant platforms, but after the mass adoption of smartphones and the connection of more elements of physical space to the internet, they are increasingly moving into our cities and homes with the same driving force to maximize their control.

As these companies expand into physical space, they also bring with them their desire for business models based on data extraction and rentierism. Not only are the existing tech monopolies trying to control the digital systems that will mediate how we interact with our homes and our communities, they also want to ensure that they control the data that is produced as we live our lives and take a cut of every transaction we make.

Tech critic Jathan Sadowski described this as the "internet of landlords," where instead of simply paying rent for our homes, the relationship between renter and landlord is extended to many more areas of society, creating a more explicit technological barrier to access that is designed to serve companies and their shareholders, not users, renters, or residents of cities where these systems are rolled out. As Sadowski described:

> The proliferation of platforms fills society with ubiquitous digital intermediaries that spread rentier relations far and

wide, at different scales and intensities, while also concentrat-
ing control over infrastructure and economic value in a small
number of large hands.[12]

The intermediary role provides the companies with an
unprecedented ability to close off access to parts of the city
if users do not have enough money or have some form of
infraction on their account; and if the experience of Uber
drivers who get kicked off the app for bad reviews with little
ability to appeal shows us anything, it is that the frictionlessness of the app-based world also provides people without
power with little means to push back when they are mis-
treated or disregarded in the process. Banks explained that
as these technologies are built into more aspects of everyday
life, "individuals would be unable to predict the behavior of
doors, queues, and prices, as these would be subject to the
whims of platform owners. One could be anywhere and suddenly find oneself outside looking in."[13]

There is a direct transfer of power from residents to the
tech companies in the app-based city, and as control over
interactions and transactions shifts to vast technological
systems, there is also a loss of accountability. In exchange
for frictionlessness for people who have reaped the benefits
of the modern economy, there are growing barriers for those
who have not—barriers that can quickly appear where they
did not previously exist, and which cannot easily be resolved
because they are controlled by algorithms instead of human
beings.

It is no surprise that the tech industry is flexing its power to
increase its control over society in service of deriving greater
profits from the outcome of that transformation, regardless of
the social consequences. This has happened many times in the
past, whether it was through constructing new communities
around streetcars, or later, much more expansive efforts to

remake cities around the automobile and suburbs to benefit automotive interests, property developers, and growing consumer goods manufacturers.

While I have discussed the role of venture capitalists and other powerful figures in tech in shepherding this ongoing transformation of our environments, they are not undertaking these efforts alone. In the same way that the US tech industry was the product of decades of public investment in educational institutions, research departments, and the sector itself, governments at various levels are essential to helping its most powerful players realize their visions for the city, for transportation, and for how we access a wide range of services.

Previous chapters have illustrated the lax regulatory environment that enabled on-demand services like ride-hailing to flourish, while in other cases city and state governments provided financing or regulatory cover to attract Tesla factories, Uber's autonomous vehicle division, or Boring Company projects. Yet these efforts are just the tip of a much larger iceberg that has been forming over decades that helped ensure cities orient themselves and their policy agendas around the tech industry.

Beginning in the 1970s, the governance practices of cities began to realign to reflect changing economic conditions. Spurred by deindustrialization, fewer restrictions on international money flows, and the 1973 recession, geographer David Harvey explained that cities adopted an "urban entrepreneurialism" where they had to compete for new industries and investment. Urban areas had to more effectively brand themselves, offer subsidy packages to entice corporations to relocate, and embrace gentrification and consumption-oriented growth. But given the new pressures on urban finances, public services and welfare programs were cut at the same moment as support for corporations increased, "producing greater polarisation in the social distribution of real income."[14] Naturally, these developments served to increase inequality and further redirect the attention of city governments away from marginalized populations toward those with power and wealth.

The entrepreneurial trends described by Harvey only deepened with time. As the tech economy was entering a new stage after the dot-com bubble had burst, cities tried to attract a particular class of worker in the hope that industries wanting to employ them would follow. The "creative class" theory, as outlined by urbanist and consultant Richard Florida, asserted that governments needed to create urban amenities and pass laws that would specifically appeal to this segment of high-demand "knowledge" workers with above-average incomes, further sidelining the residents who had already been hit by the shift to urban entrepreneurialism. In the process of importing affluent workers, cities embraced further gentrification, causing house prices to soar and urban inequality to deepen.

In line with Florida's model, sociologist Sharon Zukin explained that before the 2008 recession, cities assumed that "providing green space, bicycle paths, and cultural facilities, all much cheaper than affordable housing and more politically palatable than business subsidies, would help them to be winners in the global economy."[15] But with the post-recession growth of the tech industry, cities were positioned as "the social and cultural locus of technological innovation that makes businesses and countries winners in the global economy."[16] Guided by that strategy, there was a greater focus on providing public support to grow the sector and to ensure universities were producing both the talent and the intellectual property to form start-ups and attract industry giants.

This entrepreneurial governance model of laying out the red carpet for corporations and providing whatever was necessary to entice them while ignoring the needs of residents may have reached its apotheosis when Amazon launched a competition for its second headquarters in 2017, creating a frenzy where more than 200 cities across North America competed to sell themselves to the monopolist with large subsidy packages and embarrassing publicity stunts. After a decade and a half of selling this development strategy, Florida acknowledged its flaws that same year, while pitching a new set of ideas that promised to fix them and, presumably, attract more consulting work.

Given that governments under capitalism need to prioritize constant economic growth, they must always adapt to facilitate new strategies of capital accumulation. As the tech industry has moved beyond the network and into physical space, it has sought to further shape how we live in service of bolstering its bottom line and its level of social control. Once again, urban systems must evolve, but they are doing so to accommodate the interests of companies like Amazon and Google, not the growing class of precarious urban workers who will suffer the consequences. Any effective attempt to challenge the futures on offer by the capitalist tech industry will require a movement that can wield the power of organized residents against them, along with a vision for a hopeful, emancipatory alternative they can rally around.

9
Toward a Better Transport Future

Ursula K. Le Guin had a unique way of telling a great story that forced us to confront contradictions in the way our society is organized. She believed that empowering people to use their imaginations to think of a better world was "dangerous to those who profit from the way things are because it has the power to show that the way things are is not permanent, not universal, not necessary,"[1] and she showed this to be true through her fiction.

In 1976, Le Guin published a coming-of-age novel called *Very Far Away from Anywhere Else* that explicitly engaged with questions of mobility and the place of the automobile in American society. The protagonist of the novel was a teenage boy living in suburbia who was figuring out his identity, and finding that it clashed with the prevailing wisdom in his community. In an internal monologue, he explained, "I didn't know who I was, but I knew one thing: I wasn't the seat-fixture of an automobile." He saw himself as someone who preferred to take the bus and to walk because "I really like the streets of the city. The sidewalks, the buildings, the people you pass. Not the brake lights on the back of the car in front of yours."[2] But he was having an altogether different identity thrust upon him.

For his birthday, his father had gifted him a car, and he deeply resented it:

> You see, in giving me that car my father was saying, "This is what I want you to be. A normal car-loving American teenager." And by giving it to me he had made it impossible for me

to say what I wanted to say, which was that I had finally realized that that's what I wasn't, and was never going to be, and
I needed help finding out what I was instead. But to say that,
now, I had to say, "Take your present back, I don't want it!"
And I couldn't.[3]

In his view, foisting a car upon him was also part of a larger
pattern of pushing a particular idea of masculinity that did
not define him. His parents were engaging in an unconscious
process that happens every single day when parents normalize
the existing social conditions and downplay the harms that
accompany them to their children. But in this case, it was
not working, and that may have been a reflection of broader
social dynamics playing out in the mid-1970s.

Three years earlier, the world had experienced the first of the
oil shocks of that decade. In October 1973, the Organization of
Arab Petroleum Exporting Countries declared an oil embargo
on the countries supporting Israel in the Yom Kippur War,
including the United States, the United Kingdom, and Canada,
but it also caused the price of oil to soar even for countries
that were not embargoed. The high oil price and limited supplies naturally had wide-ranging impacts, and that included
how automobiles could be used—if they were used at all.

On January 2, 1974, President Richard Nixon signed the
Emergency Highway Energy Conservation Act, which set highway speed limits at fifty-five miles per hour—an act that was
not repealed until 1995. But due to the high energy prices that
resulted from the embargo, much more changed. Americans,
along with people in other Western countries, became more
concerned with energy use, and that was reflected in how
people lived. Rather than big, gas-guzzling vehicles, US drivers
began switching to fuel-efficient Japanese cars, and there was
a push to increase the efficiency of engines after the introduc-
tion of fuel economy standards in 1975.

By 1983, the *New York Times* was reporting that people had been using their bikes instead of their cars and going on walks to relieve their stress instead of taking long drives. People also wanted to economize on heating costs, which led them to keep their homes cooler in the winter and warmer in the summer, and the size of new homes actually shrank.[4] The oil shocks of the 1970s presented a rare opportunity for the United States to rethink how it used energy and planned communities. President Jimmy Carter, who was inaugurated in January 1977, put solar panels on the White House and invested federal funds into developing renewable energy. But the change did not take hold, as anyone can see if they visit US towns and cities today, where most people continue to depend on their cars and trucks, not so much out of choice but necessity.

Rather than entrenching and learning from the changes that took place during the 1970s, US corporate interests rejected them and doubled down on automobiles and fossil fuels. The United States extracted more oil and gas at home, and launched new wars to ensure foreign supplies were not disrupted. By the 1990s, some people were abandoning fuel-efficient cars once again for sport utility vehicles, in part because they were subject to less stringent fuel economy standards. In Texas, there was a major push to invest in coal instead of renewables in the aftermath of the oil shocks, and it even had the support of President Carter.

Instead of doubling down on suburbia and automobility, the United States could have taken another path—the path taken by parts of Europe. By the 1970s, the automobile was taking hold in Western Europe. The postwar reconstruction and economic expansion began the process of remaking European cities for the automobile by turning public spaces into parking lots, shifting street space to cars, and even leveling neighborhoods to remake them for the automobile. Europe had not adopted personal vehicles to the same degree as the United States, but the postwar period presented various corporate interests with the opportunity to imitate a process similar to that which was ongoing in the United States, and from which they would profit immensely. But they ran into trouble.

Road deaths in Europe, especially among children and young women, soared as automobile adoption increased, similar to what had happened in the United States a few decades earlier. Amsterdam, which is today known as a bicycle mecca, was not spared from this desire to transform and to modernize by making way for the car, and by 1971, 3,300 people were killed annually from cars, including 400 children.[5] In 1975, the traffic death rate in the Netherlands was 20 percent higher than in the United States.[6] Naturally, residents demanded action.

Among the groups that were formed to oppose the remaking of the city for the automobile was *Stop de Kindermoord*, which translated to "stop the child murder." The group's name was reminiscent of the evocative language that was seen on US streets in the 1910s and 1920s. Its members held demonstrations for bicycles, closed roads to allow children to play, and even occupied the sites of car crashes. They gained the ear of people in power, then received public funding and helped to develop policies to deemphasize the automobile's place in Dutch transport policy. The growing death toll was one reason for the shift, but the oil shocks also played an important role in building momentum.

After oil prices soared in 1973, the Dutch prime minister asked citizens to change the way they lived so they could conserve energy, and Sundays became car-free days. Those experiences affected policy decisions, and by the 1980s Dutch cities and towns were promoting bicycle use by giving them dedicated lanes and redesigning streets to reduce vehicle speeds. Meanwhile, across the continent governments were promoting energy efficiency and European automakers were building smaller, more efficient vehicles. Decades later, per capita energy use is lower in Europe than the United States, vehicles and homes are smaller, transit use is higher, and the automobile has not been adopted with the same fervor as in North America. The United States could have taken its foot off the pedal of auto-oriented development in the 1970s. In November 1972, the governor of Texas even called out the "wasteful use of energy in every segment of our society."[7] But instead it shifted into a higher gear as soon as the crisis had passed, with a major suburban expansion through the 1980s and 1990s at great environmental and human cost.

In a 1986 essay on the "carrier bag theory of fiction," Le Guin criticized common narratives in history and storytelling that focus on the masculine hero with his "sticks and spears and swords, the things to bash and poke and hit with, the long, hard things," but ignore the essential feminine role of the carer or gatherer with her carrier bag that was essential to human evolution.[8] She wrote that "the reduction of narrative to conflict is absurd," and explained that there is more than struggle and competition to the function of society and the improvement of the human condition. But those narratives filter out into the broader society and distort our understanding of the world around us.

Le Guin was particularly critical of what they do to the way we understand technology and science, narrowly associating those terms with high-tech fields and the "hard" sciences, which are positioned as "a heroic undertaking, Herculean, Promethean, conceived as triumph."[9] In a later essay, Le Guin argued that positioning technology in this way makes us believe it refers only to "the enormously complex and specialized technologies of the past few decades, supported by massive exploitation both of natural and human resources."[10] Instead, she wanted to see a more expansive definition, for technology to be understood as "the active human interface with the material world." As she put it:

technology is how a society copes with physical reality: how people get and keep and cook food, how they clothe themselves, what their power sources are (animal? human? water? wind? electricity? other?) what they build with and what they build, their medicine—and so on and on. Perhaps very ethereal people aren't interested in these mundane, bodily matters, but I'm fascinated by them, and I think most of my readers are too.[11]

In a moment when Silicon Valley constrains how we think about technology to serve its commercial interests, Le Guin offers us a liberatory alternative. Instead of fetishizing digitization, her broader conception allows us to embrace more mundane technologies that have stood the test of time—for instance the bicycle, the bus, and the train—and to see how they can materially improve our lives in a much more equitable way than the elite, apolitical visions on offer by the so-called visionaries of the tech industry.

The same narrative problem that Le Guin criticized in her "carrier bag" essay takes the form of the obsession with speed and domination in the realm of transportation. Mimi Sheller argued that one of the problems with auto-oriented cities in the West is that they were designed by and for influential men in positions of power without considering the needs of vulnerable road users. As Sheller put it, "White, able-bodied, middle-class, male experts and technicians dominate transport policy and urban transit agencies, hence policy, planning, and design often overlooks women's, children's, disabled people's, and poor people's perspectives, experiences, and needs, or see them as irrelevant to the sector."[12] The most vulnerable road users are disregarded in the push for faster speeds for the cars and SUVs of the most powerful, in the same way that tech's solutions give them little real consideration outside their marketing departments.

Instead of arguing for simple technological fixes such as speed limiters in every automobile, which Europe has made mandatory for all new vehicles in 2022, or vastly improving public transit to get more people out of cars, their solutions are not just to keep people in cars, but to encourage more automobile use with a range of increasingly ridiculous proposals that avoid the fact that mass automobility and the desire for vehicles to move as fast as possible are central parts of the problem. While this is frustrating, and far from helpful, it is not surprising.

In 1978, then-anarchist Murray Bookchin gave a speech where he described the language of futurism and of electronics as "the language of manipulation."[13] Bookchin argued that these powerful figures dreaming up big ideas for the future of humanity did not think critically about how society had arrived at its contemporary point and whether the social relations of the time were working for most people. To them, the future is nothing more than "the present as it exists today, projected, one hundred years from now." He expanded on that point with an example:

> Most futurists start out with the idea, "you got a shopping mall, what do you do then?" Well, the first question to be asked is, "why the hell do you have a shopping mall?" That is the real question that has to be asked. Not "what if" you have a shopping mall, then what do you do.[14]

Bookchin's example can be easily extended to the broader urban systems that made the shopping mall possible in the first place—the automobile and the community development patterns that it required to become a mass form of transportation. We must go beyond simply accepting the present as normal and assuming it should define our existence. As Bookchin said, "I just don't believe that we have to extend the present into the future. We have to change the present so that the future looks very, very different from what it is today."[15]

More than forty years later, Bookchin's point still rings true. We need much more than to extend the domination of automobiles into the future—even if they are made electric, on-demand, and autonomous with new underground roads to ferry them to their destinations. In the face of the climate crisis, along with the crises of mobility, housing, health, community, and many others, there is a dire need for a radically different kind of transportation system and urban form, and listening to Silicon Valley's tech elite will not allow us to attain it—or even to try.

Following local elections in 2015, a left-wing coalition took the reins of power in Norway's capital Oslo. The Socialist Left Party, the Labour Party, and the Greens formed a coalition with the support of the anti-capitalist Red Party, and one of their primary goals was to reduce the city's emissions, of which 39 percent came from private cars alone. Despite Norway's position as a world leader in electric vehicle sales, Oslo's new government was not content simply to see more vehicles converted to battery power. Instead, it put forward a very simple, yet radical plan: private vehicles would be banned from the city center entirely.

Even though the vehicle ownership rate was less than 12 percent in the proposed car-free zone, the response of conservatives and motorists was swift. One right-wing politician branded the plan "a Berlin Wall against motorists" and drivers claimed they felt bullied by the new city government. After a year of negotiation and attacks in the press, the left-wing coalition relented: instead of banning private vehicles, it would remove all 650 on-street parking spaces.

As the parking spaces were taken out of central Oslo, they were replaced with cycle lanes, bike parking, seating areas, places for children to play, and more social spaces. Instead of having lines of metal boxes on every street, there was infrastructure that promoted a different way of life. The physical changes still had the effect of discouraging driving, even without banning it outright, while promoting social interaction and means of mobility that allowed people to get exercise and to see one another on their journeys. The council created new incentives for people to buy bicycles and made new investments in the transit system to encourage people to get out of their cars. It even worked with the public roads administration and DHL to shift deliveries from trucks to cargo bikes. The plan was certainly not perfect, but it was a serious effort to change how people moved around their city, and one that most people supported. Oslo was not the only city to do something like this.

In September 2016, Paris announced its intention to convert a highway that ran along the Rive Droite (the Right Bank of the Seine) into a pedestrian space. The highway had been closed in the past for limited periods, but this time it was to be permanently pedestrianized as part of Socialist mayor Anne Hidalgo's strategy to get people out of cars. As in Oslo, there followed a backlash from right-wing and motorist groups to the permanent closure of the highway that carried 43,000 vehicles a day, even as a poll found that 55 percent of Parisians were in favor. The plan went to court as opponents tried to have it overturned, and while they won a legal victory in February 2018, an appeals court ruled in October that the riverbank would remain car-free.

The pedestrianization of a segment of the Rive Droite was an action that garnered a lot of attention, but it was just one piece of a much larger plan to remake Paris for its residents, instead of people who would drive in from elsewhere. This shift in urban policy did not begin with Hidalgo, but rather her Socialist predecessor Bertrand Delanoë, who became mayor in 2001. Delanoë rejected the congestion pricing that has captured the attention of US urbanists in recent years, and instead focused on altering the physical environment. He shifted road space from cars to buses, bikes, and sidewalks; introduced the Vélib' bikeshare system; provided buses with dedicated lanes and signal priority; and, in the process, cut automobile use by

20 percent in just a few years.[16] It has since fallen further as the physical environment was further transformed.

After twenty years of work and as more cities around the world were looking to Paris for an example to follow, Mayor Hidalgo introduced the next stage of her plan during her 2020 election campaign: the fifteen-minute city. At its core, this was an initiative to turn Paris into a series of walkable neighborhoods where virtually everything that people needed in their day-to-day lives would be accessible within fifteen minutes of their home. The goal was not only to further incentivize non-automotive forms of mobility, but to revive a more social and communal atmosphere that many residents (not just in Paris) feel has been lost.

The purpose of sharing these examples from Oslo and Paris is not to engage in a narrow Europhilic urbanism that believes we simply need to replicate a few highly publicized actions taken by select European governments and all the urban problems of cities in North America and other parts of the world will be solved. Even as Paris was taking these actions to make the city a better place to live, housing prices were soaring and the city center was increasingly becoming a zone for tourists, especially after the council failed to effectively stop the conversion of housing units into short-term rentals on platforms like Airbnb. This had the effect of pushing more poor and working-class residents out of the city, even as the construction of public housing accelerated under Delanoë and Hidalgo and is expected to reach 25 percent of all units by 2025. Critics have suggested the fifteen-minute city could have the effect of further fueling gentrification and providing benefits only to the wealthy.

In order to remake cities for the automobile, the power of the state had to be wielded to quite literally pave the way for the corporate interests connected to automobiles, suburban real estate, and mass consumption to reap their profits and expand their control over the population. Even if imperfect,

Paris and Oslo—among many other cities—are using their power to push back and reverse a decades-long program of encouraging automobile use, but it is not enough. As they implement policies aimed at improving the city, the forces of capital are still getting in the way to ensure they can extract value as things change, stymieing the goal of an equitable city and thus ensuring the benefits accrue primarily to those who can pay the escalating cost of admission. The more aspects of urban life are left to the private sector, the more difficult it is to make the changes that are necessary and to ensure they are equitable.

There is probably no city better known for its automotive dominance than Los Angeles. Cars took over its streets much earlier than those of other major cities in the United States, and their effects were particularly visible in the postwar period as smog gripped the region, eventually forcing the government to implement new regulations to get air pollution under control. But in recent decades, Los Angeles County has been making a concerted effort to improve its transit system and introduce reliable alternatives to the automobile—and voters support the effort.

In 2016, 72 percent of voters in Los Angeles approved Measure M, which increased the sales tax to provide an additional $120 billion over forty years for expansions to the transit system, rail network, and bike infrastructure. Additional measures in the county and across the country were passed in the following years to build on those efforts. Yet not only are they not enough, but the changes being made are not always received positively by the very people they are envisioned to help.

Los Angeles has been suffering from the general trend of increasing house prices in major cities caused by a series of factors that include the financialization of the housing market, the mass buying of housing by private equity firms after the

2008 financial crisis, and the lack of housing construction, particularly of social housing and units affordably priced for the working class. But prices increased more in areas that had greater access to transit than those that did not, leading to a form of transit gentrification that makes it more difficult for lower-income residents, particularly people of color, to remain in neighborhoods that get better transit service.[17] As a result, some of those residents oppose plans to improve transit access or bike infrastructure in their communities because they are seen as symbols of gentrification—as a sign that they will be forced out of their neighborhoods as new mobility options cause prices to increase and attract higher-income people to move in.

If we are to seriously reorient our communities, transportation systems, and way of life to address the problems that have arisen from the past century's shifting of priorities to the expansion of the automobile over the equitable expansion of public welfare, the state will need to play a significant role—at the city level, but also at the national level. However, if people feel that those changes are going to increase the prices they pay for housing and other necessities of life, they will oppose them. That means managing the transition cannot be left to the whims of the market and powerful private sector entities that put their ability to turn a profit and increase their corporate power above social goals.

An equitable urban transformation requires challenging the ideas about technology that flow from the C-suites of Silicon Valley and serve modern tech monopolies by building their systems into the urban infrastructure of the future. But it also requires us to oppose efforts by capitalists to control that infrastructure, and by extension the essentials of life, to maximize the value they can extract from society. If there was ever a time when companies paid heed to the well-being of communities, it is long past. Modern corporate culture is a parasitic force, and one that only gets worse as digital rentier services are rolled out in more aspects of our lives. Building better cities requires taking housing, transport, and other essential services out of the market altogether, and running them as public services with democratic accountability.

As explained in Chapter 1, one of the auto-oriented changes that took place in American cities in the early decades of the twentieth century was the shift in transport planners' approach to the street. Before the automobile began to take over, planners believed they should manage street space for multiple types of users, and shape its use through their decisions. They could have stepped back and let automobiles do what they wanted, but initially they tried to keep automobiles in line so that pedestrians, bicyclists, and streetcars could maintain their access to the street and remain a reliable means of getting around.

As the power of the automotive lobby increased, planners' perspectives changed. They began to see the street as a marketplace in which their role was to respond to demand—and what they perceived was being demanded was more space for cars, so that is what they facilitated. Over the course of many decades, other road users were pushed off the streets and new infrastructure was designed to serve drivers, which had the effect of creating a feedback loop until driving became the only realistic option for most residents of suburban and even urban areas. But that needs to change, and planners and lawmakers need to go back to recognizing the power of induced demand and accepting that their decisions shape how people get around. Similar to actions taken in Oslo and Paris, they need to use that power to induce a shift away from personal vehicles. But we should also go beyond that to imagine a way of organizing a transportation system that is coordinated on multiple levels and planned with democratic input for equity, accessibility, and sustainability.

On the city level, the marketization and commodification

of transportation needs to be halted, including the implementation of congestion pricing mechanisms. Instead, the focus should be on altering the physical environment and providing the necessary services to encourage residents to shift from driving their personal vehicles to using public transit, cycling, or walking to their destinations. Facilitating that transition requires a significant improvement to transit services, effectively shifting the massive subsidies currently dedicated to automobiles and their infrastructure to bolster collective mobility and build dense communities around it.

Residents must be part of that process to ensure changes address their needs. It will require more frequent services that are extended to underserved neighborhoods so that transit is reliable and people will not be stuck waiting for twenty or thirty minutes if they miss their bus or train. In some cities, it will mean a further buildout of subway systems, such as the significant expansion in China over the past several decades that has equipped twenty-five cities with metro lines; while in others, lower-cost bus rapid transit systems will be more appropriate, such as those that have swept Latin America since the Brazilian city of Curitiba built its first line in 1974. But even providing dedicated lanes on existing bus routes can make a big difference, as New York City found when its 14th Street busway increased ridership by up to 30 percent and slashed commute times by up to 47 percent.

Remembering how pedestrians were recast as "jaywalkers" in the early 1900s so that automobiles could seize the streets, it will be necessary to recast transit in the minds of much of the public to make transit the center of urban transportation. In many cities, transit has been treated as a backstop, as the last resort for marginalized groups, and that was used to justify its poor service. Yet not only do those residents deserve better, but collective mobility must improve in ways beyond service provision to get the wider public on board. Transit agencies need to ensure that bus stops have proper shelters where people are protected from the elements and that stations are truly accessible to everyone who wants to use them. The bus and subway must be seen as essential services, and that includes removing their fares to ensure equitable access.

Making such a transition will also require an active effort to teach people how to use and navigate systems they are not familiar with. For example, NBCUniversal launched a program in 2018 to encourage workers in Los Angeles to switch from driving to transit. It provided subsidized fare cards and other incentives to use non-car transport modes, then paired interested employees with mentors who used transit regularly. After six months of the program, it found that workers driving to work alone dropped from 59 percent to 14 percent, and those taking transit jumped from 19 percent to 59 percent.[18] The incentives paired with the personal support made a big difference to facilitating people's ability to reduce their car use.

To help with this goal, transit stations should also be mobility hubs, not just places to get the bus or subway. There should be ample bicycle parking so that people do not have to worry about taking their bikes with them or how to store them safely. Within the city itself, stations are ideal points to position docks for public bikeshare systems. In some instances, access to automobiles could even be facilitated through a public rental service or strictly regulated taxi service that recognizes some trips will still require them for the foreseeable future. However, even though these services would be available, road space for automobiles needs to be progressively reduced and other forms of mobility must be prioritized wherever possible.

How technology is deployed in such a system must also look very different than what is proposed by the corporate interests of Silicon Valley. Mobility should be seen not just as a service, but as a right of all residents. That could be facilitated through a public mobility app that brings together the city's transport services to provide up-to-date timetables, route information, and trip-planning functionality that encourages sustainable, collective mobility and the efficiency of the system as a whole rather than being centered on the individual. The app could also collect user data where it could help improve the service, and since the transportation system would be publicly run, data and its sales would never be treated as a business model.

At the same time, technology should not be used to automate human workers simply to impress tech utopians who fail to consider the broader impacts of its deployment. Bus drivers, for example, play a role beyond simply navigating a route; they serve a social role, they keep riders safe, they provide directions, and they are also eyes on the street who can help someone in need. There may be a place for autonomous driving systems in some instances, such as on subway trains where workers could be redirected to providing care and support in stations or on the trains themselves, but in general a comprehensive transit service should not treat workers as a cost to be cut. Their essential role in delivering mobility and extending care to their communities should be preserved and enhanced.

In *Do Androids Dream of Electric Cars?*, James Wilt laid out an expansive vision for a transportation system reoriented around public transit, and he emphasized its potential to play a transformative role in remaking social relations that have eroded under capitalism. Wilt explained that a "universal right to transportation serves as a foundation of a broader struggle against capitalist commodification and exploitation," and that the "foundational principle of radical transit politics is one of togetherness—which in turn means a coherent opposition to white supremacy, anti-migrant xenophobia, ableism, and union-busting."[19] The values embedded in such a system are the polar opposite of the individualist politics embodied by the auto-oriented status quo, and they must form the core of the future mobility system and society that we seek to build.

An expanded system of public transit should not be technocratically planned by a group of enlightened experts; rather it must be informed by the very people whose lives it is supposed to be improving to ensure schedules, services, and facilities reflect their needs. As the Untokening collective has outlined, a justice-oriented approach to mobility must

> fully excavate, recognize, and reconcile the historical and current injustices experienced by communities—with impacted communities given space and resources to envision and implement planning models and political advocacy on streets and mobility that actively work to address historical and current injustices experienced by communities.[20]

If our communities and transportation systems are currently designed around the mobility patterns and lifestyles of powerful men, an equitable and sustainable alternative must instead give priority to the people who have been marginalized by them. But planning such a system cannot end at city borders; it must be connected to an intercity transport network built around the same principles.

To tech libertarians, especially those who own personal jets and are seeking to join the coalition of automotive interests, trains seem like an outdated technology that we have long outgrown—but nothing could be further from the truth. With the environmental footprint of the aviation industry growing every year, intercity mobility needs to stop being a free-for-all for private companies. It must be planned as part of a coordinated system that prioritizes rail where it is feasible.

In recent years, China has built the largest high-speed rail system in the world, while the European Union continues to expand its high-speed links and revive night trains to make longer journeys more feasible. Yet the train systems of North America remain stuck in the twentieth century, so it is no wonder that some people there think trains are a thing of the past.

Solving this problem does not mean betting on transport fantasies such as Elon Musk's Hyperloop vision, when high-speed rail is a technology that actually exists and has been undergoing constant improvement since the 1970s. Instead of getting distracted by science fiction, national governments should develop plans for public intercity transport systems that treat rail networks as the backbone, with bus systems and air travel to fill in the gaps.

The rail network could consist of high-speed segments along high-traffic routes and between major centers. There are several proposals for the extent of such a system in North America, but the goal should be to connect clusters of larger cities in a single region to start, then connect those clusters to one another where it is feasible. But even with such high-speed expansion, the existing conventional rail network would still play an important role to provide national coverage and reach smaller cities and towns where there is not enough rider-ship to justify high-speed connections. The network, however, should not stop there.

Intercity buses are a lifeline for many people, especially those with lower incomes and without personal vehicles. In Canada, the intercity bus network has been decimated after public services like the Saskatchewan Transportation Company were shut down and Greyhound pulled out of the western part of the country in 2018, before ending service altogether in 2021. The closure of bus routes not only cut people in rural areas off from healthcare, other services, and their families, but has created a public safety crisis for Indigenous women who have to turn to hitchhiking when there are no reliable alternatives. Intercity bus services should connect people to other communities and the services they rely on, including, where possible, to the rail network so they can continue their journey. While rural areas are likely to maintain some degree of automobile use into the future, they should still have reliable public transportation within their communities and to connect them with nearby cities and towns.

Even with expanded rail and intercity bus networks, there will still be people needing to travel long distances for whom those services may not be sufficient. High-speed rail and even more frequent conventional rail services can replace some short- and even medium-haul flight routes, and the option of flying should eventually be removed where that is possible. France began to do just that in 2021 on routes with train connections of up to two and a half hours. Governments once exerted much more power over flight routes and ticket prices before the deregulation of air travel and the privatization of state airlines began in the 1970s, and greater regulation, if not renationalization, will be essential to make airlines serve the public as part of a planned transportation network that prioritizes goals of equity and sustainability.

Aviation services will still be necessary on long-haul national and international routes, and to some remote communities. Where possible, those flights should be electrified and made more efficient as the technology becomes available. But while short flights have been made with small, battery-powered airplanes, the electrification of large passenger planes or their conversion to significantly cleaner fuels is unlikely to occur in the coming decades. That means reducing emissions from air travel will come from shifting trips to rail and ultimately reducing the number of trips that are taken.

A comprehensive public transportation system that operates within cities and between them, and that places people's right to mobility before the need for corporations to turn a profit, cannot exist without the state taking an active role in planning and running it. Governments at all levels created new agencies, provided massive subsidies, rewrote the tax code, changed laws, created new regulatory systems, and spent trillions of dollars on the infrastructure that was required to facilitate mass automobility. Reorienting our transportation system and our communities away from it—and solving the problems that were created by it—will require a similar commitment.

The same effort that went into building the Interstate Highway System and local road networks should be put into building out the national rail infrastructure and public transit systems in urban, suburban, and rural communities. The subsidies and regulatory effort that went into enabling the great suburban expansion must be redirected not only to discourage suburban growth but to build public housing that is rooted in walkable, transit-accessible communities where people can easily reach the services they rely on without the need for an automobile. As part of that effort, our communities and the public services that anchor them must be reconceived for a more sustainable way of life.

The shift to suburban living in the postwar period and the mass consumption that accompanied it also contributed to the erosion of community spaces. As distances got longer and people were pushed to individually build private wealth, there was less incentive to maintain the public sphere. Wealthy and even middle-class residents had their own lawns, so they no longer went to public parks, and they got their own swimming pools to avoid community pools. They built in-home gyms to avoid public gyms, and even in-home cinema rooms are becoming a more popular alternative to visiting the movie theater.

As community spaces eroded in the face of private alternatives, only those who could afford to buy their own amenities could access their benefits. The public sphere was diminished, along with our communities and social bonds. As environmental activist George Monbiot has explained, "The expansion of public wealth creates more space for everyone; the expansion of private wealth reduces it, eventually damaging most people's quality of life."[21] The communities of the future must expand public parks and pools; build wonderful libraries that lend out books along with many other necessities; and take a whole range of basic services out of the market to provision them for public good in an effort to reverse the trend toward private luxuries. Degrowth campaigner Aaron Vansintjan called this a campaign for "public abundance," and it is a vision which we should strive to achieve.[22]

Remaking society in this way also provides the opportunity to rethink how services are delivered to best meet the needs of the public instead of letting large companies exploit them for profit. Instead of extractive food delivery apps and their ghost kitchens, there could be a new community food network that comprises local food kitchens that double as community spaces and a delivery service to bring food and other essentials to seniors, new parents, and people with limited mobility, just to give a few examples. The post office could even get involved, making it part of a coordinated delivery service using unionized workers that handles packages, grocery delivery, and other goods transfers for all shipping companies. On top of that, it is not hard to imagine using the post office as a key node to roll out other public services such as banking, telecommunications, and even cooperative technology and software development that are designed for community needs and shared around the country, if not the world.[23]

The role of technology in this future should not be to replace workers or to make their lives more precarious, but to empower them and to facilitate collective solutions to social problems. That will mean changing the way that data is produced and governed,[24] but it will also mean reversing the transfer of power from workers to algorithms. We need to avoid the scenario described by Tim Maughan where complex algorithmic systems have effectively taken away human control from aspects of the supply chain, financial markets, and other networks that affect our everyday lives in ways we often do not even realize. Instead, we need to utilize technology where it can serve us, while ensuring power remains firmly in the hands of a democratic public.

Economic historian Aaron Benanav has made the case for a form of planning that balances efficiency with qualitative goals such as justice and sustainability so the capitalist drive for infinite growth at all costs is not replicated in a socialist society. The goal must not be to create machines that operate without human input; rather they should be utilized to reduce the work that humans need to do while maintaining democratic control over production, even if that will require deliberation as communities balance various outcomes. As Benanav explained:

> If socialist planning is purely algorithmic, it executes decisions in a similar way to capitalist firms. It reiterates the logics of capitalism in a different register: what matters is the extraction of the relevant quantitative information from the mess of qualitative life. But it is only in this mess that the content of socialism can be found.[25]

Benanav rejected the depoliticization of technology and algorithms that is common in techno-utopian discourses, and instead recognized the importance of maintaining human control to determine how the technology functions, how the benefits it produces are distributed, and how its harms are lessened and mediated.

It is not difficult to imagine how this could be applied to the planned transportation system I imagined above. While there would necessarily be a role for algorithms in planning the system, decisions about how it should be built and what the schedules should look like would ultimately be decided democratically by communities that could weigh the benefits and drawbacks of different ways of organizing it to ensure it meets their needs while working as a unified whole, facilitating human connections, and reducing the environmental footprint of mobility. But it is also possible to imagine this means of planning being rolled out in other areas.

Take, for example, the problems with electric vehicles outlined in Chapter 3. If the production of vehicles and the sourcing of materials required for their construction was planned in a democratic manner, would companies and governments be able to so easily dismiss the environmental harm caused by mineral extraction in areas of the Global South and remote areas of the Global North that often affect Indigenous communities? It is very unlikely. Instead, there would have to be a dialogue about the goals of the production process, what quantity of extraction would be necessary for plans that prioritize different transportation modes, and whether placing so much emphasis on electrifying personal vehicles is an effective way of achieving those goals.

Not only would the likely outcome of that process be far different than what is currently being proposed by Western governments, it would require the consent of peoples who would be affected by extraction, which could have many outcomes: refusal, compensation, or proper environmental mediation, among others. Democratic deliberation would ensure that the need for economic growth (centered in the Global North) does not sideline certain populations with destructive effect, but instead gives them power in planning how production is undertaken.

We have been misled into believing that technology refers only to the deployment of vast new computerized systems to take over more of our lives in service of making consumption more convenient, reducing the friction of human life, and empowering the individual, often at the expense of the community. Those systems try to hide the harm and exploitation that make them possible, but that is not how technology has to function.

In 2004, Le Guin described how "'Technology' and 'hi tech' are not synonymous, and a technology that isn't 'hi,' isn't necessarily 'low' in any meaningful sense."[26] We need to stop being distracted by the Hyperloops and the Boring Companies designed to stifle investment in trains and transit; the on-demand services that decimate workers' rights in service of convenience; and the electric sports cars and SUVs that promise a green future while driving a new wave of neo-colonial exploitation.

Better futures are possible, but they will not be delivered through technological advancement alone. They require engaging with the problems of our time and recognizing that they do not exist simply because we do not have the requisite technology to solve them. Addressing the inequities and harms of our world does not require the invention of new technologies; it requires a new politics that recognizes economic growth and technological innovation do not guarantee social progress.

While the state's role in coordinating and enabling such a future is essential, it will not take those actions without an organized public that wields its collective power to demand change. We can already see countless examples of this occurring around the world. Locally, transit activists are fighting the removal of fares and for better service in their communities, while housing activists are pushing back against gentrification and demanding public housing so residents can afford to stay in their communities. In the United States, the Green New Deal galvanized climate activists to fight for an ambitious program to address the climate crisis, while empowering them to collectively imagine what an equitable and sustainable future should look like. That challenge was taken up around the world under the Green New Deal banner, but also by activists with Extinction Rebellion, School Strike for Climate, and regional initiatives like the Pacto Ecosocial del Sur in Latin America.

Meanwhile, at sites of extraction, residents are wielding their power to protect their communities and change national policy. In the Global North, Indigenous communities have been engaged in increasingly high-profile fights against extraction projects, and they are not alone. Local residents in Portugal, for example, defeated a lithium mine planned for the northern Montalegre region, and a similar campaign is ongoing in Nevada against the planned mine in Thacker Pass. These fights are also continuing in the Global South, not only through the opposition to extraction, but also by imagining what a post-extractive politics and prosperity would look like in societies like those of Latin America that have long been reliant on extractive industries.[27]

In November 1973, as oil prices were spiking, Le Guin published a short story about a utopian community called Omelas whose joy and bounty were premised on the suffering of a small child locked in a small basement broom cupboard. As the residents sang, danced, and ate their fill through the summer festival, they knew the cold and malnourished child was below, but continued on with their celebrations. When children reached the age to learn about the dark secret of their society and were taken down into the basement to peer through the door, they usually went "home in tears, or a tearless rage."[28]

Le Guin explained that over time they came to justify it, as their parents did before them—and as we so often do with the harms and inequities inherent in our own society. Yet there were some who could not square their joy with the child's plight. "These people go out into the street, and walk down the street alone," wrote Le Guin. "They keep walking, and walk straight out of the city of Omelas, through the beautiful gates," never to return.[29] But we do not have that option.

We cannot walk away from the suffering created by technological, mobility, and urban systems that leave so many without reliable transportation, roofs over their heads, and other necessities of life. We need to challenge the technological determinism and the drive for capital accumulation that seeks to remake our world in service of the tech industry. That requires building solidarity locally, nationally, and internationally to assert our collective power—not just to redesign those systems but to change the fundamental logics that drive their development. A better world is not only possible, it is essential.

Conclusion

October 17, 2017, was a big day in Toronto. Canadian prime minister Justin Trudeau and Alphabet executive chairman Eric Schmidt appeared alongside the mayor of Toronto, the premier of Ontario, and the CEOs of Sidewalk Labs and Waterfront Toronto to announce a project they promised would forever change the city for the better.

Sidewalk Labs, one of Google's sister companies, had been chosen to build a city "from the internet up" on the waterfront of downtown Toronto. Trudeau told attendees that he and Schmidt had been talking about it for a couple of years—calling into question the impartiality of the public tendering process—and asserted that the project would yield "smarter, greener, more inclusive cities"[1] by using technology for public good. What was not to like?

At the time of the announcement, it was still common for cities to roll out the red carpet for tech companies. Concern about their monopolistic practices was only beginning to gain mainstream traction, and emerging smart city companies were making bold claims about how their products would improve urban systems. Politicians still felt that embracing "innovation" was a good political strategy, especially after decades of privatizing city services. It was how things were done in the neoliberal city—but the shine quickly faded from the project.

The consultation process that the company had agreed to turned out to be little more than a sales pitch. Less than a year after Sidewalk Toronto was announced, high-profile resignations began. Saadia Muzaffar, the founder of TechGirls

Canada, who had been on Waterfront Toronto's advisory board, criticized the quasi-public body for failing to hold proper public meetings and protect the public interest. "There is nothing innovative about city-building that disenfranchises its residents in insidious ways and robs valuable earnings out of public budgets," she wrote in her resignation letter.[2] Two weeks later, Ontario's former privacy commissioner Ann Cavoukian, who served as an advisor to Sidewalk Labs, resigned after expressing significant concerns with how the company planned to treat the data it collected.

Even though the project was pitched as a big win for Toronto and its residents, it quickly became apparent that Sidewalk Labs planned to integrate a host of its own technologies into the infrastructure of Canada's largest city by using the twelve acres of land it had been contracted to transform as a beachhead, making the government and its residents dependent on them in perpetuity.

In its expansive vision document, Sidewalk Labs outlined the many ways it wished to control urban systems. It planned to build a "digital layer" that would be the interface for access to public services, community spaces, and "a neighborhood assistant tool to facilitate social cooperation and civic engagement."[3] All this would be controlled by the company, not the local government, and the access terminals would be the exclusive containers for wireless technologies. That meant that for telecommunications companies to offer network services in Sidewalk Labs' smart neighborhood, they would need its permission.

Quayside, as the site was called, would also exclude private car traffic. Instead, there would be transit service and bike lanes, along with an autonomous shuttle service through Waymo—one of Sidewalk Labs' sister companies—and access to ride-hailing services from Uber and Lyft. Notably, Google was invested in both companies. In addition, Sidewalk Labs wanted to get into healthcare through its Care Lab, control traffic with its Flow technologies, and place sensors throughout the urban landscape to run experiments through its Model Lab.

There was no indication that the residents of Toronto would have input on the decisions that Sidewalk Labs and its technocratic leaders—many of whom had worked for Michael Bloomberg when he was mayor of New York City—were imposing on them. Given Google's desire to collect as much data as possible to inform its ad targeting systems, which generated the lion's share of its revenues, there were concerns that it was moving its sophisticated infrastructure to harvest data into the urban realm—once again, with little public oversight. Residents of Toronto knew they had to fight back.

In February 2019, concerned citizens launched a group called Block Sidewalk. They demanded the city halt the project after Sidewalks Labs "orchestrated a misleading, undemocratic engagement process that harm[ed] the public interest" and leaked documents confirmed it wanted to control a much larger area of the waterfront.[4] Bianca Wylie, whose criticism of the project earned her the title of "Jane Jacobs of the smart city," called the process "thoroughly anti-democratic."[5] Instead of identifying the needs of residents, then developing or contracting for technology to meet those needs (if that was what was appropriate), the city and Waterfront Toronto were bending over backwards to allow Sidewalk Labs to impose its vision and its priorities on the residents of Toronto. Wylie, her colleagues, and a growing coalition of groups and citizens found that unacceptable.

On May 7, 2020, Sidewalk Labs finally gave in and canceled the project. The residents of Toronto had won—but they were not the only ones turning against tech companies' encroachment on urban space. Apple had to cancel prominent stores it had planned in Stockholm and Melbourne after residents opposed their placement in key public spaces. Google pulled out of a campus it had planned to open in Berlin over activists' fears it would accelerate gentrification in the Kreuzberg neighborhood. Even Amazon had to halt its plans to establish a second headquarters in New York City after public and political outrage over the $3 billion in subsidies it had been offered. Clearly, the activists in Toronto were not the only ones demanding a different vision for their communities.

After the first wave of the Covid-19 pandemic in the spring of 2020, residents of cities around the world got a taste of how different urban life could be. Car traffic was limited, opening up streets for people to walk and to cycle. Restaurants and cafés created seating areas in some of the freed-up road space. Bicycles were in short supply around the world as demand increased, and some governments put in subsidies to incentivize their purchase. Globally, air pollution plummeted, allowing the residents of many major cities to see clearer skies than they had ever seen in their lives.

In some urban areas, the measures took hold, but in others there was a strong push to get back to normal: to close the roads to pedestrians once again and restore the dominance of cars, trucks, and SUVs. As in the 1970s, there was a glaring opportunity for change, to reorient planning priorities—but the bigger question was whether cities would take it.

In March 2021, Waterfront Toronto unveiled a new vision for the space that Sidewalk Labs had abandoned. Instead of a smart city, its proposal centered on great public spaces, sustainable development, and social housing—though it was not clear how much. The tone of the new vision was much different than the tech-centered proposal that had preceded it, but there was still reason to be concerned. The agency said it wanted to create a world-class tourism attraction that would be "an important catalyst for innovation and growth," suggesting that the drive for capital accumulation would still be central to the project.[6] The plan for the waterfront had improved, but the fight was not over.

* * *

Over the course of the twentieth century, cities were reconstructed to facilitate economic expansion by incentivizing people to drive cars, move to the suburbs, and engage in mass consumption. The efforts in the first two decades of the twenty-first century to track everything that happens in cities, replace humans with artificial intelligence, and mediate our experiences through a series of apps and digital services is part of the same drive. But this time it serves a different set of commercial interests as rates of return in various sectors have shifted. Tech is where the money is, so now it has taken the wheel.

Once again, we are on the cusp of changes to the physical environment that serve capital instead of people. The tech industry may be working overtime to convince us otherwise, but that does not change the fact that the proposals for these urban technologies—for transport and beyond—are about facilitating their integration into as many facets of life as possible. Public benefit is at best an afterthought, if it is seriously considered at all outside their marketing teams.

In challenging this reality, we cannot simply focus on the technology—though we must have solid critiques of how it works and who it serves as we try to halt its deployment. We must also consider how the need for capital accumulation is driving the change, and how even if we regulate some technologies and stop others, the direction of travel will continue toward tech's vision of the city.

Think back to Jane Jacobs and Ralph Nader. Jacobs and those inspired by her work stopped some freeways from being built, while Nader and his allies undoubtedly made cars safer, saving many lives in the process. But the expansion of suburbs and the growth of automobile dependence continued with harmful consequences.

We need cities that are built for their residents, that improve their quality of life, and that consider their needs instead of opening the floodgates to technologies and gimmicks thought up by billionaires who have a very different experience of the city than most people. Technology should be built to serve the public, not to shape how they live to increase the power and profits of major corporations.

Ultimately, building better cities and improving people's lives requires challenging the very structures of capitalism itself, structures that are designed to serve profit before people. We can build transportation systems that empower people, facilitate social connections, and reduce the environmental footprint of mobility. But that requires altering social and economic relations to ensure the planning of those systems is based in community needs, not delivering financial returns.

That is a future I would like to see.

Acknowledgments

The contents of this book are the product of years of writing about cities and technology as a freelancer for a wide variety of publications and researching those same topics in my academic pursuits. I owe a debt of gratitude to the editors I have worked with over that time, especially those who gave me a chance early on and who offered constructive feedback that improved the quality of my arguments and my writing. That also goes for the faculty I worked with in the political science and geography departments at Memorial University of Newfoundland and the geography department at McGill University, in particular Yolande Pottie-Sherman, Russell Williams, Sarah Moser, Sarah Turner, and most of all my Master's supervisor Kevin Manaugh.

This book wouldn't have been possible without the work of the great team at Verso on both sides of the Atlantic, and especially my editor, Leo Hollis, who was on board with the project from the start, offered invaluable advice and feedback, and helped guide me through the publishing process. It has been a great pleasure to work with him.

I also want to thank those who provided advice and feedback throughout the process. Lizzie O'Shea gave me the push I needed to put together a proposal. James Wilt, Wendy Liu, and Gemma Milne answered my publishing questions. Jathan Sadowski, Luke Goode, Steve Matthewman, Thea Riofrancos, and Brian Merchant reviewed drafts and provided valuable notes.

Finally, a special thanks to my family and friends who listened as I talked through aspects of the book, the guests who came on my podcast so I could have thoughtful discussions with new people despite being in relative isolation on an island in the Atlantic, and to the comrades I have gotten to know on Twitter dot com from all over the world.

Notes

Introduction

1 Gregg Culver, "Death and the Car: On (Auto)Mobility, Violence, and Injustice," *ACME: An International Journal for Critical Geographies* 17:1, 2018.

1. How the Automobile Disrupted Mobility

1 John C. Falcocchio and Herbert S. Levinson, "How Transportation Technology Has Shaped Urban Travel Patterns," in *Road Traffic Congestion: A Concise Guide*, Springer International, 2015, pp. 9–17.

2 Michael Southworth and Eran Ben-Joseph, "Street Standards and the Shaping of Suburbia," *Journal of the American Planning Association* 61:1, 1995.

3 David Gartman, "Three Ages of the Automobile: The Cultural Logics of the Car," *Theory, Culture & Society* 21:4–5, 2004, p. 171.

4 André Gorz, "The Social Ideology of the Motorcar," *Le Sauvage*, September–October 1973, Unevenearth.org.

5 Ibid.

6 Peter Hall, *Cities of Tomorrow: An Intellectual History of Urban Planning and Design Since 1880*, 4th ed., Wiley Blackwell, 2014, p. 167.

7 Gregg Culver, "Death and the Car: On (Auto)Mobility, Violence, and Injustice," *ACME: An International Journal for Critical Geographies* 17:1, 2018; *New York Times*, "Fatally Hurt by Automobile," September 14, 1899, Timesmachine.nytimes.com.

8 Southworth and Ben-Joseph, "Street Standards and the Shaping of Suburbia."

9 Gartman, "Three Ages of the Automobile," p. 177.

10 Jeffrey R. Brown, Eric A. Morris, and Brian D. Taylor, "Planning for Cars in Cities: Planners, Engineers, and Freeways in the 20th

Century," *Journal of the American Planning Association* 75:2, 2009.

11 Peter D. Norton, *Fighting Traffic: The Dawn of the Motor Age in the American City*, MIT Press, 2008.

12 Culver, "Death and the Car"; Norton, *Fighting Traffic*, p. 25.

13 Norton, *Fighting Traffic*.

14 Ibid.

15 Giulio Mattioli et al., "The Political Economy of Car Dependence: A Systems of Provision Approach," *Energy Research & Social Science* 66, 2020; Norton, *Fighting Traffic*; Gregory H. Shill, "Should Law Subsidize Driving?," *New York University Law Review* 95:2, 2020.

16 Norton, *Fighting Traffic*, p. 98.

17 Ibid., p. 175.

18 Brown, Morris, and Taylor, "Planning for Cars in Cities," p. 167.

19 Ibid.

20 Ibid., p. 170.

21 Ibid., p. 162.

22 Hall, *Cities of Tomorrow*, p. 348.

23 Jan Edward Smith, *Eisenhower in War and Peace*, Random House, 2012, pp. 652–3.

24 Brown, Morris, and Taylor, "Planning for Cars in Cities," p. 171.

25 Ibid.

26 David E. Rosenbaum, "For the Highway Lobby, a Rocky Road Ahead," *New York Times*, April 2, 1972, Nytimes.com.

27 Brown, Morris, and Taylor, "Planning for Cars in Cities," p. 172.

28 Hall, *Cities of Tomorrow*.

29 Sharon Zukin, "Jane Jacobs (1916–2006)," *The Architectural Review*, October 26, 2011, Architectural-review.com.

30 Ibid.

31 Southworth and Ben-Joseph, "Street Standards and the Shaping of Suburbia," p. 73.

32 Laura Hale, "Happy 60th Birthday, Interstate Highway System!," American Society of Civil Engineers, June 29, 2016, Infrastructure reportcard.org.

33 Shill, "Should Law Subsidize Driving?"

34 See ibid. for updated figures taken from Donald Shoup, *The High Cost of Free Parking*, Routledge, 2005.

35 Ibid., p. 502.

36 World Health Organization, "Road Traffic Injuries," June 21, 2021, who.int.

37 David Shepardson, "U.S. Traffic Deaths Soar to 38,680 in 2020; Highest Yearly Total since 2007," Reuters, June 3, 2021, Reuters.com.

38 Fabio Caiazzo et al., "Air Pollution and Early Deaths in the United States. Part I: Quantifying the Impact of Major Sectors in 2005," *Atmospheric Environment* 79, 2013.

39 Eric D. Lawrence, Nathan Bomey, and Kristi Tanner, "Death on Foot: America's Love of SUVs Is Killing Pedestrians," *Detroit Free Press*, June 28, 2019, Freep.com.

40 Janette Sadik-Khan and Seth Solomonow, *Streetfight: Handbook for an Urban Revolution*, Viking, 2016, p. 29.

41 Alexa Delbosca, "Dehumanization of Cyclists Predicts Self-reported Aggressive Behaviour toward Them: A Pilot Study," *Transportation Research Part F: Traffic Psychology and Behaviour* 62, 2019, p. 685.

42 Gorz, "The Social Ideology of the Motorcar."

43 John Urry, "The 'System' of Automobility," *Theory, Culture & Society* 21:4–5, 2004, p. 28.

44 Gorz, "The Social Ideology of the Motorcar."

45 Gartman, "Three Ages of the Automobile," p. 192.

46 Ibid.

2. Understanding the Silicon Valley Worldview

1 Margaret O'Mara, *The Code: Silicon Valley and the Remaking of America*, Penguin Books, 2020, p. 7.

2 Ibid., p. 15.

3 AnnaLee Saxenian, *Regional Advantage: Culture and Competition in Silicon Valley and Route 128*, Harvard University Press, 1996.

4 O'Mara, *The Code*, pp. 75–6.

5 Tom Wolfe, "The Tinkerings of Robert Noyce," *Esquire*, December 1983, Classic.esquire.com.

6 Fred Turner, *From Counterculture to Cyberculture: Stewart Brand, the Whole Earth Network, and the Rise of Digital Utopianism*, University of Chicago Press, 2006, p. 31.

7 Ibid., p. 73.

8 Ibid., p. 76.

9 Ibid., p. 14.

10 Richard Barbrook and Andy Cameron, "The Californian Ideology," *Science as Culture* 6:1, 1996, imaginaryfutures.net.

11 Saxenian, *Regional Advantage*, p. 90.

12 O'Mara, *The Code*, p. 214.

13 Ibid., p. 226.

14 Peter Thiel, "The End of the Future," *National Review*, October 3, 2011, Nationalreview.com.

15 Tom Simonite, "Technology Stalled in 1970," *MIT Technology Review*, September 18, 2014, Technologyreview.com.
16 David Graeber, "Of Flying Cars and the Declining Rate of Profit," *The Baffler* 19, March 2012, Thebaffler.com.
17 O'Mara, *The Code*, pp. 90–1.
18 Tim Maughan, "The Modern World Has Finally Become Too Complex for Any of Us to Understand," *OneZero*, November 30, 2020, Onezero.medium.com.
19 Ibid.
20 Senator Gore, speaking on S. 1067, 101st Congress, 1st sess., *Congressional Record* 135, May 18, 1989, S 9887.
21 Daniel Greene, *The Promise of Access: Technology, Inequality, and the Political Economy of Hope*, MIT Press, 2011.
22 Madeline Carr, *US Power and the Internet in International Relations: The Irony of the Information Age*, Palgrave Macmillan, 2016, p. 58 (author's emphasis).
23 Turner, *From Counterculture to Cyberculture*, p. 194.
24 John Perry Barlow, "A Declaration of the Independence of Cyberspace," February 8, 1996, Eff.org.
25 Turner, *From Counterculture to Cyberculture*, p. 209.
26 Ibid., p. 222.
27 Ibid.
28 Mariana Mazzucato, *The Entrepreneurial State: Debunking Public vs. Private Sector Myths*, Anthem Press, 2013.
29 Carmen Hermosillo, "Pandora's Vox: On Community in Cyberspace," 1994, Gist.github.com.
30 Jennifer S. Light, "Developing the Virtual Landscape," *Environment and Planning D: Society and Space* 14:2, 1996, p. 127.
31 Ibid., pp. 127–9.
32 Benjamin Peters, "A Network Is Not a Network," in *Your Computer Is on Fire*, MIT Press, 2020, p. 87.
33 Ibid., p. 85.
34 Evgeny Morozov, *To Save Everything, Click Here: The Folly of Technological Solutionism*, PublicAffairs, 2013, p. 6.
35 Ibid., p. 5.
36 Jarrett Walker, "The Dangers of Elite Projection," *Human Transit* (blog), July 31, 2017, Humantransit.org.
37 Adrian Daub, *What Tech Calls Thinking: An Inquiry into the Intellectual Bedrock of Silicon Valley*, FSG Originals, 2020, p. 36.
38 Luis F. Alvarez León and Jovanna Rosen, "Technology as Ideology in Urban Governance," *Annals of the American Association of Geographers* 110:2, 2020, p. 500.
39 "Instagram Boss Adam Mosseri on Teenagers, Tik-Tok and Paying Creators," Recode Media, September 16, 2021.

3. Greenwashing the Electric Vehicle

1 David A. Kirsch, *The Electric Vehicle and the Burden of History*, Rutgers University Press, 2000, p. 30.
2 Ibid., p. 63.
3 Kirsch, *The Electric Vehicle and the Burden of History*, p. 6.
4 Annie Kelly, "Apple and Google Named in US Lawsuit over Congolese Child Cobalt Mining Deaths," *Guardian*, December 16, 2019, Theguardian.com.
5 Elsa Dominish, Sven Teske, and Nick Florin, *Responsible Minerals Sourcing for Renewable Energy*, report prepared for Earthworks by the Institute for Sustainable Futures, University of Technology Sydney, 2019, Earthworks.org.
6 Siddharth Kara, "I Saw the Unbearable Grief Inflicted on Families by Cobalt Mining. I Pray for Change," *Guardian*, December 16, 2019, Theguardian.com.
7 Kirsten Hund et al., "Minerals for Climate Action: The Mineral Intensity of the Clean Energy Transition," The World Bank, 2020, Worldbank.org.
8 "Turning Down The Heat: Can We Mine Our Way out of the Climate Crisis?," Mining Watch Canada, November 2020, Miningwatch.ca.
9 "The Role of Critical Minerals in Clean Energy Transitions," International Energy Agency, May 2021, Iea.org.
10 Ibid.
11 Dominish, Teske, and Florin, "Responsible Minerals Sourcing for Renewable Energy."
12 "Mineral Commodity Summaries 2021," U.S. Geological Survey, 2021, Usgs.gov.
13 Thea Riofrancos, "What Green Costs," *Logic Magazine*, December 7, 2019, logicmag.io.
14 Thea Riofrancos, "Brine to Batteries," Harvard Radcliffe Institute, April 22, 2021, YouTube.com.
15 See Ernest Scheyder, "To Go Electric, America Needs More Mines. Can It Build Them?," Reuters, March 1, 2021, Reuters.com; Julie Cart, "Will California's Desert Be Transformed into Lithium Valley?," *Cal Matters*, February 25, 2021, Calmatters.org; Kirk Siegler, "These Tribal Activists Want Biden to Stop a Planned Lithium Mine on Their Sacred Land," NPR, September 2, 2021, Npr.com; Maddie Stone, "The Battle of Thacker Pass," *Grist*, March 12, 2021, Grist.org.
16 Ernest Scheyder and Jeff Lewis, "Exclusive: U.S. Looks to Canada for Minerals to Build Electric Vehicles—Documents," Reuters, March 18, 2021, Reuters.com.

17 "Roadmap for a Renewed U.S.-Canada Partnership," Office of the Prime Minister of Canada, February 23, 2021, pm.gc.ca.

18 Caitlin Stall-Paquet, "The Hidden Cost of Rechargeable Batteries," *The Walrus*, June 8, 2021, thewalrus.ca.

19 Emilee Gilpin, "Tilhqot'in Nation Sends Mining Company Home in Peaceful Protest," *National Observer*, July 2, 2019, National observer.com.

20 Benjamin K. Sovacool et al., "Energy Injustice and Nordic Electric Mobility: Inequality, Elitism, and Externalities in the Electrification of Vehicle-to-Grid (V2G) Transport," *Ecological Economics* 157, 2019, p. 211.

21 Dave Fickling, "Elon Musk Should Come Clean: Tesla's Emissions Are Rising," *Bloomberg*, February 17, 2021, Bloomberg.com.

22 Fabio Caiazzo et al., "Air Pollution and Early Deaths in the United States. Part I: Quantifying the Impact of Major Sectors in 2005," *Atmospheric Environment* 79, 2013.

23 Sovacool, "Energy Injustice and Nordic Electric Mobility," p. 211.

24 Riofrancos, "What Green Costs."

4. Uber's Assault on Cities and Labor

1 Carlos A. Schwantes, "The West Adapts the Automobile: Technology, Unemployment, and the Jitney Phenomenon of 1914–1917," *Western Historical Quarterly* 16:3, 1985, p. 314.

2 Ross D. Eckert and George W. Hilton, "The Jitneys," *Journal of Law and Economics* 15:2, 1972, p. 296.

3 Ibid.

4 Travis Kalanick, "Uber's Plan to Get More People into Fewer Cars," TED, February 2016, Ted.com.

5 "Fireside Chat with Travis Kalanick and Marc Benioff," Salesforce, September 2015, Salesforce.com.

6 Sam Harnett, "Words Matter: How Tech Media Helped Write Gig Companies into Existence," in *Beyond the Algorithm: Qualitative Insights for Gig Work Regulation*, ed. Deepa Das Acevedo, Cambridge University Press, 2021.

7 Dana Rubinstein, "Uber, Lyft, and the End of Taxi History," *Politico*, October 30, 2014, Politico.com.

8 Gregory D. Erhardt, "Do Transportation Network Companies Decrease or Increase Congestion?," *Science Advances* 5:5, 2019, p. 11.

9 "TNCs Today: A Profile of San Francisco Transportation Network Company Activity," San Francisco County Transportation Authority, 2017, Sfcta.org.

10 Bruce Schaller, "Empty Seats, Full Streets: Fixing Manhattan's Traffic Problem," Schaller Consulting, 2017, Schallerconsult .com.

11 Bruce Schaller, "The New Automobility: Lyft, Uber and the Future of American Cities," Schaller Consulting, 2018, Schallerconsult .com.

12 Michael Graehler Jr., Richard Alexander Mucci, and Gregory D. Erhardt, "Understanding the Recent Transit Ridership Decline in Major US Cities: Service Cuts or Emerging Modes?," Transportation Research Board 98th Annual Meeting, January 2019.

13 Regina R. Clewlow and Gouri Shankar Mishra, "Disruptive Transportation: The Adoption, Utilization, and Impacts of Ride-Hailing in the United States," Institute of Transportation Studies, 2017.

14 Steven R. Gehrke, Alison Felix, and Timothy Reardon, "Fare Choices: A Survey of Ride-Hailing Passengers in Metro Boston," Metropolitan Area Planning Council, 2018, Mapc.org; Mischa Young and Steven Farber, "The Who, Why, and When of Uber and Other Ride-Hailing Trips: An Examination of a Large Sample Household Travel Survey," *Transportation Research Part A: Policy and Practice* 119, 2019.

15 Graehler, Mucci, and Erhardt, "Understanding the Recent Transit Ridership Decline in Major US Cities."

16 Don Anair et al., "Ride-Hailing's Climate Risks: Steering a Growing Industry Toward a Clean Transportation Future," Union of Concerned Scientists, 2020, Ucsusa.org.

17 Clewlow and Mishra, "Disruptive Transportation."

18 Young and Farber, "The Who, Why, and When of Uber and Other Ride-Hailing Trips."

19 V.B. Dubal, "The Drive to Precarity: A Political History of Work, Regulation, & Labor Advocacy in San Francisco's Taxi & Uber Economies," *Berkeley Journal of Employment and Labor Law* 38:1, 2017, p. 109.

20 Hubert Horan, "Can Uber Ever Deliver? Part Nine: The 1990s Koch Funded Propaganda Program That Is Uber's True Origin Story," *Naked Capitalism* (blog), March 15, 2017, Naked capitalism.com.

21 Corky Siemaszko, "In the Shadow of Uber's Rise, Taxi Driver Suicides Leave Cabbies Shaken," *NBC News*, June 7, 2018, Nbc news.com.

22 Doug Schifter, Facebook post, February 5, 2018, facebook.com/ people/Doug-Schifter/100009072541151.

23 Christine Lagorio-Chafkin, "Resistance Is Futile," *Inc*, July–August 2013, Inc.com.

24 Hubert Horan, "Can Uber Ever Deliver? Part One—Understanding Uber's Bleak Operating Economics," *Naked Capitalism* (blog), November 30, 2016, Nakedcapitalism.com.

25 Ibid.

26 Anthony Ha, "California Regulator Passes First Ridesharing Rules, a Big Win for Lyft, Sidecar, and Uber," *TechCrunch*, September 19, 2013, Techcrunch.com.

27 Ken Jacobs and Michael Reich, "The Uber/Lyft Ballot Initiative Guarantees Only $5.64 an Hour," UC Berkeley Labor Center, October 21, 2019, Laborcenter.berkeley.edu.

28 Wilfred Chan, "Can American Labor Survive Prop 22?," *Nation*, November 10, 2020, Thenation.com.

5. Self-Driving Cars Did Not Deliver

1   James Niccolai, "Self-driving Cars a Reality for 'Ordinary People' within 5 Years, Says Google's Sergey Brin," *Computer World*, September 25, 2012, Computerworld.com.

2   John Paczkowski, "Google's Self-Driving Cars Now Legal in California," *All Things D*, September 25, 2012, Allthingsd.com.

3   Nicholas Carlson, "Uber Is Planning for a World Without Drivers—Just a Self-Driving Fleet," *Business Insider*, May 28, 2014, Businessinsider.com.

4   Kara Swisher, "Self-Driving into the Future: Full Code Conference Video of Google's Sergey Brin," *Recode*, June 11, 2014, Vox.com.

5   Ibid.

6   Adrienne LaFrance, "Your Grandmother's Driverless Car," *Atlantic*, June 29, 2016, Theatlantic.com.

7   Doc Quigg, "Reporter Rides Driverless Car," *Press-Courier*, June 7, 1960, News.google.com.

8   "A Brief History of Autonomous Vehicle Technology," *Wired*, n.d., Wired.com.

9   Robert D. Leighty, "DARPA ALV (Autonomous Land Vehicle) Summary," U.S. Army Engineer Topographic Laboratories, March 1986, Apps.dtic.mil.

10 Robert A. Ferlis, "The Dream of an Automated Highway," *Public Roads* 71:1, July–August 2007, Fhwa.dot.gov.

11 Charles Duhigg, "Did Uber Steal Google's Intellectual Property?," *New Yorker*, October 15, 2018, Newyorker.com.

12 Ibid.

13 Peter D. Norton, *Fighting Traffic: The Dawn of the Motor Age in the American City*, MIT Press, 2008.

14 Kelcie Ralph et al., "Editorial Patterns in Bicyclist and Pedestrian Crash Reporting," *Transportation Research Record: Journal of the Transportation Research Board* 2673:2, 2019.

15 Russell Brandom, "Self-driving Cars Are Headed toward an AI Roadblock," *Verge*, July 3, 2018, Theverge.com.

16 Eric A. Taub, "How Jaywalking Could Jam Up the Era of Self-Driving Cars," *New York Times*, August 1, 2019, Nytimes.com.

17 Ibid.

18 Matthew Sparkes, "Should We All Wear Sensors to Avoid Being Run Over by Driverless Cars?," *New Scientist*, March 5, 2021, Newscientist.com.

19 Edward Taylor, "Volkswagen Says Driverless Vehicles Have Limited Appeal and High Cost," Reuters, March 5, 2019, Reuters.com.

20 Daisuke Wakabayashi, "Uber's Self-Driving Cars Were Struggling Before Arizona Crash," *New York Times*, March 23, 2018, Nytimes.com.

21 "Collision between Vehicle Controlled by Developmental Automated Driving System and Pedestrian, Tempe, Arizona, March 18, 2018," Highway Accident Report NTSB/HAR-19/03 prepared by the National Transportation Safety Board, 2019, pp. 43–5, Ntsb.gov.

22 Ibid.

23 Ibid.

24 Lora Kolodny, "Tesla Faces Another NHTSA Investigation after Fatal Driverless Crash in Spring, Texas," CNBC, April 19, 2021, Cnbc.com.

25 Shara Tibken, "Waymo CEO: Autonomous Cars Won't Ever Be Able to Drive in All Conditions," CNET, November 13, 2018, Cnet.com.

26 A. Khalid, "Ford CEO Says the Company 'Overestimated' Self-driving Cars," *Engadget*, April 11, 2019, Engadget.com.

27 Connie Lin, "Tesla Admits It May Never Achieve Full-Self-Driving Cars," *Fast Company*, April 28, 2021, Fastcompany.com.

6. Making New Roads for Cars

1 Joe Cortright, "Reducing Congestion: Katy Didn't," *City Observatory*, December 16, 2015, Cityobservatory.org

2 Patrick Sisson, "Houston's $7 Billion Solution to Gridlock Is More Highways," *Curbed*, August 5, 2019, Archive.curbed.com.

3 Aaron Short, "A Great Big Freeway—Thanks to Induced Demand," *Streetsblog USA*, May 8, 2019, Usa.streetsblog.org.

4 Jeff Speck, *Walkable City: How Downtown Can Save America,*

One Step at a Time, North Point Press, 2012, p. 83.

5 Gilles Duranton and Matthew A. Turner, "The Fundamental Law of Road Congestion: Evidence from US Cities," *American Economic Association* 101:6, 2011.

6 Ashlee Vance, *Elon Musk: Tesla, SpaceX, and the Quest for a Fantastic Future*, HarperCollins, 2015.

7 "The Boring Company Event Webcast," The Boring Company, December 19, 2018, YouTube.com.

8 Ibid.

9 Aarian Marshall, "Elon Musk Reveals His Awkward Dislike of Mass Transit," *Wired*, December 14, 2017, Wired.com.

10 Ibid.

11 "The Boring Company Event Webcast," The Boring Company.

12 Laura J. Nelson, "Elon Musk Unveils His Company's First Tunnel in Hawthorne, and It's Not a Smooth Ride," *Los Angeles Times*, December 18, 2018, Latimes.com.

13 Dennis Romero, "Vintage Roller Coaster Fans See Familiar Tech in Elon Musk's Loop Tunnel," *NBC News*, December 28, 2018, Nbcnews.com.

14 Alissa Walker, "Stop Calling Elon Musk's Boring Tunnel Public Transit," *Curbed*, January 8, 2020, Archive.curbed.com.

15 "The Boring Company Event Webcast," The Boring Company.

16 Jenna Chandler and Alissa Walker, "Elon Musk First Envisioned Double-Decker 405 before Tunnel Idea," *Curbed*, November 9, 2018, La.curbed.com.

17 E.V. Rickenbacker, "Flying Autos in 20 Years," *Popular Science Monthly* 105:1, July 1924, p. 30.

18 Dave Hall, "Flying Cars: Why Haven't They Taken Off Yet?," *Guardian*, June 19, 2018, Theguardian.com.

19 "Urban Air Mobility—Closer Than You Think," Uber, June 27, 2019, YouTube.com.

20 "UBERAIR: Closer Than You Think," Uber, November 8, 2017, YouTube.com.

21 "Fast-Forwarding to a Future of On-Demand Urban Air Transportation," white paper from Uber Elevate, October 27, 2016, 62, Uber.com.

22 Elizabeth Rosner, Olivia Bensimon, and David Meyer, "We Pit the Uber Copter Vs. Public Transit in a Race to JFK—Here's Who Won," *New York Post*, October 6, 2019, Nypost.com; Ray Parisi, "Battle of the Airport Commute: CNBC Tests Lyft, Uber Copter, Blade Helicopter and Mass Transit in Race to NYC's Busiest Airport," CNBC, August 19, 2018, Cnbc.com.

23 Megan Rose Dickey, "This Is Uber's Plan to Deliver on Flying 'Cars,'" *TechCrunch*, February 10, 2018, Techcrunch.com.

24 Elon Musk, "The Future We're Building—and Boring," TED, April 2017, Ted.com.

25 André Gorz, "The Social Ideology of the Motorcar," *Le Sauvage*, September–October 1973, Unevenearth.org.

26 Mimi Sheller, *Mobility Justice: The Politics of Movement in an Age of Extremes*, Verso Books, 2018, pp. 78–9.

7. The Coming Fight for the Sidewalk

1 Sarah Goodyear, "How Women Rode the Bicycle into the Future," *Grist*, March 25, 2011, Grist.org.

2 Roff Smith, "How Bicycles Transformed Our World," *National Geographic*, June 17, 2020, Nationalgeographic.com.

3 Kathleen Pender, "Electric Scooters for Grown-Ups Now Available for Rent in SF, San Jose," *San Francisco Chronicle*, March 27, 2018, Sfchronicle.com.

4 Kathleen Pender, "Scooters Descend on San Francisco Sidewalks," *San Francisco Chronicle*, March 29, 2018.

5 Michael Cabanatuan, "As Complaints Roll in, San Francisco Considers Action over Wave of Motorized Scooters," *San Francisco Chronicle*, April 9, 2018, Sfchronicle.com.

6 Aaron Gordon, "How Uber Turned a Promising Bikeshare Company into Literal Garbage," *Vice*, June 23, 2020, Vice.com.

7 Ibid.

8 Ibid.

9 Aarian Marshall, "As Tech Invades Cycling, Are Bike Activists Selling Out?," *Wired*, January 15, 2019, Wired.com.

10 Alison Griswold, "Shared Scooters Don't Last Long," *Quartz*, March 1, 2019, Qz.com.

11 Sam Dean and Jon Schleuss, "Can Bird Build a Better Scooter Before It Runs Out of Cash?," *Los Angeles Times*, May 5, 2019, Latimes.com.

12 Mark Sussman, "Five Graphs That Show How Dockless Bikeshare and CaBi Work in DC," *Greater Greater Washington* (blog), September 5, 2018, Ggwash.org.

13 Joseph Hollingsworth, Brenna Copeland, and Jeremiah X Johnson, "Are E-scooters Polluters? The Environmental Impacts of Shared Dockless Electric Scooters," *Environmental Research Letters* 14, 2019.

14 Anne de Bortoli, "Environmental Performance of Shared Micromobility and Personal Alternatives Using Integrated Modal LCA," *Transportation Research Part D: Transport and Environment* 93, April 2021.

15 Sussman, "Five Graphs That Show How Dockless Bikeshare and CaBi Work in DC."

16 Julia Carrie Wong, "Delivery Robots: A Revolutionary Step or Sidewalk-clogging Nightmare?," *Guardian*, April 12, 2017, Theguardian.com.

17 Aaron Kinney, "Redwood City Ready to Debut Futuristic Delivery Robots," *Mercury News*, November 21, 2016, Mercurynews.com.

18 Emily Ackerman, "My Fight with a Sidewalk Robot," *CityLab*, November 19, 2019, Bloomberg.com.

19 Ibid.

20 Haben Girma, "The Robots Occupying Our Sidewalks," *TechCrunch*, August 11, 2020, Techcrunch.com.

21 Ibid.

22 Ryan Deto, "Pennsylvania Legalizes Autonomous Delivery Robots, Classifies Them as Pedestrians," *Pittsburgh City Paper*, December 2, 2020, Pghcitypaper.com.

23 Jennifer A. Kingston, "Sidewalk Robots Get Legal Rights as 'Pedestrians'," *Axios*, March 4, 2021, Axios.com.

24 Timothy B. Lee, "The Pandemic Is Bringing Us Closer to Our Robot Takeout Future," *Ars Technica*, April 24, 2020, Arstechnica.com.

25 Julia Carrie Wong, "San Francisco Sours on Rampant Delivery Robots: 'Not Every Innovation Is Great,'" *Guardian*, December 10, 2017, Theguardian.com.

8. The Real Futures That Tech Is Building

1 Eric Levitz, "America Has Central Planners. We Just Call Them 'Venture Capitalists,'" *Intelligencer*, December 2, 2020, Nymag.com.

2 Martin Kenney and John Zysman, "Unicorns, Cheshire Cats, and the New Dilemmas of Entrepreneurial Finance," *Venture Capital* 21:1, 2019, p. 39.

3 Megan Cerullo, "Uber Loses an Average of 58 Cents Per Ride—and Says It's Ready to Go Public," *CBS News*, May 6, 2019, Cbsnews.com.

4 Mark O'Connell, "Why Silicon Valley Billionaires Are Prepping for the Apocalypse in New Zealand," *Guardian*, February 15, 2018, Theguardian.com.

5 Kate Aronoff et al., *A Planet to Win: Why We Need a Green New Deal*, Verso Books, 2019, p. 108.

6 Charlie Jarvis, "A Shopper's Heaven," *Real Life*, March 29, 2021, Reallifemag.com.

7 Adam Forrest, "'It's Scary': Shoppers Give Verdict on Amazon's Futuristic Till-Free Supermarket," *Independent*, March 4, 2021, Independent.co.uk.

8 Chris Gilliard, "Pedagogy and the Logic of Platforms," *Educause Review* 52:4, July 3, 2017.

9 Chris Gilliard, "Friction-Free Racism," *Real Life*, October 15, 2018, Reallifemag.com.

10 Lauren Smiley, "The Shut-In Economy," *Matter*, March 25, 2015, Medium.com.

11 David A. Banks, "Subscriber City," *Real Life*, October 26, 2020, Reallifemag.com.

12 Jathan Sadowski, "The Internet of Landlords Makes Renters of Us All," *Reboot*, March 8, 2021, Thereboot.com.

13 Banks, "Subscriber City."

14 David Harvey, "From Managerialism to Entrepreneurialism: The Transformation in Urban Governance in Late Capitalism," *Human Geography* 71:1, 1989, p. 12.

15 Sharon Zukin, "Seeing Like a City: How Tech Became Urban," *Theory and Society* 49, 2020, p. 948.

16 Ibid., p. 942.

9. Toward a Better Transport Future

1 Ursula K. Le Guin, "A War Without End," *Verso Books* (blog), January 24, 2018 [2004], Versobooks.com.

2 Ursula K. Le Guin, *Very Far Away from Anywhere Else*, Harcourt, 2004 [1976], p. 14.

3 Ibid., pp. 28–9.

4 N. R. Kleinfield, "American Way of Life Altered by Fuel Crisis," *New York Times*, September 26, 1983, Nytimes.com.

5 Renate van der Zee, "How Amsterdam Became the Bicycle Capital of the World," *Guardian*, May 5, 2015, Theguardian.com.

6 Ben Fried, "The Origins of Holland's 'Stop Murdering Children' Street Safety Movement," *Streetsblog USA*, February 20, 2013, Usa.streetsblog.org.

7 Jim Malewitz, "1 Energy Crisis, 2 Futures: How Denmark and Texas Answered a Challenge," *Texas Tribune*, November 21, 2016, Texastribune.org.

8 Ursula K. Le Guin, "The Carrier Bag Theory of Fiction," in *Dancing at the Edge of the World*, Grove Press, 1986, Theanarchist library.com.

9 Ibid.

10 Ursula K. Le Guin, "A Rant about 'Technology'," *Ursula K. Le Guin* (blog), 2004, Ursulakleguinarchive.com.

11 Ibid.

12 Mimi Sheller, *Mobility Justice: The Politics of Movement in an Age of Extremes*, Verso Books, 2018, p. 46.

13 Murray Bookchin, "Utopia, Not Futurism: Why Doing the Impossible Is the Most Rational Thing We Can Do," lecture at Toward Tomorrow Fair in Amherst, Massachusetts, trans. Constanze Huther, October 2, 2019 [August 24, 1978], Unevenearth.org.

14 Ibid.

15 Ibid.

16 Ben Fried, "How Paris Is Beating Traffic without Congestion Pricing," *Streetsblog USA*, April 22, 2008, Usa.streetsblog.org.

17 Laura Bliss, "Los Angeles Passed a Historic Transit Tax. Why Isn't It Working?," *CityLab*, January 17, 2019, Bloomberg.com.

18 Alissa Walker, "We Don't Need More Dedicated Places Where Cars Can Go Fast," *Curbed*, December 20, 2018, Archive.curbed .com.

19 James Wilt, *Do Androids Dream of Electric Cars?: Public Transit in the Age of Google, Uber, and Elon Musk*, Between the Lines Books, 2020, pp. 193–205.

20 Untokening, "Untokening 1.0—Principles of Mobility Justice," *The Untokening* (blog), November 11, 2017, Untokening.org.

21 George Monbiot, "Public Luxury for All or Private Luxury for Some: This Is the Choice We Face," *Guardian*, May 31, 2017, Theguardian.com.

22 Aaron Vansintjan, "Public Abundance Is the Secret to the Green New Deal," *Green European Journal*, May 27, 2020.

23 For specific proposals, see Callum Cant, *Riding for Deliveroo: Resistance in the New Economy*, Polity Press, 2019; Dan Hind, "The British Digital Cooperative: A New Model Public Sector Institution," *Common Wealth*, September 20, 2019, Common-wealth.co.uk; "Our Plan," *Delivering Community Power*, n.d., Deliveringcommunitypower.ca; Paris Marx, "Build Socialism Through the Post Office," *Jacobin*, April 15, 2020, Jacobinmag. com.

24 See Salomé Viljoen, "Data as Property?," *Phenomenal World*, October 16, 2020, Phenomenalworld.org.

25 Aaron Benanav, "How to Make a Pencil," *Logic Magazine*, December 20, 2020, Logicmag.io.

26 Le Guin, "A Rant About 'Technology.'"

27 Thea Riofrancos, *Resource Radicals: From Petro-Nationalism to Post-Extractivism in Ecuador*, Duke University Press, 2020.

28 Ursula K. Le Guin, "The Ones Who Walk Away from Omelas,"

in *New Dimensions 3*, ed. Richard Silverberg, Nelson Doubleday, 1973, p. 6.
29 Ibid., p. 7.

Conclusion

1 "Announcing Sidewalk Toronto: Press Conference Live Stream," Sidewalk Labs, October 17, 2017, YouTube.com.
2 Saadia Muzaffar, "My Full Resignation Letter from Waterfront Toronto's Digital Strategy Advisory Panel," *Medium*, October 8, 2018, Medium.com.
3 "Vision Sections of RFP Submission," *Sidewalk Labs*, October 17, 2017, Sidewalklabs.com.
4 "Concerned Torontonians Launch #BlockSidewalk Campaign," *Block Sidewalk*, February 25, 2019, Blocksidewalk.ca.
5 Laura Bliss, "Meet the Jane Jacobs of the Smart Cities Age," *CityLab*, December 21, 2018, Bloomberg.com.
6 Dave Yasvinski, "Waterfront Toronto Releases New Vision for 12 Acres Abandoned by Sidewalk Labs," *National Post*, March 10, 2021, Nationalpost.com.

Index